Contemporary Issues in Financial Institutions and Markets

This book showcases recent academic work on contemporary issues in financial institutions and markets. It covers a broad range of topics, highlighting the diverse nature of academic research in banking and finance. As a consequence the contributions cover a wide range of issues across a broad spectrum, including: capital structure arbitrage, credit rating agencies, credit default swap spreads, market power in the banking industry and stock returns. This timely collection offers fresh insights and understandings into the ongoing debates within and between the academic and professional finance communities.

This book was originally published as a special issue of *The European Journal of Finance.*

Claudia Girardone is Professor of Banking and Finance at the Essex Business School, University of Essex, UK. Her research interests focus on modelling efficiency and productivity of financial institutions, bank mergers and acquisitions, bank corporate governance, competition issues and banking integration. She has published widely in international peer-reviewed journals and co-authored a textbook entitled *Introduction to Banking* (2/e forthcoming 2015). She is on the editorial board of several journals including the *Journal of Banking and Finance* and *The European Journal of Finance.*

John O.S. Wilson is Professor of Banking and Finance and Director for the Centre for Responsible Banking & Finance at the University of St Andrews, UK. His research focuses on the areas of industrial organization, banking and credit unions. He is the author/co-author of books, a monograph, chapters and articles. His books include *European Banking: Efficiency, Technology and Growth*, *Industrial Organisation: An Analysis of Competitive Markets*, *The Economics of Business Strategy* and *Industrial Organization: Competition Strategy and Policy* (now in its fourth edition with translations in Italian and Greek). John edited a Routledge Major Works, *Banking*. He also co-edited the *Oxford Handbook of Banking* (with Allen Berger and Phil Molyneux). John is Associate Editor at the *Journal of Money, Credit and Banking*, *European Journal of Finance* and *British Accounting Review*, and serves on the editorial boards of the *Journal of Business Finance and Accounting* and *Journal of Financial Economic Policy.*

Philip Hamill is Dean of The Institute of Banking, Ireland. His research involves theoretical and empirical analysis of financial markets with a specific focus on modelling stock market volatility, security valuation and corporate governance. During his academic career he has been seconded to work in the financial services sector and has been a consultant to both public and private sector organisations. His research has been published in a range of leading academic journals, books and professional periodicals including the *Journal of Empirical Finance*, *Global Finance Journal*, *The Financial Review* and the *British Accounting Review.*

Contemporary Issues in Financial Institutions and Markets

Volume II

Edited by
Claudia Girardone, Philip Hamill and John O.S. Wilson

Routledge
Taylor & Francis Group
LONDON AND NEW YORK

First published 2015 by Routledge

2 Park Square, Milton Park, Abingdon, Oxon, OX14 4RN
605 Third Avenue, New York, NY 10017

Routledge is an imprint of the Taylor & Francis Group, an informa business

First issued in paperback 2020

British Library Cataloguing in Publication Data
A catalogue record for this book is available from the British Library

ISBN 13: 978-1-138-80993-2 (hbk)
ISBN 13: 978-0-367-73904-1 (pbk)

Typeset in Times New Roman
by RefineCatch Limited, Bungay, Suffolk

Publisher's Note
The publisher accepts responsibility for any inconsistencies that may have arisen during the conversion of this book from journal articles to book chapters, namely the possible inclusion of journal terminology.

Contents

Citation Information vii
Notes on Contributors ix

1. Introduction 1
Claudia Girardone, Philip A. Hamill, John O.S. Wilson

2. Are there benefits to being naked? The returns and diversification impact of capital structure arbitrage 5
Giovanni Calice, Jing Chen and Julian M. Williams

3. The path to impairment: do credit-rating agencies anticipate default events of structured finance transactions? 31
Matthias Bodenstedt, Daniel Rösch and Harald Scheule

4. The determinants of bank CDS spreads: evidence from the financial crisis 51
Laura Chiaramonte and Barbara Casu

5. The impact of market power and funding strategy on bank-interest margins 78
Mohammed Amidu and Simon Wolfe

6. An examination of investor sentiment effect on G7 stock market returns 99
Deven Bathia and Don Bredin

Index 129

Citation Information

The chapters in this book were originally published in *The European Journal of Finance*, volume 19, issue 9–10 (October–November 2013). When citing this material, please use the original page numbering for each article, as follows:

Chapter 1
Editorial
Claudia Girardone, Philip A. Hamill, John O.S. Wilson
The European Journal of Finance, volume 19, issue 9–10 (October–November 2013) pp. 811–814

Chapter 2
Are there benefits to being naked? The returns and diversification impact of capital structure arbitrage
Giovanni Calice, Jing Chen and Julian M. Williams
The European Journal of Finance, volume 19, issue 9–10 (October–November 2013) pp. 815–840

Chapter 3
The path to impairment: do credit-rating agencies anticipate default events of structured finance transactions?
Matthias Bodenstedt, Daniel Rösch and Harald Scheule
The European Journal of Finance, volume 19, issue 9–10 (October–November 2013) pp. 841–860

Chapter 4
The determinants of bank CDS spreads: evidence from the financial crisis
Laura Chiaramonte and Barbara Casu
The European Journal of Finance, volume 19, issue 9–10 (October–November 2013) pp. 861–887

Chapter 5
The impact of market power and funding strategy on bank-interest margins
Mohammed Amidu and Simon Wolfe
The European Journal of Finance, volume 19, issue 9–10 (October–November 2013) pp. 888–908

Chapter 6

An examination of investor sentiment effect on G7 stock market returns
Deven Bathia and Don Bredin
The European Journal of Finance, volume 19, issue 9–10 (October–November 2013) pp. 909–937

Please direct any queries you may have about the citations to clsuk.permissions@cengage.com

Notes on Contributors

Mohammed Amidu, Department of Accounting, University of Ghana Business School, Ghana.

Deven Bathia, School of Business and Management, Queen Mary University London, UK.

Matthias Bodenstedt, Judge Business School, University of Cambridge, UK.

Don Bredin, UCD Smurfit Graduate Business School, Co Dublin, Ireland.

Giovanni Calice, Department of Economics, University of Birmingham, UK.

Barbara Casu, Cass Business School, City University London, UK.

Jing Chen, School of Economics and Business, Swansea University, UK.

Laura Chiaramonte, Department of Economics, Catholic University of Milan, Italy.

Daniel Rösch, Institute of Banking and Finance, Leibniz University of Hannover, Germany.

Harald Scheule, School of Finance and Economics, University of Technology, Sydney, Australia.

Simon Wolfe, School of Management, University of Southampton, UK.

Julian M. Williams, Business School, Durham University, UK.

Introduction

Contemporary issues in financial markets and institutions

The second Emerging Scholars Conference in Banking and Finance took place at Cass Business School, City University, London, on 9 December 2010. It was jointly organised by The British Accounting and Finance Association's Financial Markets and Institutions-Special Interest Group (FMI-SIG) and the Centre for Banking Research at Cass Business School. A key objective of the FMI-SIG is to provide opportunities for emerging scholars to debate their work in a constructive collegial environment and to support early-career scholar's transition into the academic community. To that end, the emerging scholars' conference was accompanied by a special issue of the *European Journal of Finance*. The theme for the conference was contemporary issues in financial institutions and markets. It was deliberately general to reflect the diversity of research across FMI, and to encourage as broad a submission as possible from emerging scholars with the overriding objective of promoting the best work at the conference and in the special issue.

Two excellent plenary sessions complemented the emerging scholar's papers. Dr Peter Hahn (City University) opened the proceedings with a critique of evolving remuneration policy in the financial services sector entitled *Regulation of Executive Compensation*. Professor Thorsten Beck's (European Banking Centre; Tilburg University) keynote address – *Villain or Solution? Cross-border Banking and the Global Crisis* – discussed the contribution of cross-border banking to the financial crisis and concluded by arguing that the geographic outreach of banks should be matched with a corresponding regulatory and resolution framework. From over 50 submitted papers, 12 were chosen from the refereeing process for presentation at the conference with 5 published in this special issue. The first three selected papers share *credit* as a common overarching theme; the first paper investigates the returns from investing in naked credit default swaps (CDS), the second introduces a new test of credit rating agency's performance, while the third paper evaluates the determinants of CDS spreads and whether CDS spreads can be considered a good proxy for bank risk. The fourth paper investigates the implications of market power and funding strategies for bank interest margins for emerging and developing countries. The final paper assesses how a range of sentiment proxies affects returns of value and growth stocks, and aggregate markets returns, across G7 economies. The remainder of this editorial summarises the key insights from each paper.

Because of its speculative nature, trading in naked CDS has been subject of intense debate over the last few years, and not just in relation to the 2007–2009 financial turmoil but also for the more recent Eurozone crisis.[1] An interesting insight into CDS and capital structure arbitrage is given by Giovanni Calice, Jing Chen and Julian Williams in the article entitled: 'Are there benefits to being naked? The Returns and Diversification Impact of Capital Structure Arbitrage'. The study proposes a novel testing framework to establish whether the inclusion of naked CDS positions in an optimised portfolio is replicable by a large set of alternative assets. More specifically, the method uses first and second moments and co-moments to assess replicability of asset returns under different portfolio optimisation regimes. The data sample spans from January 2004 to August 2010 and most estimated results are divided over two sample periods (pre- and post-2007) to account for the recent financial crisis. The empirical analysis reveals that investing in naked CDS yields significant excess returns of approximately 28% per annum. It also suggests that these systematic abnormal returns are inherently unstable and could potentially initiate a bubble in CDS prices. On the one hand, this study gives solid evidence that that there are considerable potential gains for speculative traders and investors for trading in naked CDS. On the other hand, it raises concerns about the potential economic and social benefits deriving from naked CDS contracts.

Normally, rating agencies play a pivotal role in financial markets globally through the production and dissemination of credit information. Their ability to produce timely and accurate ratings is valued by investors while at the same time enhancing the credibility of the best performing agencies in a competitive market (Güttler and Wahrenburg 2007; Alsakka and ap Gwilym 2010). Soon after the onset of the financial crisis in 2007, it became clear that many credit ratings were suspect. There is no doubt that overly optimistic ratings, due to unrealistic model inputs and the conflict of interest that arose as rating agencies received relatively higher fees from issuers for rating structured products, exacerbated the banking crisis (Crouhy, Jarrow, and Turnbull 2008; Brunnermeier 2009). Given this backdrop, the paper *The Path to Impairment: Do Credit Rating Agencies Anticipate Default Events of Structured Finance Transactions?* by Matthias Bodenstedt, Daniel Rösch and Harald Scheule assesses the ability of credit rating agencies to adjust their ratings prior to impairment of structured finance transactions, and develop a new metric – *the anticipation coefficient* – which quantifies a rating agency's performance in advance of defaults. The advantage of the anticipation coefficient is its ability to incorporate ratings information for a 1-year period which contrasts with the typical focus on ratings at origination or at the beginning of the year. Utilising ratings by Moody's Investor Service for 13,679 structured finance transactions with impairments between 2001 and 2008, the authors show that Moody's ability to identify higher levels of impairment risk deteriorated significantly in the global financial crisis. And that differences in Moody's performance could be partially explained by deal-specific and macroeconomic factors. Overall, the findings from this paper suggest that ratings do not consistently reflect increased risk prior to impairments and factors including deal volume, asset type, time since origination and the overall economic situation should be considered in tandem with ratings.

CDS are thought to have played a significant role during the recent financial crisis (Stulz 2010). CDS are contracts that make it possible to isolate and transfer credit risk, and as such have become useful as indicators of an organisation's credit risk (Hull, Predescu, and White 2004). These instruments have also led to investors to bet on the likelihood of bankruptcy or default of a given organisation and in some cases led to contagion effects within the financial system (Jorion and Zhang 2007). Recent evidence suggests that CDS spreads could provide regulators and investors with important information with respect to the risk of individual financial institutions (Völz and Wedow 2011). The paper *The Determinants of Bank CDS spreads: Evidence from the financial crisis* by Laura Chiaramonte and Barbara Casu investigate the determinants of CDS spreads for a sample of large international banks over three time periods comprising: a pre-crisis period; a crisis period; and a less acute crisis. The results of the empirical analysis conducted by the authors suggest that bank CDS spreads reflect the risk captured by bank balance sheet ratios. Furthermore, the determinants of bank CDS spreads vary through time with general economic and bank-specific conditions (such as liquidity).

Market failure or anti-competitive behaviour on the part of banks has far-reaching implications for productive efficiency, consumer welfare and economic growth. In recent years, a literature that is largely confined to developed countries has sought to explain the importance of competition (or market power) for bank performance (Carbó Valverde and Rodriguez Fernandez 2007; Goddard et al. forthcoming). The paper entitled *The impact of market power and funding strategy on bank interest margins* by Mohammed Amidu and Simon Wolfe examines the implications of market power and funding strategies for bank interest margins (net interest margin, NIM). Utilising a large sample of banks located in emerging and developing countries over the period 2000–2007, the authors find a negative relationship between size and cost to income ratio and NIM, and a positive relationship between credit risk and NIM. Furthermore, the type of funding plays an important role in explaining variations in NIM.

An ongoing debate within, and between, the academic and professional finance communities is the extent to which stock returns and well-documented anomalies can be explained by the traditional risk-return trade-off paradigm or explanations offered by behavioural finance. Mostly, the US centric empirical evidence identifies factors unrelated to fundamentals as important determinants of stock returns (Baker and Wurgler 2006; Barber and Odean 2008; Green and Hwang 2009; Tetlock 2011). Understanding the influence of relevant factors across markets is important for global investors. The paper *An Examination of Investor Sentiment Effect on G7 Stock Market Returns* by Deven Bathia and Don Bredin investigates how sentiment proxies (consumer confidence index, equity fund flow, closed-end equity fund (CEEF) discount and the equity put-call ratio) affect value and growth stock returns, and aggregate market returns for G7 (US, Canada, UK, France, Germany, Italy and Japan) capital markets from January 1995 to December 2007. Assessing how a range of sentiment proxies affects returns, not only for aggregate markets returns, but also value and growth stocks across markets in a noticeable gap in the literature motivates this paper. The first insight reported is the disproportionate influence of survey sentiment on value stocks relative to growth. The authors also provide evidence of price pressure on value stocks and the market due to an increase in equity fund flow. In contrast to the US evidence, the authors also report that CEFF discount enters into the returns generating process with a narrowing of the CEFF discount associated with an increase (decrease) in value (growth) stocks returns. Collectively, these findings confirm the efficacy of both variables as valid sentiment proxies and highlight the significant influence of individual investors in affecting returns. The final sentiment variable, the equity put-call ratio, was only significantly correlated with value stocks. The authors conclude by arguing that their findings support the contention that investors' behaviour is consistent with the adaptive expectations hypothesis.

This collection of papers reflects the work of emerging scholars who are completing their doctoral studies or have been in an academic post for 3 years or less. Julian Williams, Matthias Bodenstedt, Laura Chiramonte, Mohammed Amidu, Deven Bathia and their co-authors address important issues in the FMIs literature. We look forward to reading further contributions as their careers develop.

Claudia Girardone
Essex Business School, University of Essex

Philip A. Hamill
Department of Business, Retail and Financial Services, University of Ulster

John O.S. Wilson
School of Management, University of St Andrews

Acknowledgements

The Guest Editors thank the Editor, Professor Chris Adcock, for commissioning this special issue and for providing advice and guidance throughout the process and Pat Anderson at the *European Journal of Finance* for administrative assistance. They also thank Peter Hahn and Thorsten Beck for excellent plenary sessions, Peter for his opening plenary session debating the merits of regulation and executive compensation in the financial services sector and Thorsten Beck for his closing keynote address critiquing of the merits of cross-border banking and its contribution to the financial crisis. We are also indebted to the discussants: Anna Sarkisyan, Simon Wolfe, Francesca Arnaboldi, Elena Beccalli, Andreas Hoepner, Richard Payne, Phil Molyneux, Jonathan Williams, Meziane Lasfer Jerry Coakley and Steve Haberman for chairing the keynote session. Conference organisation was overseen by a scientific committee comprising, in addition to the Guest Editors of this special issue, Barbara Casu, Shelagh Heffernan, Phil Molyneux, Elena Kalotychou, David McMillan, Anna Sarkisyan and Sotris Staikouras. Without papers and presenters, a conference is not possible. It, therefore, remains for us to thank all of the presenters for sharing their work at the second Conference for Emerging Scholars in Banking and Finance. Finally, this event would not have been possible without generous financial assistance from the sponsors: Cass Business School, the British Accounting and Finance Association (BAFA), the Institute of Chartered Accountants of Scotland (ICAS), Bangor University, BNY Mellon and Citi. On behalf of everyone involved, the Guest Editors thank them for the support. The usual disclaimer applies.

Note

1. At the time of writing (October 2011), European Union lawmakers are moving closer to a ban on naked CDS on sovereign debt.

References

Alsakka, R., and O. ap Gwilym. 2010. Leads and lag in sovereign credit rating. *Journal of Banking & Finance* 34: 2614–26.

Baker, M., and J. Wurgler. 2006. Investor sentiment and the cross-section of stock returns. *Journal of Finance* 61: 1645–80.

Barber, M.B., and T. Odean. 2008. All that glitters: The effect of attention and news on the buying behaviour of individual and institutional investors. *Review of Financial Studies* 21, no. 2: 785–818.

Brunnermeier, M. 2009. Deciphering the liquidity and credit crunch 2007–2008. *Journal of Economic Perspectives* 23: 77–100.

Carbó Valverde, S., and F. Rodriguez Fernandez. 2007. The determinants of bank margins in European banking. *Journal of Banking & Finance* 31: 2043–63.

Crouhy, M., R. Jarrow, and S. Turnbull. 2008. The subprime credit crisis of 07. *Journal of Derivatives* 16: 81–110.

Green, T.C., and B.H. Hwang. 2009. Price-based return co-movement. *Journal of Financial Economics* 93: 37–50.

Goddard, J., H. Liu, P. Molyneux, and J.O.S. Wilson. Forthcoming. Do bank profits converge? *European Financial Management*.

Güttler, A., and M. Wahrenburg. 2007. The adjustment of credit ratings in advance of defaults. *Journal of Banking & Finance* 31: 751–67.

Hull, J., M. Predescu, and A. White. 2004. The relationship between credit default swap spreads, bond yields, and credit rating announcements. *Journal of Banking & Finance* 28: 2789–811.

Jorion, P., and G. Zhang. 2007. Good and bad credit contagion: Evidence from credit default swaps. *Journal of Financial Economics* 84: 860–83.

Tetlock, P.C. 2011. All the news that's fit to reprint: Do investors react to stale information? *Review of Financial Studies* 24: 1481–512.

Stulz, R.N. 2010. Credit default swaps and the credit crisis. *Journal of Economic Perspectives* 24: 73–92.

Völz, M., and M. Wedow. 2011. Market discipline and too-big-to-fail in the CDS market: Does banks' size reduce market discipline? *Journal of Empirical Finance* 18: 195–210.

Are there benefits to being naked? The returns and diversification impact of capital structure arbitrage

Giovanni Calice[a], Jing Chen[b] and Julian M. Williams[c]

[a] *Management School, University of Southampton, Southampton, UK;* [b] *School of Economics and Business, Swansea University, Swansea, UK;* [c] *Business School, Edward Wright Building, University of Aberdeen, Old Aberdeen, Aberdeen AB24 3QY, UK*

In a naked credit default swap (CDS) position, a party pays an income stream to a seller of protection to swap away default risk on an underlying defaultable security without actually holding this reference instrument. Using mark-to-market returns on a large cross section of CDS positions, held independent from their reference entity, we implement a novel test to establish whether their inclusion in an optimised portfolio is replicable by a large set of alternative assets. Overall, we find significant excess returns of over 28% per annum against an optimised benchmark, we speculate that it is these characteristics that could be driving a bubble in the CDS market.

1. Introduction

An entirely sensible view of a credit default swap (CDS) contract is to regard it as being equivalent to a short position in a defaultable bond. As such, in a complete market consisting of a very large cross section of assets from various different classes, the mark-to-market returns on a naked CDS contract should be redundant.

There is, however, growing theoretical and empirical evidence rejecting this canonical representation. It is suggested, by practitioners, academics and politicians that the perverse incentives generated by the ability to trade protection on a defaultable claim results in an instrument with pricing and co-movement characteristics deviant from its synthetic origins. It is very difficult to directly observe these properties from quoted financial data; however, certain artefacts will appear in the price evolution as the market develops. This paper provides evidence about the structure of returns on traded CDS positions. More specifically, we attempt to understand whether the inclusion of these assets in portfolios of more conventional assets significantly changes the risk-return profile. Our argument being that systematic excess returns and decoupling (negative correlation trends) over and from standard asset classes provide the *prima facie* evidence for uniqueness argument and divergence from the complete market representation of this contract. In ethos, our approach is most similar to Longstaff et al. (2010), albeit we concentrate on a much broader profile of CDS contracts on corporate debt.

Our title is somewhat facetious in the sense that a systematic divergence from market completeness, while evidently beneficial for those holding the contract, could be extremely damaging for social welfare as a whole. Consider a consumption model of default risk, if CDS are traded as an asset and an anticipated discount factor is applied then the meaning of this in terms of a naked short position is ambiguous. A non-zero expectation of mark-to-market returns (i.e. the change in the spreads) on a short naked CDS positions has profound implications for the market as a whole, given the explicit structure of the contract. Evidence for a lack of replication and returns on holdings inconsistent with other assets lend credence to the argument that the dead weight costs associated with CDSs matter more than the actual design of the contract.

The salient point is that if the credit event-generating process *is* inherently coupled to the value of the contract then a stable long-run pricing equilibrium cannot exist. In reality this would redoubtably lead to a sudden collapse in the CDS spreads, as the implied level of default risk would be inherently intolerable with respect to the underlying social contract. Effectively, the social welfare implications of a runaway CDS market would lead to its inherent failure.

In this paper, we document the growth in the value of CDS contracts over the 1 January 2004 to 2 April 2010 period. We show that the payoff of mean variance optimised portfolios that include traded CDS positions exhibit a substantially different return and correlation structure than portfolios where the CDS positions are excluded. We utilise the entire CMA-DataStream data set of single name corporate CDS positions in addition to a large cross section of alternative assets. We then construct a total sample of 1.240 million return-day observations and compute mean variance optimised *ex ante* rolling portfolios, with and without traded CDS positions.

We employ random resampling and replacement to construct bootstrap intervals to test this hypothesis for a large collection of assets from a wide variety of classes. We advocate that our results are empirically indicative of the leverage cycle with CDS suggested by Geanakoplos (2009). In this context, the deepening of a financial crisis and the associated increase in default risk benefit the capital structure arbitrager by antagonising the naturally occurring misalignment of incentives between speculative traders and net providers of leverage. We document the potential profits that can be made from this misalignment *ex ante* by recursive analysis. Additionally, we test the significance of the restriction of CDS positions by comparing a systematic restriction of CDS versus a random restriction on a broad set of alternative assets on the weighted and unweighted correlation profile of a fund of fund portfolio.

The notional value of underlying assets *protected* by CDS positions is typically far larger than the total value of the underlying debt. Holding default protection on a bond without actually holding the underlying bond, i.e. being naked in the CDS position, is in effect a bet on the deterioration in credit quality of the underlying reference entity. Holding a CDS position with a variety of assets other than a fully default offsetting position in the underlying name is often referred to as capital structure arbitrage. Generally, the alternative offsetting assets are equity although the strategy can encompass many alternative combinations.[1]

This paper makes three main contributions to the literature. We believe that this is the first paper to robustly estimate the level of excess returns on mark-to-market CDS positions and the changes in the correlation structure with respect to various alternative assets. We also show that there is a very high degree of diversification of capital risk in a large portfolios of alternative assets.

Second, we measure these affects using a novel portfolio bootstrapping approach that generated very large combinations of portfolios and then computes average correlation and return statistics for broad cross sections of assets at relatively (end of day) high-frequency observations.

Finally, we document a large variety of statistical evidence about the unique time period between 2003 and 2010. During this time period, the financial sector has seen the wide spread adoption of standardised credit derivatives contracts, several correlated asset bubbles, a collapse in the liquidity of the financial market and finally the insolvency and bailout of multiple financial institutions. The CDS market has been singled out as a conduit for credit risk transfer (CRT).

For example, our results indicate that immediately after the Lehman Brothers default, the average block cross correlations between collections of CDS and equities dropped from around -10% to under -15% and, for the 2040 block correlations estimated each day, the maximum observed block correlations between CDS and equity also fell from around 20% towards zero. We believe that this result is of significant interest to academics and practitioners working on portfolio diversification in the presence of financial crises. Third, we fill a gap in the empirical literature on capital structure arbitrage with CDSs, reconciling this trading approach with theoretical models of market completeness and documenting the potential returns of this type of strategy.

The remainder of this paper is organised as follows. Section 2 adds some background discussion and reviews some of the related literature in this area. Section 3 discusses a trading position in CDS and the associated payoff structure and unit of account. Furthermore, we introduce the idea of a complete market with exogenous risk and demonstrate why the CDS has an exactly computable price when default risk is exogenous. Section 4 describes the data sample and presents our empirical methodology for building portfolios based on a mean variance optimisation framework. We then introduce our return and correlation diagnostics to test whether the CDS position is replicative relative to a broad cross section of alternatives. Section 6 contains our results, analysis and discussion while Section 7 concludes.

2. Background and related literature

Initial over the counter trading in CDSs originated in the mid-1990s as a means through which banks could reduce their holdings of certain types of expensive core capital. As Shadab (2009, 411: 2) notes 'CDSs were born in regulatory sin'. Bolton and Ochmke (2010) also suggest that when debtors can buy protection on their own debt, the empty creditor problem could result in the perverse preference to instigate default. However, Bolton and Ochmke (2010) conclude that CDS serve a useful purpose in providing a means of facilitating appropriate levels of credit to debtors and reducing the 'anxiety' of the creditor, in the Geanakoplos (2009) parlance. As such, the classical representation of the spread on a CDS as pricing the expectation of default driven by an exogenous stochastic default time is inappropriate. Default risk would, in practice, exhibit a nonlinear state-dependent correlation with its own spread as payoffs tipped in various directions. Thus, the returns on CDS positions would exhibit a state-dependent correlation with other assets in the market and would at times decouple completely from their underlying positions (Figure 1).

The ability to effectively leverage short positions on default risk has proved controversial. On 10 March 2010, the president of the European Commission, Jose Manuel Barroso, suggested that the EU would examine whether naked CDS positions should be banned. This pronouncement follows the July 2009 comments by the Chairman of the United States House of Representatives Financial Services Committee, Barney Frank, who stated that a prohibition on trades of naked CDS positions was 'on the cards'. This attempted prohibition was eventually watered down to 'a ban on abusive trades'.[2] The most direct action against the short selling of sovereign debt instruments occurred on 18 May 2010 when the German financial regulator BaFin banned the trade in naked CDS on Eurozone government debt in Germany. However, CDS markets in the major trading centre's of New York and London were unaffected. These assaults on the CDS market are primarily driven by political ire at the speculative short selling of sovereign default risk and subsequent perceived distortions of the sovereign debt market. It is interesting to note that, in the main, the notional

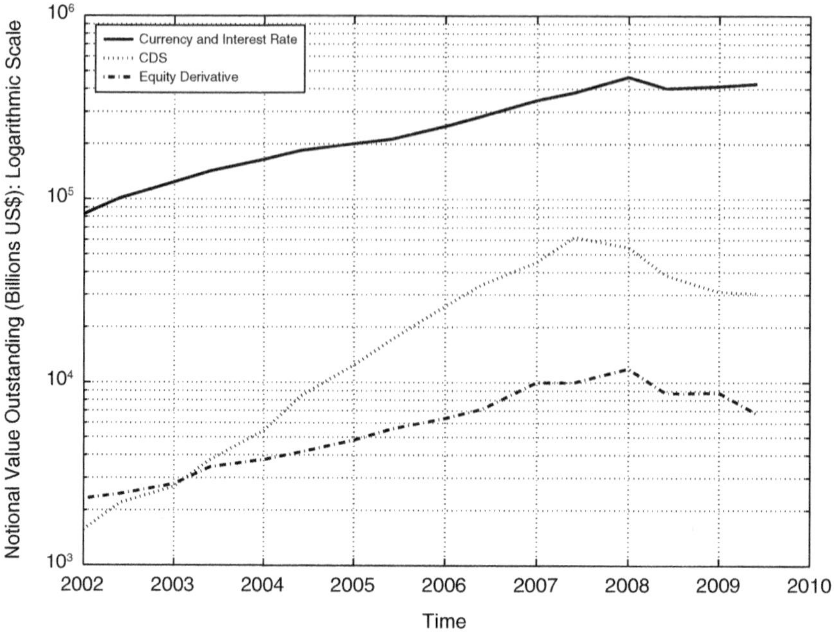

Figure 1. Comparison between the aggregate notional amounts outstanding on interest rate/FX, credit (CDS) and equity derivatives.
Source: ISDA.

amount protected by CDS positions on sovereign debt are not generally in excess of the actual issued debt; however, corporate CDS positions usually are. As such, political protestations have not, however, been restricted simply to speculative trade in sovereign debt CDSs.

Trading in naked CDS positions on corporate debt and other asset-backed securities has been an ongoing source of controversy since the mid-2000s. On 16 April 2010, Goldman Sachs was in receipt of a 'Wells notice' of intended enforcement action by the US Securities and Exchange Commission for alleged activity in relation to the structuring of a collateralised debt obligation (CDO) in conjunction with a hedge fund. Essentially, the hedge fund purchased protection against default risk within the CDO without holding any stake in it. This protection position (in essence, a naked CDS) was a bet on the downgrading of the various tranches within the CDO, most of which were subsequently downgraded.[3] In this context, the underlying transaction from which the lawsuit originates, underscores some of the ethical questions over the role of naked protection positions in facilitating potentially fraudulent activity. The event of the lawsuit itself neatly illustrates the effectiveness of a capital structure arbitrage position. On 16 April 2010, Goldman Sachs' listed share price had fell by nearly 13%, while simultaneously the CDS spreads on Goldman Sachs 5-year bonds had widened by 19%. Under these circumstances, a capital structure arbitrager holding a naked CDS position in Goldman Sachs bonds would have more than offset the loss in the stock price. In fact, the arbitrager would have obtained roughly a 5% return if the value of the respective positions were precisely offset. We discuss the theory underlying the presence of protection on defaultable debt in a complete market in Section 3.[4]

This anecdotal and empirical evidence that CDS positions *do more* than simply act as a short bond position has negative as well as positive connotations. Several recent articles, such as Hu and

Black (2008) and Bolton and Oehmke (2010), have suggested that the trading of CDS positions results in an empty creditor problem. In this case, the debt holder acquires default protection but retains various control rights in the event of default. Once the value of the insurance has been established, the creditor may proactively seek default to trigger the payoff. At a macro-level, this may result in the contagious manipulation of credit markets to drive default risk higher and allow speculators to book profits on default protection purchased at a cheaper rate.

Furthermore, a relevant implication of the analysis provided in Geanakoplos (2009) is that the CDS is no longer serving as a redundant asset replicating the payoff of a short position in defaultable debt. The major reason posited for this divergence from its synthetic roots is that the CDS was introduced part way through the leverage cycle, an economic cycle first introduced in Geanakoplos (1997) and further developed in Fostel and Geanakoplos (2008). An important element for validating this approach is establishing whether the CDS is actually a separate asset class or simply a redundant linear combination of alternative assets.

In this paper, we investigate empirically whether buying a broad baskets of short naked CDS positions provides a significant offsetting of capital risk and potential returns in a large portfolio of different assets.[5] In particular, we postulate a fund that buys and holds a set of naked CDS positions at a particular set of spreads for one day and then either sells or offsets it with the following day's market spreads. The difference is then reinvested into the same strategy. Hence, the value of the fund tracks the change in spreads of the underlying assets. If a credit event occurs then the position returns the notional value invested and this is invested into alternative positions within the fund's portfolio. For the alternative assets, we follow the ethos of Pesaran, Schleicher, and Zaffaroni (2009) by choosing a broad set of investible assets that span multiple asset classes with daily data, albeit in our case across a far larger cross section. Pesaran, Schleicher, and Zaffaroni (2009) solve for portfolios and test the efficacy of multiple dynamic covariance models. Yet, the cross-sectional magnitude of our portfolios is far larger and it is computationally impractical to optimise across multiple model classes. Hence, in our framework we use an exponentially weighted moving average and optimise across the single decay parameter.

We initially take an agnostic view on the morality of such positions and simply seek to quantify the potential gains associated with these positions. To our knowledge, this is the first paper of its type and our results are of relevance to investors, issuers and regulators involved with the CDS market, which as of August 2009, had a total notional amount under protection of approximately 31 trillion US dollars.[6] We utilise the entire CMA database provided by Thompson Reuters from 2004 onwards and build sector-level portfolios of CDS positions for the US, UK, European Monetary Union (EMU) and Japan. The portfolios can be regarded as exchange-traded funds (ETFs) with exposure to changes in the spreads on protection of the underlying corporate debt. We mix these CDS funds into a larger pool of funds covering five other asset classes. We take the position of a fund of funds rebalancing its portfolio across these available assets, using a standard mean variance approach. As a reference portfolio, we then build an alternative fund of funds with the CDS positions restricted to a zero holding and rebalancing across the remaining unrestricted instruments.

For brevity, we liberally interchange between 'fund' and 'basket'. In both senses we are referring to an individual collection of tradeable positions. For example, we can think of an individual synthetic fund investing in CDSs of varying maturities on bonds issued by EMU automotive firms. In this sense, basket refers to the collection of tradeable positions and fund refers to the dollar return on those positions. The complete list of funds/baskets included in this study is reported in Table A3 and its construction is discussed in more detail in Section 3. We also refer to a block of funds in terms of *asset class*, e.g. CDS or equity. However, this again is slightly disingenuous as, for example, the commodities and foreign exchange funds are tracking indices that include a variety of spot, forward and future rates. Furthermore, we divide most of our estimated results over two sample periods: from 1 January 2004 to 31 July 2007 and from 1 August 2007 to 2 April 2010. While there is not a clear-cut consensus as to the exact starting point of the financial crisis, the summer of 2007 seems to be a reasonable choice to partition our analysis and *prima facia* evidence from the evolution of our portfolios supports this assumption.

To the best of our knowledge, empirical work on portfolio diversification and CDS as tradeable assets is non-existent. Although CDSs can introduce an extra diversification component in portfolios, an argument against CRT via CDSs is that it leads to greater retention by financial institutions of 'toxic waste' assets that are particularly illiquid and vulnerable to macroeconomic performance. Wagner (2007) shows that the increased portfolio diversification possibilities introduced by CRT can increase the probability of liquidity-based crises. The reason is that the increased diversification leads banks to reduce the amount of liquid assets they hold and increase the amount of risky assets. It has also been suggested, for example, by Acharya and Johnson (2007) that because a bank typically has inside information regarding a borrower's credit quality, the bank could use CRT to exploit sellers of credit protection.

Our results show that holding CDS positions without actually holding the equivalent amount of reference entity to the notional can provide an effective hedging tool against a negative shock to instruments unrelated to the actual CDS reference entity. The effect of a significant increase in default risk in a single reference entity has implications for many correlated instruments. Therefore, the required capital gain associated with the holding of a CDS position against default risk typically far outweighs the total value of the reference entities issued bonds. Consequently, holding a broad cross section of naked CDS positions seems to offer an offsetting device against both default and capital risk. In particular, we show that for a log-utility maximising investor over the sample period from 1 January 2004 to 2 April 2010 (effectively the longest sample period available for CDS on corporate bonds), the inclusion of a broad set of CDS baskets in a mixed portfolio offsets capital risk by approximately 10% and increases risk-adjusted returns by 28% per annum.

For all of our simulated investment strategies, the risk-adjusted returns are higher when the CDS basket is included. In the case of a simple equally weighting investor, the portfolio with CDS positions outperforms the restricted reference portfolio by nominally 8%, with a corresponding 17% increase in standard deviation. However, the low correlation between the portfolios results in a β of only 19% and a risk-adjusted excess return of just over 13%. An additional benefit is that for all strategy types and rebalancing frequencies, the inclusion of the CDS baskets reduces total portfolio turnover even when 46 extra fund baskets are included. This result clearly demonstrates that fund of funds portfolio compositions are more stable when naked CDS positions are included.

The intuition for these findings is that, in the event of a downturn/crisis, equity prices and commodities will decline as pressure is placed on dividends and bankruptcy risk increases. Capital flight to sovereign bonds in reserve currencies, such as the dollar and the yen, and the increased risk of default will depress sovereign bond yields and cause the required rate of return on corporate debt to increase. However, the CDS premium will widen on both sovereign and corporate debt and hence naked CDS positions will naturally hedge many other asset classes while additionally protecting against default risk. In the case of foreign exchange (FOREX) exposures, the naked CDS positions assist in hedging volatility risk as differential impacts on sovereign bond yields will lead to more volatile exchange rates. To exemplify, an investor is compensated for the rise in exchange rate volatility through an increase in returns on the traded CDS positions. Anecdotal evidence suggests that, under adverse market conditions, this volatility feedback results in a rise in spreads on non-reserve debt instruments. In the case of an upturn, the inverse is also true. Equity price rises will increase the implied value of assets relative to the value of liabilities, leading to a fall in the probability of default. This in turn, will cause a narrowing of the spread and results in a reduction in the value of CDS positions.

We model the returns on naked CDS positions to capture the day-to-day variation in the quoted spreads. The profits and losses on these rolled positions are reinvested back into the fund. As such, in effect it tracks a weighted average of the constituent spreads. Several CDS indices following this approach and a variety of ETFs are available to buy exposure to these indices. Deutsche Bank provides ETFs on a number of short positions tracking the iTraxx five-year total return index on the spreads of 125 underlying names. A large number of investment banks provide spread trackers for both long and short positions. In terms of direct implementation of CDS arbitrage opportunities, at present 28 hedge funds out of 8359 listed on the HedgeFund.net data set (2009) of North American hedge funds list *capital structure arbitrage* as a primary or secondary strategy. In addition to these, 138 hedge funds list themselves as fixed income arbitragers. Our analysis restricts itself to addressing the viable returns from the current available CDS positions on the CMA database.

3. Mark-to-market returns on CDS positions

In a CDS transaction, the buyer makes periodic payments to the seller and in return receives a payoff if the underlying instrument defaults. Another way of viewing this transaction is that the buyer is acquiring the right to protect the notional value of the underlying asset at a particular payment rate (quoted in basis points per fixed amount of the underlying notional).

In this paper, we specifically focus on the mark-to-market returns on the CDS. It is important to observe that we have deliberately excluded default events as these are impossible to quantify in a portfolio without explicitly identifying the notional amount protected by the position.

We begin our discussion with a simple example to illustrate our approach to CDS trading. We then provide a more complete description of the market and demonstrate why in theory CDS should be a redundant asset in the market. We consider a hedge fund called *Pessimist* that wishes to speculate on the deterioration in the credit quality of a basket of corporate bonds. The *Pessimist* fund wishes to invest a fixed amount $V = \$1$ million in this position. For simplicity, we assume that the corporate bonds belong to a sector that contains one hundred named entities issuing corporate debt with very long maturities. As such, these securities are in effect perpetuities. Note that at this stage, we do not consider the required rate of return on the defaultable bonds.

For an equally weighted basket of CDS in these one hundred reference entities, the offered CDS spread is $\kappa_t^{\text{offered}} = 200$ basis points. Moreover, we assume that the *Pessimist* fund has private information that suggests that the basket will be trading at $\kappa_t^{\text{ask}} = 215$ basis points tomorrow. The *Pessimist* fund buys a notional amount of naked protection on a $\text{Notional}_t = \$50$ million of the reference name. This is an agreement to pay a quarterly cash flow of $\text{Payment}_t = \$1$ million for the period until the end of the maturity of the CDS, deferred by one quarter. For brevity, suppose that this is a perpetual arrangement with a global risk-free rate of $\beta = 2.5\%$. The present value of this cash flow to the counterparty is approximately $V(\text{Payment}) = \$40$ million.

The *Pessimist* fund then waits for a period of time – in this case one day – and re-enters the market and sells protection to fully offset the notional naked position. Note that since we assume an interval of one day we do not discount the notional. Additionally, let us assume the following: the *Pessimist* fund was correct in its expectations; the market perception of the creditworthiness underlying bonds has deteriorated and the spread is now being asked at $\kappa_t^{\text{ask}} = 215$ basis points.

Assuming also that the time period is reasonably short, the trader now enters the market and sells protection on a $\text{Notional}_{t+1} = \$50$ million at $\kappa_t^{\text{ask}} = 215$, which is an agreement to receive $\text{Income} = \$1,075,000$ at every future quarter from $t+1$. Again for simplicity, this is assumed to be a perpetuity. The value of this income stream is approximately $V(\text{Income}) = \$43$ million. The *Pessimist* fund can now enter into an exercise of portfolio compression, whereby the matched pair of CDS positions is sold onto to a third party for the difference in $V(\text{Income})$ and $V(\text{Payment})$. We can see that the profit on the exercise is 7.5%, i.e. the difference in investing in a perpetual risk-free rate at 2.5% and the cash flow from the CDS transactions.[7]

In this case no cash has been paid upfront. Hence, the issue to be explored in details is how the $V = \$1$ million is invested. To buy the original naked position, a certain amount of collateral needs to be pledged. In such a manner, the fund can show its commitment to honour its contractual obligations. We postulate that for an ongoing contract, the hedge fund needs to put on cash in the first quarter similar to the case of a first payment upfront in a CDS contract. The fund would not wish to enter into a contract to continuously pay the protection leg. Therefore, the pessimist will offset her position against a brief calender spread. By contrast, another fund, the *Optimist*, expects a contraction in the default spread. As a result, it will enter into the opposing position. In the case of a contraction in the spread to $\kappa_t^{\text{ask}} = 185$, then the *Pessimist* fund will not be able to fully offset the outflow from the protection leg of the first transaction and the present value of the back-to-back transaction will be approximately $V(\text{Income}) = \$37$ million. Therefore, the rate of return on the initial pledge of $V = \$1$ million is -7.5%. The change in value of each unit of currency thus is proportional to the percentage change in the calender spread, adjusting for the spread bid and spread offered.

In accounting for the value of this protection, a naked CDS position is booked at mark to market using the same approach as if it were continually offset (albeit from the mid price ignoring the liquidity component). In the event of a default, the value of the notional amount protected is released. This is booked as a return over the present value of the promised cash flow. In the case of the *Pessimist* fund, in the event of a default before the offsetting position is enacted, the accounting profit booked would be \$50 million − \$1 million = \$49 million.

3.1 *CDS in a complete market*

Above we have illustrated an example of a strategy by which CDSs can be used to speculate on the deterioration of creditworthiness of the underlying instruments. Next, we demonstrate how CDSs fit into a complete market of alternative non-redundant assets in a more general context. To justify the construction of our nominal returns on a naked CDS contract, we follow an adaptation of the model of Bielecki and Rutkowski (2002) and Bielecki, Jeanblanc, and Rutkowski (2005). Adopting the notation scheme in Musiela and Rutkowski (2005), we define a random default time τ on a filtered probability space $(\Omega, \mathcal{G}, \mathbb{Q})$ with jump process $H_t = \mathbf{1}_{\tau \leq t}$. The associated jump filtration $\mathbb{H}$ is generated by this default time process. Furthermore, we define an auxiliary stochastic process with filtration $\mathbb{F}$ such that $\mathcal{G}_t = \sigma(\mathcal{H}_t, \mathcal{F}_t)$ for every $t \in \mathbb{R}_+$. For a defaultable claim with promised payoffs X, promised dividends A and recovery process Z, designated (X, A, Z, τ) maturing at time T, X is an $\mathcal{F}_T$ measurable random variable, A is an adapted process with finite variation and filtration in $\mathbb{F}$ and Z is an $\mathbb{F}$-predictable process. The cash flows of a dividend process D maturing at time T is

$$D_t = X\mathbf{1}_{\tau>T}\mathbf{1}_{t>\infty}(t) + \int_0^t (1 - H_u)\,\mathrm{d}A_u + \int_0^t Z_u\,\mathrm{d}H_u, \tag{1}$$

where $\mathbf{1}$ is the indicator function and the premium at $t = 0$ is considered, by convention, to be equal to zero. If $A_t = -\kappa t$ for some constant $\kappa > 0$, then the price of the CDS is the continuously credit default spread or premium. Typically, in a CDS contract the promised payoff, X, is zero and Z is determined with reference to a specific recovery rate, for example, 25%. This is represented by

$$\int_0^t (1 - H_u)\, \mathrm{d}A_u = \int_0^t \mathbf{1}_{\tau > u}\, \mathrm{d}A_u = A_{\tau-}\mathbf{1}_{(\tau \leq t)} + A_\tau \mathbf{1}_{(\tau > t)}. \tag{2}$$

In the event of a default, the remaining promised dividend $A_t - A_{t-}$ can be disregarded. Therefore,

$$\int_0^t Z_u\, \mathrm{d}H_u = Z_{\min(\tau,t)}\mathbf{1}_{(\tau \leq t)} = Z_\tau \mathbf{1}_{(\tau \leq t)}. \tag{3}$$

For an investor purchasing a defaultable claim at t, $D_u - D_t$, $u \in [t, T]$, denotes all cash flows received from the defaultable claim over the time frame u. For a risk neutral probability measure $\mathbb{Q}^*$, such that $\mathbb{Q}$ is on $(\Omega, \mathcal{G}_t)$, the value of a unit of account $B = S^k$ is $B_t = \exp \int_0^t r_u\, du$ for a continuous interest rate r_t. The discounted price of an asset S^{i*} is $S_t^{i*} = S_t^i B_t^{-1}$, for $i \in 1, \dots, k-1$ assets with nominal price S^i on a filtered probability space $(\Omega, \mathbb{G}, \mathbb{Q})$, where $\mathbb{Q}$ is the observed measure. Note that this is the complete market with arbitrage-free pricing described in Karatzas (1996), Karatzas (2006). To this setup, we add the traded security of a defaultable claim, with price S, by convention considered to be asset zero. We now introduce a process $x \in \mathbb{R}^{k+1}$ measured on $\mathbb{G}$ representing a trading strategy, where x_t^j is the investment weighting of a $j \in 0, \dots, k$ indexed Arrow–Debreu asset held at time t.

3.2 *Trading protection in a complete market*

We can think of the combination of a fully protected portfolio of a defaultable bond and insurance as a synthetic risk-free rate. A natural question that arises is whether a fully replicating position is possible to short a default. Brigo and Mercurio (2006) suggest that it is not fully replicating unless a position is constructed by which one can borrow at the defaultable rate and signal the intention to default in a manner that is synchronised with the reference asset. The CDS instrument completes this aspect of the market by allowing the creation of a position that replicates the intention to issue defaultable cash flow with default characteristics identical to the reference defaultable without actually being the reference entity. The information conveyed by the traded price of the CDS is in the form of $\mathcal{G}_t$. We need to extract this information from the quoted data to understand whether the CDS price is completing the market.

At time $t = 0$, one unit of S is purchased at an initial price S_0 and it is held until expiration T. Following Brigo and Mercurio (2005) and Bielecki, Jeanblanc, and Rutkowski (2005), if all the proceeds from the savings account are reinvested in B, i.e. $x = \{x_0 = 1, x_{k+1} = x^k\}$, the wealth process $U(x)$ is $U_t(x) = S_t + x_t^k B_t, \forall t \in [0, T]$. As with a conventional derivative, the self-financing value of the portfolio is driven by a differential equation, $\mathrm{d}U_t(x) = \mathrm{d}S_t + \mathrm{d}D_t + x_t^k\, \mathrm{d}B_t$. Therefore, for every $t \in [0, T]$, the nominal wealth is

$$U_t(x) - U_0(x) = S_t - S_0 + D_t + \int_0^t x_u^k\, \mathrm{d}B_u \tag{4}$$

and the relative wealth is

$$U_t^*(x) = U_t^*(x) + S_t^* - S_t^* + \int_0^t S_u(S^*)^{-1}\, \mathrm{d}D_u. \tag{5}$$

Bielecki, Jeanblanc, and Rutkowski (2005) derive the ex-dividend continuous price process of the defaultable claim at $t \in [0, T]$ as

$$S_t = B_t \mathbb{E}_{Q^*}\left(\int_t^T B_u^{-1}\,\mathrm{d}D_u \,\middle|\, \mathcal{G}_t\right). \tag{6}$$

If we now consider a CDS, with spread κ, this is a defaultable claim $(0, A, Z, \tau)$, where $Z_t = \delta(t)$, $A = -\kappa t$ for every $t \in [0, T]$, $\delta : [0, T] \to \mathbb{R}$ is a càdlàg function that represents the protection payment and κ denotes the spread or the premium of a CDS. Bielecki and Rutkowski (2002) provide a simple model of default where the filtration $\mathbb{G} = \mathbb{H}$ is generated by a counting process $H_t = \mathbf{1}_{\{\tau \le t\}}$. For a survival probability function $G = 1 - F$, where F is a cumulative distribution of the default time τ under $\mathbb{Q}^*$, such that $G(t) > 0$, $\forall t \in [0, T]$. For the purposes of our analysis, suppose that the CDS position is being rolled over every day. Therefore, we assume that the interest $r \to 0$. From this setup, the ex- dividend price of the CDS is

$$S_t(\kappa) = \mathbb{E}_{\mathbb{Q}^*}(\delta(\tau)\mathbf{1}_{\{t<\tau\le T\}} - \mathbf{1}_{\{t<\tau\}}\kappa(\min(\tau, T) - t)|\mathcal{H}_t). \tag{7}$$

Hence, the ex-dividend price at time $t \in [s, T]$, for a CDS instigated at some time s before t, is

$$S_t(\kappa) = \mathbf{1}_{\{t<\tau\}}\frac{1}{G(t)}\left(-\int_t^T \delta(u)\,\mathrm{d}G(u) - \kappa\int_t^T G(u)\,\mathrm{d}u\right). \tag{8}$$

We now present an important definition for the nominal return calculation on a CDS contract with changing spread. The spread $\kappa(s, T)$ of a CDS at the inception of the contract is determined by $S_s(\kappa(s, T)) = 0$. For the T maturity market spread, the value of the contract is the solution to

$$\int_s^T \delta(u)\,\mathrm{d}G(u) + \kappa(s, T)\int_s^T G(u)\,\mathrm{d}u = 0 \tag{9}$$

and therefore for a traded CDS for $s \in [0, T]$, the spread is

$$\kappa(s, T) = \int_s^T \delta(u)\,\mathrm{d}G(u)\left(\int_s^T G(u)\,\mathrm{d}u\right)^{-1}. \tag{10}$$

The difference $v(t, s) = \kappa(t) - \kappa(s)$ represents the calendar spread between s and t and for a rolled over position such that $t - s$ is a short time period where $v(t, s)$ represents the nominal return on the naked-only position. In the next section, we provide an alternative implementation of the problem under investigation by letting the portfolio weights rebalance across a very broad set of assets. We define a vector process of dollar positions (normalised as weights) $x(t) = [x'(t)_{\text{CDS}}, x'(t)_{\text{Alt}}]'$ for the CDS and alternative asset funds.

3.3 *Trading strategies and unit of account*

Consider a quoted naked CDS spread at time t with offered spread $\kappa_t^{\text{offered}}$, spread ask κ_t^{ask} and transacted spread κ_t^{trans}. The contract inception is at $t_0 < t < T$ and the discounted value of the outflows is given by $\pi(\kappa_{i,t}^{\text{trans}}, V_t, T - t)$ for protection held, where V_t is the notional amount under protection. We now consider a fund that purchases protection at t and then sells protection at $t + \Delta t$. This generates a cash flow with the expected value

$$\tilde{\Lambda}_{i,t} = B_{\Delta t}^{-1}(\pi_{t+\Delta t}(\kappa_{i,t}^{\text{trans}}, B_{\Delta t}^{-1}V_t, T - t, B_t) - \pi_t(\kappa_{i,t}^{\text{trans}}, V_t, T - t, B_t)). \tag{11}$$

The period Δt is the short exposure time on the CDS position. Suppose this a very short period, say a day, and assuming no default event, the value of the cash flow is approximated by the spread bid to spread offered in the market. Then if $B_{\Delta t}^{-1} \to 1$ and the variation is driven by an affine transformation of $\kappa_{i,t}^{\text{trans}}$, the price at which counterparties are willing to buy or sell protection in the market is equal to

$$\tilde{\Lambda}_{i,t} \approx \kappa_{t+\Delta t}^{\text{offered}} - \kappa_t^{\text{ask}}. \tag{12}$$

We term this the realised calender spread. The trader can leverage the position $\tilde{\Lambda}_{i,t}$ by a factor V_t. The initial trade is of course costless. However, with the offset position, the variation in $\kappa_{t+\Delta t}^{\text{offered}} | \kappa_t^{\text{ask}}, \kappa_t^{\text{offered}}, \kappa_t^{\text{trans}}$ provides the account payoff risk.

4. Empirical methodology and data

Conceptually, traded protection instruments such as CDSs have a particular payoff structure that in some way could be replicated by combinations of other instruments within a large market of alternatives. In this section, our aim is to determine whether CDS positions, aggregated as fund baskets, have a replicable return and risk diversification profile relative to a large set of alternative assets. The short available sample is generally unsuitable for more traditional long-run covariance/regression analysis such as the approach suggested in Campbell, Serfaty-De-Madeiros, and Viciera (2010). Consequently, we restrict our approach to an analysis of portfolio returns and portfolio correlation structures, via bootstrap resampling. Following the theoretical framework presented in Section 3 whereby prices are set in the risk neutral universe, we operationalise our empirical approach from the viewpoint of a risk-averse fund management. This reduces the portfolio problem to a smooth mean variance optimisation procedure and this is critical when dealing with such a large assets universe.

Alternative approaches to identifying the correct benchmark return would be to derive the specific replicating portfolio specifically for each individual contract from the partial differential equation suggested in Section 3. The drawback here is identical to the issue faced when analysing the correct futures hedge. It is impractical to precisely match individual spot and derivative contracts. Therefore, the replicating hedge is not easily identifiable. We choose to benchmark our CDS positions against restricted portfolios using a historical mean variance optimisation approach, in the spirit of Kroner and Sultan (1993), but incorporating a randomised robustness check. In other words, we view the problem as a risk-averse mean variance optimiser and if substantial and excess returns are observed when CDS positions are included in the portfolio relative to a restricted benchmark then we conclude that the portfolio cannot be replicating in this manner.

The general orientation of the optimisation problem is from the view of the second-order expansion of a smooth at least twice differentiable utility function of wealth, $u(w_t)$, whereby the expected utility at a terminal time period T, is given by

$$\mathbb{E}(u(w_T;\theta)) = u(w_0;\theta) + u'(w_0;\theta)\mathbb{E}(w_t - w_0) + \tfrac{1}{2}u''(w_0;\theta)\mathbb{E}(w_t - w_0)^2, \tag{13}$$

where the first two moments of the wealth-generating process are

$$\mathbb{E}(w_t - w_0) = w_0 \exp\left(\int_0^t x'(t)\mathbb{E}(r(t))\,\mathrm{d}t\right), \tag{14}$$

$$\mathbb{E}(w_t - w_0)^2 = w_0^2 \exp\left(\int_0^t x'(t)\Sigma(t)x(t)\,\mathrm{d}t\right). \tag{15}$$

The optimisation problem is of the form $\max_{x(t)} \mathbb{E}(u(w_T;\theta))$. Where θ is a vector of utility function parameters, $x(t)$ is the vector of portfolio weights, $r(t)$ is the vector portfolio returns process and

$\Sigma(t)$ is a time-varying variance covariance matrix. The expected utility maximisation problem can be orientated to maximise directly 14. Or by constraining the problem by setting a target level of risk, which is indeed a common hedge fund strategy.

We utilise three strategies. First, we impose a power utility with unit risk aversion. Thus, the utility function simplifies to $u(w_t;\theta) = \log(w_t)$ and the expected utility maximisation is

$$\max_{x(t)} \int_0^t x'(t)\mathbb{E}(r(t))\,\mathrm{d}t - \frac{1}{2}\int_0^t x'(t)\Sigma(t)x(t)\,\mathrm{d}t. \tag{16}$$

For a target risk level σ^2, the optimisation is

$$\max_{x(t)} \mathbb{E}(u(w_T;\theta)) \left| \int_0^t x'(t)\Sigma(t)x(t)\,\mathrm{d}t = \sigma^2. \right. \tag{17}$$

And finally for a target minimum variance level

$$\max_{x(t)} \mathbb{E}(u(w_T;\theta)) \left| \min \int_0^t x'(t)\Sigma(t)x(t)\,\mathrm{d}t. \right. \tag{18}$$

The simple objective here is to randomly impose asset class restrictions and then run the portfolios recursively over the large cross section of assets and compare this to the systematic restriction.

Having set the investor portfolio optimisation conditions, we construct broad highly diversified portfolios consisting of funds drawn from six asset classes: CDS, equity, corporate bonds, sovereign bonds, FOREX and commodities. These asset classes are further decomposed into sub-baskets of simulated funds that consist of a very large number of underlying positions. The components of these funds are weighted by asset class convention: equal weights for the CDS baskets, capitalisation weights for equity baskets, equal weights for bonds, trade weights for FOREX and production weights for commodities. The full list of 255 funds is presented in Table A3. We define 'broad' as an individual fund that invests in more than 12 underlying instruments. Our approach simulates a set of dollar funds investing in these baskets and a fund of funds that optimises across these individual funds.

To analyse the return structure of CDS positions within this large cross section of alternative assets, we employ a large-scale *ex-ante* back-tested optimisation, whereby we construct simple rolling mean variance forecasts for the broad cross section of assets that are optimised recursively. We then apply systematic and random restrictions on various assets and re-apply the back testing on the restricted set. For each portfolio, we record the daily returns and variances as well as the internal correlation structures. We then compare the properties of the randomly restricted portfolios with the systematic restrictions.

Our empirical strategy is to consider a single class of CDS positions for a given sector consisting of equally weighted naked CDS positions for all available maturities. For a change in the spread $\Delta\kappa_t$, we compute a nominal change in the value of a single unit position following the definitions set out in Equations (7)–(10). For a back-to-back trade over $t + \Delta t$, where we assume Δt is one day, the fund is adjusted on a daily basis to capture the return on the changing spread. For simplicity, we assume that the overnight unit of account is stored as cash and therefore the interest rate is zero. This trading strategy in CDS positions results in a large number of outstanding contracts. At regular intervals, hedge funds and other investment vehicles undertake a process of 'portfolio compression', whereby the notional size and number of outstanding contracts are reduced by terminating contracts and then replacing them with a smaller number of trades with the same payoff structure.

We equally weight 2846 CDS positions into 51 sector funds for the US, UK, EMU and Japan. We include all available corporate CDS positions for the US, UK, EMU and Japanese corporate bonds traded for the period from 1 January 2004 to 2 April 2010. Note that certain CDS position data are available from 1 January 2003. However, the early spreads exhibit stale pricing effects. Hence, our sample begins on 1 January 2004. Additionally, we simulate ETFs that invest in all the US, UK, EMU and Japanese listed equities and construct 40 funds defined by country and sector. All available US, UK, EMU and Japanese corporate bonds are grouped by country and sector into 60 funds. All available US, UK, EMU and Japanese sovereign bond yields for 2-, 3-, 5-, 7-, 10-, 15-, 20- and 30-year maturities are divided into 30 macro-funds, classified by country and maturity. To include foreign exchange exposures, we use trade-weighted indices for 46 currencies and we also include 28 broad commodity indices consisting of multiple futures positions. These instruments are then placed into 255 funds and weighted in the fund of fund portfolio optimisation.

Table A3 describes each asset class.[8] To derive returns on these fund baskets, we adopt the following approach. First, CDS returns are equally weighted and quoted as spread bid to spread ask. Second, equities are indexed in terms of total return, adjusted for dividends, the bid–ask spread and weighted by market capitalisation. Third, corporate and sovereign bonds are equally weighted and indexed as total returns, with all gross coupons reinvested. Fourth, currency baskets are computed in returns at trade weights. Finally, commodities' indices are computed from production-weighted portfolios, adjusted for the bid–ask spread. All instruments returns are in US dollars. Table 1 provides summary information for our total return methodologies and for all the aggregated underlying positions and funds by asset class.

Our sample period starts on 1 January 2004 and runs daily until 2 April 2010. This yields 1621 trading days of data. We utilise the first 100 days of the sample to initialise the econometric analysis of the expected mean and variance for the portfolio weights optimisation. Our portfolio optimisations are assumed to be dynamic over the period, rebalancing over a time horizon of s days at set periods, $t_1, t_2, \ldots, t_3$.

4.1 *Portfolio construction*

We define a vector of nominal daily returns on CDS positions and alternative asset positions as being $r_t = [r'_{\text{CDS},t}, r'_{\text{Alt},t}]'$, where $r_{\text{Alt},t}$ is the collection of non-CDS assets

$$r_{\text{Alt},t} = [r'_{\text{Equity},t}, r'_{\text{Forex},t}, r'_{\text{Corp},t}, r'_{\text{Sov},t}, r'_{\text{Comms},t}]'. \tag{19}$$

We refer to this as the reference portfolio. The time t expected returns, conditional on the current information set Ω_t, is therefore $\mathbb{E}_t(r_t|\Omega_t) = \mu_t$. The time t residuals are $r_t - \mu_t = u_t$ and hence the time t conditional covariance matrix can be written as

$$\Sigma_{t|t=1,\ldots,t=t-1} = \mathbb{E}_t((r_t - \mu_t)(r_t - \mu_t)'|\Omega_t) \tag{20}$$

For the three rebalancing regimes, weekly, monthly and quarterly for a set of portfolio weights x_t, such that the realised portfolio returns are $r_{p,t} = x'_t r_t$, the expected portfolio returns and portfolio conditional standard deviations are defined respectively as

$$\mathbb{E}_t(r_{p,t}) = x'_t \mu_t, \quad \sigma_p = (x'_t \Sigma_t x_t)^{1/2}. \tag{21}$$

We confine our analysis to three investor types with corresponding portfolio optimisation problems. First, the minimum variance portfolio-targeting investor who rebalances her portfolio with

Table 1. Summary of fund positions and valuations.

Asset class	Positions	Fund baskets	Daily obs.	Total obs. (bid, ask, transacted)
CDS	2846	51	1621	248,013
Equities	25,922	40	1621	194,520
Corporate bonds	10,545	60	1621	291,780
Sovereign bonds	2886	30	1621	145,890
FOREX[a]	46	46	1621	223,698
Commodities[b]	314	28	1621	136,164
Total	42,559	255		1,240,065

Notes: For the FOREX and commodities' funds, we use the existing broad-based baskets that are currently available to benchmark several ETFs. These are provided by J.P. Morgan and Standard & Poor's/Goldman Sachs, respectively. The remaining four asset classes are subdivided into fund baskets aggregated from individual tradeable positions. In essence, for each basket we conceive of an available ETF that tracks the positions, transaction cost adjusted. CDS returns are equally weighted and quoted as spread bid to spread ask and the motivation for this return calculation is described in Section 3. Defaults are recorded, but we assume that they are fully offset. Therefore, we are only interested in the return on the realised calender spread (see Section 3). For the equity positions, we consider funds that are exposed to the complete cross section of the US, UK, EMU and Japanese stocks. The indices are total return in the sense that dividends are assumed to be reinvested in the fund. Moreover, transaction costs are adjusted on a daily basis via the daily average bid–ask spread. Returns on corporate bonds are computed using the Merrill Lynch-Bank of America bond index total return methodology. This methodology assumes that gross coupons are reinvested into the bonds. For a basket of k bonds, the total return is

$$RI_t = RI_t\left(\frac{\sum_{i=1}^{k}(P_{i,t}+A_{i,t}+CP_{i,t})N_{i,t-1}}{\sum_{i=1}^{k}(P_{i,t-1}+A_{i,t-1}+CP_{i,t-1})N_{i,t-1}}\right),$$

where P is the clean price of the ith bond at time t, adjusted for any partial serial redemptions. A is the accrued interest to the 'normal' settlement date. N is the nominal value of amount outstanding, if known, otherwise the issued amount and CP is an adjustment made for bonds that have ex-dividends. The discrepancy between the number of fund baskets for the CDS, equity and corporate bond baskets is due to the industry classification used to identify each instrument. For the CDS positions, the industry identifier is derived from the underlying corporate bond. In total, there are 60 unique available country–sectors identified on the CMA database, from which we draw 51 CDS positions. For equities, one digit SIC codes are used and this generates 40 unique fund baskets. Unfortunately, the level of overlap for each country–sector is not perfectly uniform for the SIC codes. The total return on sovereign bond baskets is computed in the same way as the return on corporate baskets and we include all of the bonds in the Merrill Lynch-Bank of America bond tracker funds.
Source: Thomson Reuters and Bank of America.
Source: J.P. Morgan Broad Trade Weighted Indices Methodology 2010. S&P GSCI Index Methodology 2010.
[a]FOREX funds are supposed to track the J.P. Morgan Broad Trade Weighted Index. These indices are designed to be tracked by ETFs and consist of a basket of multiple forward rates, trade weighted over a basket of currencies.
[b]Commodities' funds are supposed to track the Standard and Poor's-Goldman Sachs commodity index (S&P GSCI). This is a production-weighted index of liquid futures positions over multiple maturities. These indices track the complete 12-month futures curve and are computed over 30,000 individual contracts per annum. Several ETFs are available to track these indices. In total, we utilise 42,559 individual data series to construct 255 funds for which we can compute nominal returns. Nevertheless, the total number of actual underlying positions is in excess of 100,000 depending on the inclusion criteria for the FOREX and commodities' baskets.

objective function

$$\sigma_{\min,p} \triangleq \min_{x_t}(x_t'\Sigma_t x_t)^{1/2}, \tag{22}$$

where $x_{\min,t}$ are the target weights for the minimum variance portfolio. We follow standard hedge fund covenants and set a 6% concentration limit in each of the 255 funds. The second investor type targets a logarithmic utility function and as such seeks to maximise the following:

$$\mathbb{E}_t(u(r_t)|x_{\text{util},t}) = \max_{x_t}(x_t'\mu_t - \tfrac{1}{2}x_t'\Sigma_t x_t). \tag{23}$$

The final investor type targets the maximum return subject to a particular annualised standard deviation $\bar{\sigma}_p$. The objective function is therefore

$$\mathbb{E}_t(r_{p,t}|x_{\text{risk},t}) \triangleq \max_{x_t} x_t'\mu_t \quad \text{subject to } (x_t'\Sigma_t x_t)^{1/2} = \bar{\sigma}_p. \tag{24}$$

In addition to the actively rebalanced portfolios, we construct an equally weighted benchmark portfolio r_{eq} as an alternative reference entity.

Optimisation criterion	Reference portfolio designation	Test portfolio designation
Minimum variance	$r_{p,\text{minex}}$	$r_{p,\text{min}}$
Logarithmic utility	$r_{p,\text{utilex}}$	$r_{p,\text{util}}$
Variance targeting	$r_{p,\text{riskex}}$	$r_{p,\text{risk}}$
Equally weighted	$r_{p,\text{equalex}}$	$r_{p,\text{equal}}$

4.2 *Robust covariance estimation*

Kyj, Ostdiek, and Ensor (2010) introduce a shrinkage estimator on high-frequency data and we follow strictly this approach to ensure that the portfolio weights are derived from a well-conditioned matrix. The basic conditional covariance matrix is constructed from an exponentially weighted moving average model with bandwidth α and lagged kernel weighting $h_i = (1-\alpha)^i, \forall i \in \{1, \ldots, l\}$ to compute the expected returns and covariances. The number of lags containing the $\lambda = 99\%$ mass is $l = \log(1-\lambda)/\log(1-\alpha)$. The optimal bandwidth parameter for the mean model is computed via the minimum mean- squared error. A further important attribute of our analysis is that we set the expected return $\mu_t = \sum_{i=1}^{l} h_i r_{t-i}$ and then collect the sequence of past abnormal returns $u_{t-1}', u_{t-2}', \ldots, u_{t-u}'$. Due to the high dimensionality of the system, the conditioning of the covariance matrix is an issue. Therefore, we optimise the covariance estimation over the bandwidth parameter h

$$\Sigma_t = \sum_{i=1}^{l} h_i u_{t-i} u_{t-i}'. \tag{25}$$

Table 2. Block covariances and correlations.

	CDS	Equities	Corporate bonds	Sovereign bonds	FOREX	Commodities
CDS	2601	2040	3060	1530	2346	1428
Equities		1600	2400	1200	1840	1120
Corporate bonds			3600	1800	2760	1680
Sovereign bonds				900	1380	840
FOREX					2116	1288
Commodities						784

Notes: The total number of block covariances $\Sigma_t = [\Sigma_{i,j,t}]$ and correlations $R_t = [R_{i,j,t}]$ are estimated daily using the exponentially weighted moving average methodology outlined in Section 5, $i, j = \{$CDS, Equities, Corporate bonds, Sovereign bonds, FOREX, Commodities$\}$ index the asset classes. The decay factor for the EWMA is computed using maximum likelihood over the whole sample period. Weights are partitioned $x_t = [x_{i,t}]$, where i indexes the asset class. Optimised portfolios generate weighting matrices $X_{i,j,t} = x_{i,t}x_{j,t}'$ from the quadratic optimisations reported in Section 6. The summations of the daily-weighted correlation matrices $X_{i,j,t} \circ R_{i,j,t}$ are reported in Section 6. These averages are computed via $\rho_{i,j,t} = x_{i,j,t}' R_{i,j,t} x_{i,j,t}$.

The p conditioning number is calculated as follows:

$$\varsigma_t = \|\Sigma_t\|_p \|\Sigma_t^{-1}\|_p. \tag{26}$$

Values of $\varsigma_{p,t}$ near 1 indicate a well-conditioned matrix. Poorly conditioned matrices often have multiple non-convergent solutions. To overcome this issue, we propose the following optimisation procedure. First, we adjust the bandwidth parameter h and hence the $u_{t-i}, \forall i \in \{1, \ldots, l\}$ to generate a set of matrices $U_{j,t}, \forall j \in \{1, \ldots, J\}$. Next, for each matrix we compute the corresponding covariance matrix $\Sigma_{i,t}$ and conditioning number $\varsigma_{i,t}$. Finally, we identify a point at which the reduction in the conditioning number flattens.

5. Portfolio performance and correlation measures

For each portfolio selection strategy, we construct a reference portfolio excluding the CDS baskets, the total number of block correlations is outlined in Table 2. For each portfolio return series, we then utilise a set of conventional portfolio performance tests to compare the relative performance of the test versus the reference portfolios.

5.1 *Total return and risk-adjusted evaluation*

Consider the observed returns of the reference portfolio $r_{\text{ref},t}$ and test portfolio $r_{\text{test},t}$. The mean return is computed by $\mu_{\text{ref}} = T^{-1}\sum_{t=1}^{T} r_{\text{ref},t}$ and $\mu_{\text{test}} = T^{-1}\sum_{t=1}^{T} r_{\text{test},t}$ and the heteroskedasticity and autocorrelation consistent (HAC) variance for each portfolio is determined by $\sigma_{\text{ref}}^2 = h'\Gamma_{\text{ref}}h$ and $\sigma_{\text{test}}^2 = h'\Gamma_{\text{test}}h$, where Γ is the autocovariance matrix and h is the vector of kernel weights with bandwidth parameter λ. Setting ρ to be the unconditional correlation between the reference and test portfolios, we can assume the following: $\text{cov}(r_{\text{ref}}, r_{\text{test}}) = \sigma_{\text{test,ref}} = \rho\sigma_{\text{ref}}\sigma_{\text{test}}$ and $\beta_{\text{test,ref}} = \sigma_{\text{test,ref}}/\sigma_{\text{ref}}^2 = \rho\sigma_{\text{ref}}^{-1}\sigma_{\text{test}}$. We can now set out the conventional portfolio evaluation measures in terms of our notation as

$$\Lambda_{\text{norm1}} = \mu_{\text{test}} - \beta_{\text{test,ref}}\mu_{\text{ref}}, \quad \Lambda_{\text{norm2}} = \frac{\sigma_{\text{test}}}{\sigma_{\text{ref}}}. \tag{27}$$

The excess return Λ_{norm1} captures the risk-adjusted differences in expected and realised returns for the test and reference portfolios. The volatility ratio Λ_{norm2} simply measures the difference between the standard deviations of the test and reference portfolios.

5.2 *Average correlation evaluation*

In the previous section, we have presented performance evaluation tests for the aggregate returns on the reference and test portfolios. We now introduce an alternative and useful measure that focuses on the weighted and unweighted correlations of the reference baskets within the portfolio structure. The test portfolio covariance and correlation matrices are partitioned relative to the reference portfolio as follows:

$$\Sigma_t = \begin{bmatrix} \Sigma_{\text{CDS},t} & \Sigma_{\text{ref,CDS},t} \\ \Sigma_{\text{ref,CDS},t} & \Sigma_{\text{ref},t} \end{bmatrix}, \quad R_t = \begin{bmatrix} R_{\text{CDS},t} & R_{\text{ref,CDS},t} \\ R_{\text{ref,CDS},t} & R_{\text{ref},t} \end{bmatrix}, \tag{28}$$

where $\Sigma_{\text{ref,CDS},t}$ and $R_{\text{ref,CDS},t}$ are the canonical covariance and correlations between the CDS portfolio and the reference portfolio, respectively. Setting the weighting matrix for the reference and test portfolios as $X_{\text{ref},t} = x_{\text{ref},t}x'_{\text{ref},t}$ and $X_{\text{test},t} = x_{\text{test},t}x'_{\text{test},t}$, where for the reference portfolio $x'_{\text{ref},t} = [0', x'_{\text{exCDS}}]'$, we can then develop a weighted average measure of the correlations as follows:

$$\xi_{\text{ref},t} = e'\text{ivech}((R_t - I) \circ X_{\text{ref},t}), \tag{29}$$

$$\xi_{\text{test},t} = e'\text{ivech}((R_t - I) \circ X_{\text{test},t}), \tag{30}$$

where I is an identity matrix of size n_{ref} and n_{test} respectively, $\circ$ is the Hadamard product, n_{ref} is the number of assets in the reference portfolio and n_{test} is the number of elements in the test portfolio. The ivech operator stacks the elements of the upper triangular part of the matrix in a vector. Hence, the weighted correlation test statistic is

$$\Lambda_{\text{corr}} = -T^{-1}\sum_{t=1}^{T} \xi_{\text{ref},t} - \xi_{\text{test},t}. \tag{31}$$

For inference, we use bootstrap resampling to compute the empirical distribution of Λ_{norm1}, Λ_{norm2} and λ_{corr}. This proceeds by resampling with replacement of the vector of time observations $t = 1, \ldots, T$ and computing the empirical 1%, 5% and 10% significance bounds. For comparison, we take the following approach. First, we recompute the test and reference portfolios with each asset class systematically restricted, i.e. $x'_{\text{ref},t} = [0', x'_{\text{exAlt}}]'$, Alt $\in$ {Equity, Forex, Corp, Sov, Comms} and compute Λ_{corr} for each restriction. To ensure robustness, we then repeatedly and randomly restrict m assets where $m \in \{1, \ldots, n\}$, which are randomly sampled from a uniform distribution. We can test whether the change in correlation structure from a systematic restriction of a given asset class is significantly different from a random restriction. This is accomplished by repeating the random restrictions N times and then sorting the resultant Λ_{corr} to compute the appropriate critical bounds. The procedure originates from the method suggested by Muirhead (1981). However, our approach differs from Muirhead (1981) in that we test for the differential correlation between two alternative average measures rather than testing the average correlation against zero. Finally, it is important also to note that we bootstrap resample the correlation test statistics for significance utilising a modification of the correlation bootstrap, as suggested in Hatemi and Roca (2006). Evidence for the stability of the test statistics from Monte-Carlo simulations is available from the authors.

6. Empirical results

Tables A1 and A2 present the descriptive statistics and correlations for the six portfolios aggregating by equally weighted asset classes (designated as the naïve portfolios). The first striking result that we observe is the size of the comparative average annualised returns for each asset class. The CDS baskets are averaging 35.7% per annum over the sample period. Overall this finding is in line with anecdotal evidence for the very large speculative returns to investments in naked CDS positions. The equity and commodities' portfolios reveal an average annualised aggregate return of 8.6% and 6.8%, respectively. Note that these aggregate measures, grouped by asset classes, are useful guidelines in assessing the relative performance of the alternative actively managed portfolios.

The linear correlation between the naïve CDS and equity portfolios is −12.4%. Importantly, this average correlation is stable over the sample period. Accordingly, capital arbitrage strategies are able to generate significant returns by exploiting miss-pricing relative to this negative correlation. As expected, the returns on the CDS portfolios are positively correlated with corporate and sovereign bond portfolios, but are significantly negatively correlated with the FOREX and commodities' portfolios. This measurement is economically important in the sense that the row-wise aggregate correlation with the other five asset classes is −0.72, i.e. an average of −14.4% across asset classes. Therefore, the *long-run* correlations are globally negative. Remarkably, this evidence suggests that overall investments in naked CDS positions do hedge capital risk (as well as default risk) across a wide variety of assets.

6.1 *Risk-adjusted returns versus reference portfolio*

Table 3 reports the results across the 10 portfolios for the comparative risk-adjusted returns set out in test λ_{norm1}. Table 3 shows that the risk-adjusted returns for *every* strategy and rebalancing frequency are higher for the test portfolios. Furthermore, only three portfolios exhibit a standard deviation ratio greater than one. The first is the equally weighted portfolio, while the other two are the weekly and quarterly variance-targeting portfolios, which appear unable to accurately target a particular risk level. Additionally, we bootstrap resample the results reported in column five of Table 3 and find that the positive excess returns are significant at 1% for all the portfolio strategies and rebalancing frequencies. The uniformity of improvement in the portfolios is remarkable and unambiguous. The inclusion of the CDS positions in actively managed portfolios yields substantially higher risk-adjusted returns. More importantly, for higher risk strategies, the return to risk of investing in CDS positions increases. The log-utility portfolios exhibit a 31.32%, 28.00% and 24.45% annualised risk-adjusted excess return over the reference portfolio.

6.2 *Weighted correlations test versus reference portfolio*

Table 4 reports the results for the differences in weighted average correlations between the reference and test portfolios. The first column presents the difference in weighted average correlations when the weights on the CDS funds are restricted to zero, the second column for equity and so on. The table is divided into three sections, namely the weighted difference in correlations over

Table 3. Linear risk adjustments test versus reference portfolios.

	$\hat{r}_{test}$	$\hat{r}_{ref}$	$\beta_{test,ref}$	$\bar{r}_{test}$	$\hat{r}_{test} - \bar{r}_{ref}$	$\frac{\sigma_{test}}{\sigma_{ref}}$
Min. var weekly	0.0338	0.0237	0.7967	0.0189	0.0148	0.9029
Min. var monthly	0.0319	0.0223	0.8089	0.0181	0.0138	0.9195
Min. var quarterly	0.0331	0.0242	0.8081	0.0196	0.0135	0.9283
Log-utility weekly	0.3103	0.1136	−0.0255	−0.0029	0.3132	0.9780
Log-utility monthly	0.2791	0.0985	−0.0099	−0.0009	0.2800	0.9451
Log-utility quarterly	0.2474	0.0912	0.0316	0.0028	0.2445	0.8909
Variance target weekly	0.0481	0.0306	0.8231	0.0252	0.0229	1.0316
Variance target monthly	0.0464	0.0295	0.7985	0.0235	0.0228	0.9964
Variance target quarterly	0.0397	0.0245	0.8289	0.0203	0.0194	1.1386
Equally weighted	0.1466	0.0614	0.1927	0.0118	0.1347	1.1775

Notes: Columns one and two report the respective average nominal returns per annum on the test versus reference portfolios. Column three reports the HAC beta for each portfolio. Column four presents the annualised risk-adjusted expected return on the portfolio relative to the reference benchmark. Column five reports the difference between the reference and test portfolios, Λ_{norm1}. Finally, column six presents the ratio of the HAC standard deviations, Λ_{norm2}. Bootstrap resampling of the return vectors with replacement suggests that all the elements of columns six are significantly different from zero at the 1% level and the elements of column six are all different from one, again at the 1% level.

Table 4. Weighted average correlation differences: test versus reference portfolios.

	Whole sample								
	$x_{\text{CDS}} = 0$	$x_{\text{Equity}} = 0$	$x_{\text{CorpBonds}} = 0$	$x_{\text{SovBonds}} = 0$	$x_{\text{FOREX}} = 0$	$x_{\text{comms}} = 0$	$\alpha = 1\%$	$\alpha = 5\%$	$\alpha = 10\%$
Min. var weekly	0.07348	0.00306	−0.00347	−0.00505	0.04478	0.00219	0.01307	0.01308	0.01309
Min. var monthly	0.07376	0.00306	−0.00343	−0.00505	0.04493	0.00218	0.01318	0.01320	0.01321
Min. var quarterly	0.07547	0.00307	−0.00335	−0.00493	0.04376	0.00218	0.01329	0.01331	0.01331
Log-utility weekly	0.06032	0.02458	0.00326	0.00015	0.00336	0.00944	0.01584	0.01589	0.01592
Log-utility monthly	0.06055	0.02440	0.00340	0.00014	0.00331	0.00930	0.01603	0.01608	0.01610
Log-utility quarterly	0.06085	0.02419	0.00310	0.00014	0.00336	0.00928	0.01642	0.01645	0.01646
Variance target weekly	0.01726	0.00411	−0.00491	−0.00720	0.06190	0.00199	0.00862	0.00869	0.00873
Variance target monthly	0.01675	0.00396	−0.00502	−0.00749	0.06229	0.00194	0.00795	0.00797	0.00799
Variance target quarterly	0.00100	0.00298	−0.00598	−0.00802	0.06423	0.00123	0.00814	0.00815	0.00816
Equally weighted	0.04634	0.01263	−0.00246	−0.00509	0.01375	0.00499	0.00516	0.00517	0.00517
1 January 2004 to 31 July 2007									
Min. var weekly	0.09306	0.00306	−0.00288	−0.00536	0.04858	0.00219	0.01095	0.01100	0.01103
Min. var monthly	0.09372	0.00305	−0.00278	−0.00534	0.04852	0.00217	0.01096	0.01102	0.01104
Min. var quarterly	0.09627	0.00303	−0.00259	−0.00529	0.04722	0.00216	0.01076	0.01081	0.01084
Log-utility weekly	0.04648	0.00907	0.00282	0.00024	0.00484	0.00464	0.01099	0.01109	0.01115
Log-utility monthly	0.04595	0.00894	0.00319	0.00024	0.00474	0.00457	0.01091	0.01102	0.01107
Log-utility quarterly	0.04686	0.01002	0.00272	0.00025	0.00478	0.00477	0.01118	0.01129	0.01135
Variance target weekly	−0.00555	0.00468	−0.00305	−0.00626	0.01292	0.00261	0.00839	0.00850	0.00855
Variance target monthly	−0.00545	0.00446	−0.00304	−0.00687	0.01425	0.00256	0.00850	0.00858	0.00864
Variance target quarterly	−0.00687	0.00419	−0.00335	−0.00662	0.01540	0.00249	0.00859	0.00869	0.00875
Equally weighted	0.05399	0.00988	−0.00273	−0.00553	0.01337	0.00456	0.00499	0.00501	0.00502

(Continued)

Table 4. Continued

	Whole sample								
	$x_{CDS}=0$	$x_{Equity}=0$	$x_{CorpBonds}=0$	$x_{SovBonds}=0$	$x_{FOREX}=0$	$x_{comms}=0$	$\alpha=1\%$	$\alpha=5\%$	$\alpha=10\%$
1 August 2007 to 2 April 2010									
Min. var weekly	0.04745	0.00307	−0.00427	−0.00464	0.04303	0.00220	0.01320	0.01323	0.01325
Min. var monthly	0.04723	0.00307	−0.00430	−0.00467	0.04344	0.00219	0.01326	0.01329	0.01331
Min. var quarterly	0.04782	0.00312	−0.00436	−0.00446	0.04246	0.00221	0.01314	0.01318	0.01320
Log-utility weekly	0.07871	0.04520	0.00385	0.00003	0.00139	0.01583	0.02360	0.02376	0.02385
Log-utility monthly	0.07996	0.04495	0.00368	0.00002	0.00142	0.01559	0.02372	0.02389	0.02397
Log-utility quarterly	0.07944	0.04302	0.00360	0.00000	0.00147	0.01528	0.02321	0.02338	0.02346
Variance target weekly	0.02032	0.00336	−0.00739	−0.00844	0.01385	0.00117	0.00968	0.00986	0.00996
Variance target monthly	0.02137	0.00330	−0.00765	−0.00830	0.01296	0.00113	0.00955	0.00970	0.00979
Variance target quarterly	0.02009	0.00136	−0.00947	−0.00989	0.01597	−0.00043	0.00859	0.00876	0.00887
Equally weighted	0.03617	0.01628	−0.00210	−0.00452	0.01426	0.00555	0.00602	0.00605	0.00606

Notes: For comparison, we repeat the calculation of the weighted average daily correlations Λ_{corr} with each of the six asset classes systematically restricted from the portfolio optimisations. Confidence intervals under the null of no improvement are computed by drawing 1000 random integers $m \in \{1 \dots n\}$ and then again with equal weight randomly suppressing m assets and repeating the portfolio optimisation. The recomputed test statistics of Λ_{corr} are sorted and the 1%, 5% and 10% critical bounds are computed. The results in the table can be interpreted as follows. A positive number indicates a decrease in the weighted internal correlation within the portfolio, i.e. improves diversification given the relaxation of the restriction. A negative number suggests an increase in the correlation when the restriction is relaxed. The absolute magnitude of the change in correlation must be greater than the test statistic to reject the null of equality between the weighted internal correlations of the test and the reference portfolios. The upper part of the table presents evidence for the whole sample. The middle part reports the results for the sub-period 1 January 2004 to 31 July 2007 and the lower part for the sub-period from 1 August 2007 to 2 April 2010. The restriction on the CDS portfolio has a significant impact for all portfolios over the whole sample and 1 August 2007 to 2 April 2010. However, the variance-targeting portfolio fails to reject the null of equality for the sub-period 1 January 2004 to 31 July 2007. The only other asset that reports a robust λ_{corr} that is more significant than the random replacement is the restriction on the foreign exchange basket of funds. This result corresponds to the findings of Campbell, Serfaty-De-Madeiros, and Viciera (2010), who find that equity portfolios and foreign exchange rates exhibit persistent negative correlations in their returns.

the whole sample and for two partitioned sub-samples over the periods 1 January 2004 to 31 July 2007 and 1 August 2007 to 2 April 2010. The final three columns present resampling results for random imposed restrictions on different funds.

This allows comparison to check whether the difference in weighted correlations between the test and restricted reference portfolios is statistically dissimilar from a randomly imposed restriction. The results also show that for the whole sample and both sub-samples, the weighted correlation of the portfolios is lower when the naked CDS positions are included (i.e. benefits the most from the relaxation of the portfolio weights restriction). The reduction in weighted correlation within the portfolio is greatest for the higher risk portfolios, indicating that funds of funds targeting higher expected returns can benefit substantially from allowing the inclusion of the naked CDS funds. The difference in weighted correlations for a restriction on sovereign and corporate bond portfolios is also significantly different from a random restriction. Nevertheless, the magnitudes are substantially smaller.

The results of the weighted correlation test indicate that the inclusion of the CDS funds reduces, on average, correlation, across rebalancing frequencies, by approximately 7% for the minimum variance portfolio, 6% for the log-utility portfolio and 1.5% for the variance-targeting portfolio. For the first two strategies, the inclusion of CDS funds produces statistically significant reductions in the weighted correlations within the portfolio. This result clearly indicates that utilising naked CDS positions in basic mean variance strategies with standard objective functions does improves the diversification of risk within the portfolio. Bootstrap resampling suggests that this result is significant at 10%, 5% and 1% significance.

6.3 *Portfolio performance and block correlations*

Figure A1 in Appendix A (Appendix is available in the online version of the article) plots the comparative evolution of the overall equally weighted (i.e. equally weighted in class and equally weighted across asset classes) test (solid line) and reference (dashed line) portfolios. The portfolios' returns reflect the information contained in Table A1. The naïve portfolio that includes the naked CDS baskets outperforms the naïve portfolio without the CDS position. However, visual inspection of the period 1 January 2004 to 31 July 2007 suggests that the naïve portfolio including the CDS positions tracks very closely the naïve portfolio netted of the CDS positions. The major bounce in the CDS spreads and subsequent increase in portfolio performance occurred before September 2008, when Lehman Brothers default, an event that has a substantial impact on the value of the naïve portfolio with the CDS positions removed.

The naïve portfolios offer some interesting insights in the timing of the hedging effect across asset classes of the CDS portfolios. However, the short sample period does not offer a significant long-term scrutiny into the impact of the inclusion of the CDS positions, via for example parametric regression style analysis. Consequently, we must restrict our analysis to the dynamics of the cross section and the impact of mean variance optimising across the asset classes and semi-analysis of the parametric correlation structures.

Figures A2 and A3 in Appendix A present the evolution of the three portfolios strategies optimising the cross section and rebalancing weekly (solid line), monthly (long dashed line) and quarterly (dotted line). It can be seen that the frequency of rebalancing does not substantially change the trajectory of the portfolios. Moreover, there is no evidence of bid–ask spread penalty for more frequent rebalancing. The portfolio descriptive statistics in Table A7 also describe the portfolio turnovers as a cumulative percentage (100% represents a complete turnover of the portfolio by value). All portfolios including the CDS positions exhibit lower turnover than their corresponding reference portfolios.

For all rebalancing strategies, the inclusion of the CDS positions in the fund structure reduces the variance and increases returns substantially, although this finding is expected given the inherent nature of the CDS instruments. The magnitude of the change for the log-utility investor is substantial: the standard deviations decline, the skewness increases and the kurtosis decreases (i.e. first-order stochastic dominance) for all rebalancing frequencies. The log-utility investor obtains a 31.03% average return per annum over the 2004–2010 period with a 14.50% standard deviation for the test portfolio versus an 11.36% average annualised portfolio return and a 14.82% standard deviation for the reference portfolio. However, more critically, the skewness of the reference portfolio is negative while the skewness of the test portfolio is positive and the level of excess kurtosis in the test portfolio is almost half that of the reference portfolio for a weekly rebalancing frequency.

Figures A4–A6 display the time evolution of the block correlations among the six asset classes (i.e. across the 255 portfolios and the constituent underlying assets grouped by asset class). Several key aspects emerge from these plots. First, the block correlations are obviously not stable through time and the effect of the financial crisis permeates into the correlation moving average. Second, the dynamics of the minimum correlations, as illustrated in Figure A5 show that certain positive correlations are highly persistent after mid-2007.

We can see several major changes in the average block correlations over the sample period. Of particular note are the correlation adjustments that occur after the 2007 closure of two hedge funds run by the French bank BNP Paribas. After this event, the correlations between the CDS and equity fund returns begin to trend downwards, from approximately −10% to −20%. Furthermore, this trend continued after the Lehman Brothers default event, before stabilising at a level below −20%.

CDS and FOREX positions both exhibit low-average correlations with equity. However, the FOREX returns increase rapidly after the onset of the crisis, while the CDS correlations sharply decrease, suggesting that in the short-term FOREX positions during times of financial distress may not be as useful as a hedging tool as in non-crisis periods. The average unweighted block correlations do not appear to be informative, whereas the maximum correlations provide useful signals for risk management practices. For example, throughout the sample, a number of the equity and FOREX funds exhibit returns close to one in correlation. On the other hand, the estimated correlations for the CDS and commodities asset classes are never above 30%.

Of the 2040 daily correlations between the returns on the 51 CDS and 40 equity funds, the highest correlation is approximately 12% over the entire sample period. The profitability of capital structure arbitrage positions result from this low correlation risk, which is highly persistent throughout the whole crisis period. The average cross correlation is −0.15%. Hence, this persistent level of diversification is responsible for the lower average correlations in the optimised portfolios. These findings clearly indicate that rebalancing to the lowest block correlations can yield very important gains in terms of risk-return tradeoffs within the macro-portfolios of available assets.

Our estimates show that the gain from the inclusion of the CDS funds is not symmetric across strategy types. From Table A7, we can see that, for a log-utility investor rebalancing weekly, the inclusion of CDS funds in the fund of fund mix produces a risk-adjusted abnormal return of 31.32% on a per annum basis relative to the reference portfolio. By contrast, a risk-targeting portfolio (targeting a 3% standard deviation per annum) yields a risk-adjusted excess return over the reference portfolio of only 2.29% per annum for the weekly rebalanced portfolio and 1.94% for the quarterly rebalanced portfolio.

Interestingly, we find that the mean variance optimisation algorithm with a 3% objective standard deviation consistently undershoots the targeted level of risk. More specifically, from Table A7 we can see that the minimisation of risk in the test portfolios is greater than in the reference portfolios. Yet, the standard deviation of the risk-targeting test portfolios for weekly and quarterly rebalancing, which are 1.86% and 2.07% respectively, still undershoots their target.

A further key finding that emerges from the analysis is the very high level of kurtosis for low-risk targeting portfolios. The kurtosis for the weekly reference and test portfolios for the variance-targeting strategy is 21.764 and 18.250, respectively, and this is the highest level of kurtosis observed in any of the portfolios. This finding implies that variance targeting underscores standard deviation as a risk measure and subjects the portfolio to higher levels of variation in standard deviation. This is a highly undesirable feature. Both these portfolios are dominated, in terms of first-order stochastic dominance, by all of the log-utility strategies while, in the second-order stochastic dominance, by simple targeting the available minimum variance portfolio (note that the minimum variance portfolio has a variable standard deviation as a reference point). This finding is potentially of interest to academics and market participants and is consistent with the anecdotal evidence that hedge funds typically adopt risk-targeting strategies for portfolio optimisation.

The minimum variance test portfolio exhibits a 1.48% , 1.38% and 1.35% risk-adjusted excess returns for the weekly, monthly and quarterly rebalancing. The portfolios exhibit first-order stochastic dominance, with lower variance as well as higher returns for the test portfolios over the reference portfolios. Additionally, targeting the minimum variance portfolio does not result in the kurtosis penalties exhibited by the variance-targeting portfolios.

Tables A4–A6 in Appendix A also offer interesting insights into the discrepancies between the average correlations from the aggregate equally weighted portfolios presented in Table A2. Noticeably, the skewness of the unweighted block CDS and equity are negatively skewed. However, in the post 1 August 2007 period the skewness is positive, although the average block correlation decreases from −13.42 to −20.03%.

6.4 *Discussion*

Our results provide strong empirical evidence that a CDS is not priced as a linear combination of alternatives in the market. Sequential restriction tests and bootstrap resampling indicate that the CDS trading position outlined in Section 3 do not tally with the broad cross-section of alternative assets in the sample. The results from the correlation analysis are of remarkable magnitude. For instance, the average block correlation with corporate debt is virtually zero. Holding corporate debt is generally considered to garner a risk premium. If CDS positions were in effect equivalent to a short position in corporate debt, the correlation and replacement correlations would be expected to be negative and approaching unity. However, this result does not hold. In addition, we see that equity returns are negatively correlated with CDS positions. And remarkably, this correlation is both strong and persistent.

In a recent contribution, Stulz (2010) argues that CDS positions were not responsible for the credit crisis and that their radical shifts in price were symptomatic of a transitory mispricing of the intrinsic value of the underlying asset and hence the derivative contract. In a similar fashion, we would expect that as the prices of the underlying assets are adjusted to account for the changing risk vectors, the prices of the derivative instruments would adjust in a synchronised manner. This pattern, however, is not observable in our data set, which encompasses most of the single name trades in corporate CDSs.

Furthermore, our empirical evidence appears to contradict this view as it suggests that the returns on CDS positions are uncorrelated with their reference entities and exhibit unstable positive and negative time-varying correlations with a variety of other assets across the market. Interestingly, we show that relative to a linear reference benchmark, the CDS positions offer roughly a 28% return in excess for a log-utility maximising investor rebalancing weekly. Investors in effect do not receive an adequate risk premium for holding debt, but they are compensated with a substantial premium for holding the equivalent protection (i.e. being short in the debt). The fact that the portfolio returns, comprising CDS, are not replicable by any other linear combination is indicative of this decoupling.

From these results we conclude that a traded CDS position can be regarded as a unique Arrow–Debreu asset over the 2004–2010 period. Furthermore, the notion that the returns on CDS positions have decoupled post mid-2007 lends supports to the arguments put forward by Geanakoplos (2009), suggesting that the introduction of CDSs midway through the leverage cycle allowed speculators to drive default risk higher via the excessive trading of CDS positions. This trading boom resulted in the explosive increase in the notional amounts of defaultable bonds protected by these instruments, via the trading mechanism suggested in Section 3. Furthermore, once the feedback mechanism created by the separation of ownership between creditors and insurers had been enshrined, default risk became a marketable and desirable outcome for speculators in this asset class.

In summary, we find strong evidence to suggest that the introduction of CDS contracts in late 2004 does appear to have resulted in a contagious decoupling of the CDS spreads from their reference assets. Over the financial crisis period, the evolution of CDS spreads defined a class of assets with unique asset price dynamics, relative to other alternatives. In this case, the financial benefit is asymmetric as the holders of naked protection enjoy a substantial premium that affects multiple asset classes across the spectrum of available assets.

7. Conclusions

The contribution of this paper is to show that the introduction of naked CDS positions in a broad highly diversified fund of funds portfolios results in a substantial adjustment in the portfolio's return and risk profile. Specifically, the results show that investing in a naked CDS position yields an excess return of roughly 28% per annum and a corresponding important reduction in correlation.

We find that the degree of risk diversification is highly significant. In addition, we show that the effect in terms of risk return of an exclusion of the CDS returns in relation to a broad set of portfolios in alternative assets cannot be replicated and is significantly different from a random restriction.

To overcome the limitation of a relatively short sample period, we utilise a very broad cross section of assets and compute average cross correlations. We find significant and robust evidence of negative correlations between the returns on baskets of CDS positions and a variety of equity, commodity and foreign exchange baskets. We document that portfolios that include all of the available CDS positions, over the period 1 January 2004 to 2 April 2010, exhibit first-order stochastic dominance over portfolios with a restricted set of instruments.

The risk-return properties of this class of assets appear to be substantially at odds with the rest of the market. In particular, the low block correlation (average of a large number of cross correlations between asset classes) between the CDSs and bond sub-portfolios indicates that the price evolution of the CDS spreads appears to have decoupled from the fundamental structure of their underlying contracts.

Collectively, the empirical results presented here raise a key question of market policy: are naked CDS contracts beneficial? Our results provide empirical support for the view that CDS positions can offer additional benefits beyond their natural purpose. Therefore, these findings have at least two noteworthy implications. First, these systematic abnormal returns are inherently unstable and could potentially initiate a bubble in CDS prices. Second, the evolution of risk premia appears to hedge out exposure to the leverage cycle and the return profile realistically reflects default risk.

Taken together, our findings highlight the potential benefits of CDS contracts for speculative investors, whereas the social benefits are evidently questionable. It is clear that the leveraging of short positions produces effects beyond the originally conceptualised design of a CDS contract. Whether centralised clearing houses and a more transparent mark-to-market price would result in greater social benefits is still unclear. Going forward, nevertheless, it appears likely that clearing house margins and collateral arrangements will reduce the incentive problem inherent in such a highly leveraged transaction.

Acknowledgements

An internet appendix containing supplementary figures and tables is available from http://www.abdn.ac.uk/~acc138. We have received helpful input from Mike Adams, Mike Bowe, Stuart Hyde, Christos Ioannidis, Con Keating and seminar participants at the University of Aberdeen Business School, the Eastern Finance Association 2011 Annual Meeting (Savannah), the 29th SUERF Colloquium: New Paradigms in Money and Finance? (Brussels), the 2nd Humboldt - Copenhagen Conference in Financial Econometrics (Copenhagen), the EFFAS European Bond Commission Meeting (St. Andrews) and the Fifth Annual Risk Management Conference (Singapore). We are particularly grateful for the comments and suggestions of two anonymous referees. All remaining errors are our own.

Notes

1. Generally, practitioners refer to capital structure arbitrage as holding, for example, a short naked CDS position and an equivalent sized position in the equity of the same firm. However, we extend this definition to simply holding a large cross section of CDS and alternative instruments. A better description for this paper could be macro-structure arbitrage as we include a very wide variety of money market and other investment instruments across the financial spectrum.
2. Source: Bloomberg, *news wire* 11 March 2010, 'Naked Swaps Crackdown in Europe Rings Hollow Without Washington', by Ben Moshinsky and Aaron Kirchfield, US House of Representatives Committee of Financial Services Hearing. 17 July 2009, Serial No. 111-62, 5-17.
3. *Wall Street Journal*, 17 April 2010 'Goldman Sachs Charged With Fraud' by Gregory Zuckerman, Susanne Craig and Serena Ng. By 2008, 99% of the underlying assets and hence the majority of the tranches in this CDO product had been downgraded.
4. Source: CMA Vision, 20 April 2010.
5. Capital risk is the variation in the value of a portfolio due to market fluctuations in the constituent assets.
6. Depository Trust & Clearing Corporation, August 2009 CDS Market Report.
7. For the fictional perpetual protection case it is $\text{Notional}_t \times \kappa_t^{\text{ask}}/\beta$. Recall that the value of a perpetuity with a coupon of \$1 million at 2.5% is \$40 million.
8. We gratefully acknowledge the assistance of Thomson Reuters and CMA in assisting in building the instrument baskets. Thomson Reuters DataStream CMA currently provides sector-level basket data using the cross section of assets available in the CMA database and we use this list to build our CDS sector funds.

References

Acharya V.V., and C.T. Johnson. 2007. Insider trading in credit derivatives. *Journal of Financial Economics* 84, no. 1: 110–41.

Bielecki, T.R., M. Jeanblanc, and M. Rutkowski. 2005. Pricing and trading credit default swaps under deterministic intensity. Unpublished working paper, Isaac Newton Institute for Mathematical Sciences, Cambridge, MA.

Bielecki, T.R., and M. Rutkowski. 2002. *Credit risk: Modeling valuation and hedging*. Berlin: Springer-Verlag.

Bolton, P. and M. Oehmke, 2010. Credit default swaps and the empty creditor problem. Columbia University Working Paper Series, Columbia University, NY.

Brigo, D., and F. Mercurio, 2005. *Interest rate models – theory and practice*. 2nd ed. Berlin, Heidelberg: Springer Finance.

Campbell, J.Y., K. Serfaty-De-Madeiros, and L.M. Viciera. 2010. Global currency hedging. *Journal of Finance* 65, no. 1: 87–123.

Fostel, A., and J. Geanakoplos. 2008. Leverage cycles and the anxious economy. *American Economic Review* 98, no. 4: 1211–44.

Geanakoplos, J. 1997. Promises, promises. In *The economy as an evolving complex system, II*, ed. W.B. Arthur, S. Durlauf, and D. Lane, 285–320. Reading MA: Addison-Wesley.

Geanakoplos, J. 2009. The leverage cycle. In *NBER macroeconomics annual 2009*, ed. D. Acemoglu, K. Rogoff, and M. Woodford, vol. 24, 1–65. Chicago: University of Chicago Press.

Hatemi, J.A., and E. Roca. 2006. A re-examination of international portfolio diversification based on evidence from leveraged bootstrap methods. *Economic Modelling* 6, no. 22: 993–1007.

Hu, H.T.C., and B. Black. 2008. Debt, equity, and hybrid decoupling: Governance and systematic risk implications. *European Financial Management* 14, no. 4: 663–709.

Karatzas, I. 1996. *Lectures on the mathematics of finance*. CRM Monograph Series, vol. 8, 148. Providence, RI: American Mathematical Society. The Andre Aisenstadt Lectures at the University of Montreal, May 1996.

Karatzas, I. 2006. *A survey of stochastic portfolio theory*. The Eugene Lukacs Lectures, Bowling Green University, May–June 2006.

Kroner, K., and J. Sultan. 1993. Time varying distributions and dynamic hedging with foreign currency futures. *Journal of Financial and Quantitative Analysis* 28, no. 4: 535–51.

Kyj, L.M., B. Ostdiek, and K. Ensor. 2010. Covariance estimation in dynamic portfolio optimization: A realized single factor model. American Finance Association 2010 Atlanta Meetings Paper.

Longstaff, F.A., J. Pan, L.H. Pedersen, and K.J. Singleton. 2010. How sovereign is sovereign credit risk? *American Economic Journal: Macroeconomics*, 3, no. 2: 75–103.

Muirhead, R.J. 1981. *Aspects of multivariate statistical theory*. New Jersey: John Wiley & Sons.

Musiela, M., and M. Rutkowski. 2005. *Martingale methods in financial modelling*. Berlin: Springer-Verlag.

Pesaran, M.H., C. Schleicher, and P. Zaffaroni. 2009. Model averaging in risk management with an application to futures markets. *Journal of Empirical Finance* 16, no. 2 280–305.

Shadab, H.B. 2009. Guilty by association: Regulating credit default swaps. *Entrepreneurial Business Law Journal* 4, no. 2: 407–66.

Stulz, R.M. 2010. Credit default swaps and the credit crisis. *Journal of Economic Perspectives* 24, no. 1: 73–92.

Wagner, W. 2007. The liquidity of bank assets and banking stability. *Journal of Banking and Finance* 31: 121–39.

The path to impairment: do credit-rating agencies anticipate default events of structured finance transactions?

Matthias Bodenstedt[a], Daniel Rösch[b] and Harald Scheule[c]

[a]*Judge Business School, University of Cambridge, Trumpington Street, CB2 1AG Cambridge, UK;* [b]*Institute of Banking and Finance, Leibniz University of Hannover, Königsworther Platz 1, 30167 Hannover, Germany;* [c]*School of Finance and Economics, University of Technology, Sydney, PO Box 123, Broadway, NSW 2007, Australia*

The global financial crisis (GFC) has led to a general discussion of the accuracy and declining standards of credit-rating agency ratings. Substantial criticism has been directed towards the securitisation market, which has been identified as one of the main sources of the crisis. This study focuses on the ability of rating agencies to adjust their ratings prior to impairments of structured finance transactions. We develop a new measure that quantifies a rating agency's performance in advance of defaults. By analysing a large number of impaired transactions rated by Moody's Investors Service, we find that rating quality deteriorated during the GFC. Furthermore, we identify tranche-specific and macroeconomic factors that explain differences in Moody's performance.

1. Introduction

The structured finance market has become an increasingly important part of the financial system. Just a few years ago, securitisation was widely regarded as the 'instrument of the future' (Kothari 2006). The ability of structured finance to pool a large number of risky assets and to sell them to investors with various risk preferences led to a tremendous growth in the issuance of structured securities, which are also known as securitisations. Among the beneficiaries of the growing securitisation market were the credit-rating agencies (CRAs). Moody's Investors Service, for example, reported in 2006 that its structured finance earnings accounted for 44% of its revenues. A large proportion of securitisation deals received investment-grade ratings, suggesting a low risk involved in these transactions.

The global financial crisis (GFC), however, led to a general discussion of the accuracy and declining standards of CRA ratings. The Bank for International Settlements (2009) summarises as follows:

> A bank should conduct analyses of the underlying risks when investing in structured products and must not solely rely on the external credit ratings assigned to securitisation exposures by

> the CRAs. A bank should be aware that external ratings are a useful starting point for credit analysis, but are no substitute for full and proper understanding of the underlying risk, especially where ratings for certain asset classes have a short history or have been shown to be volatile.

One striking feature of the GFC is that a large fraction of highly rated securitisations were impaired. Between 1981 and 2006, only 0.02% of investment-grade structured finance transactions defaulted. In 2008, this figure reached a historical maximum of 1.03%. Given the important role of external ratings, the question as to how well ratings are suited to serve as an indicator for impairment risk is of particular interest for investors and regulators.

The aim of this paper is to answer whether CRAs anticipate impairment events of structured finance transactions. In the context of this work, the term *rating quality* is defined by a CRA's ability to adjust its ratings in a timely manner to increased risk prior to impairment. Our first contribution is the development of the *anticipation coefficient* which quantifies a rating agency's performance in advance of defaults. This is an important contribution as this new metric incorporates the whole adjustment process before impairment. Previous research concentrates on the rating at single points in time such as the time of origination or one year prior to default in order to analyse differences in the forecasting ability of rating agencies. Important parts of the adjustment process are ignored in these contributions.

Using the anticipation coefficient, we empirically analyse ratings by Moody's Investors Service for 13,679 structured finance transactions with impairment between 2001 and 2008. Our analysis is divided into three parts. The first part looks at how credit ratings are adjusted in general. Our study shows that Moody's adjusted its ratings gradually in advance of defaults. In 2008, a significant amount of downgrading took place 180 days prior to impairment. Moreover, the analysis reveals that in the context of the GFC, Moody's carried out systematic changes to its rating models, resulting in an overall downgrading of most securitisations.

The second part addresses the question as to whether the general criticism towards CRAs of having poorly anticipated impairments during the GFC is justified. We observe a decline in Moody's rating quality during the GFC that can be explained by two main factors: first, a poorer anticipation of defaults of securities that initially received investment-grade ratings and, second, a higher proportion of defaults of initially highly rated securities.

The third part analyses the impact of tranche-specific and macroeconomic factors on a rating agency's ability to adjust its ratings in a timely manner. Previous research suggests that CRAs may assign inflated ratings due to issuer shopping (Bolton, Freixas, and Shapiro, forthcoming). Our analysis indicates that this conflict of interest is less severe for transactions with a higher deal volume. Potentially, reputational pressure is higher for these securities. Moreover, we find that Moody's ratings become more valuable over time and that they better reflect increased risk prior to impairments when other CRAs evaluate the same security. Finally, the empirical analysis suggests that rating quality in the securitisation market strongly depends on the state of the US real estate market.

The remainder of this work is organised as follows: Section 2 provides a brief overview of the relevant literature. Section 3 develops a new measure to quantify a rating agency's ability to adjust ratings in advance of impairments. Section 4 analyses how credit rating quality changes over time and which tranche-specific and macroeconomic factors influence the forecasting ability of structured finance ratings. Section 5 summarises the findings and discusses the major ramifications of the empirical results.

2. Literature review

This paper is related to several strands of literature. One part of the research deals with the pricing and the risk parameters of structured finance transactions. Duffie and Gârleanu (2001), Longstaff and Rajan (2008), and Hull and White (2004) focused on explaining the observed market prices of credit default swap indices such as the North American CDX and the European iTraxx. The central point of their research was the specification of dependency structures of portfolio assets. Relevant parameters for the risk of loan portfolios include default probabilities, loss rates given default, and dependency parameters among the portfolio's assets, such as correlations, or more general copulas. Among others, Merton (1974), Longstaff and Schwartz (1995), and Leland and Toft (1996) addressed the probabilities of default. Altman et al. (2005), Acharya, Bharath, and Srinivasan (2007), and Qi and Yang (2009) provided an analysis of the recovery rates of defaulted securities. Li (2000) and Schönbucher and Schubert (2001) focused on the dependency structures of default events. The CRAs estimate these parameters to assess the risk inherent in structured finance transactions.

With regard to the GFC, Coval, Jurek, and Stafford (2009) showed how modest imprecision in these parameter estimates can cause AAA-rated securities to default with reasonable likelihood. Porras (2008) emphasised the impact of underestimated correlation during the GFC. Rösch and Scheule (2010) and Ashcraft, Goldsmith-Pinkham, and Vickery (2010) found that structured finance ratings do not include all factors explaining securitisation impairment risk. Benmelech and Dlugosz (2009) empirically analysed the rating quality of structured debt.

One of the major critiques of the rating industry argues that CRAs have an incentive to assign inflated ratings as they receive their fees from the issuer. Support for this hypothesis was given by Griffin and Tang (forthcoming), who analysed the impact of subjectivity on collateralised debt obligation (CDO) ratings and found that rating agencies divert from their own models by assigning better ratings than a neutral risk assessment would suggest. Bolton, Freixas, and Shapiro (forthcoming) introduced a model based on microeconomic assumptions, suggesting that competition among CRAs increases the problem of issuer shopping. Löffler (2009), on the other hand, analysed Moody's stock price and argued that market discipline may be sufficient to prevent CRAs from assigning inflated ratings. Mathis, McAndrews, and Rochet (2009) examined this reputation argument and showed that its validity depends on the share of income that a CRA generates with the rating of complex products. A comprehensive discussion on the causes of the GFC was given by Crouhy, Jarrow, and Turnbull (2008), who argued that CRAs were at the centre of the crisis as many investors relied on their ratings for complex products. Likewise, a report by the Committee on the Global Financial System (2008) highlights the impact of structured finance ratings on the GFC. Finally, several studies have addressed the adequacy of external ratings in determining financial institutions' capital requirements for securitisations (Calem and LaCour-Little 2004; Rösch and Scheule, forthcoming).

Altman and Rijken (2004) and Amato and Furfine (2004) addressed the aim of CRAs to achieve rating stability (through-the-cycle approach). Löffler (2005) found that rating agencies react slowly to new information. This is explained by assuming that CRAs set different thresholds for each rating migration step. Altman and Kao (1992) detected a positive serial autocorrelation in agency ratings when the initial rating change is a downgrade. A study that analyses the adjustment of credit ratings in advance of defaults was presented by Güttler and Wahrenburg (2007). However, in contrast to our study, they examined corporate bond rather than structured finance ratings and their main focus was on how rating agencies react to rating transitions by other rating agencies. Violi (2008) analysed rating transitions of corporate and structured ratings and found significant differences in the rating mobility across structured finance products.

3. Rating quality framework and hypothesis development

3.1 *Rating quality framework*

One of the research objectives of this study is to provide insights into the adjustment process of ratings prior to impairment. This section develops a new measure that allows assessing the quality of ratings in advance of a default. In order to analyse the work of CRAs not only qualitatively but also quantitatively, it is essential to assign numerical values to ratings. Although rating agencies claim that their ratings are ordinal measures of risk, it is common practice among academics and regulatory authorities to transform ratings into a cardinal scale (Cantor and Packer 1997; Jorion, Liu, and Shi 2005). In the following, we use a mapping scale that converts Moody's rating classes into 21 integers, starting with Aaa = 1 to C = 21. A higher value consequently means that the rating agency considers a security to be more risky.

Moreover, our rating quality framework draws on the event study methodology. Fama et al. (1969) first introduced this methodology in the context of market efficiency tests. Traditionally, event studies focus on the impact of an event on the price of a firm (MacKinlay 1997). The main idea of an event study is to define a central event as day 0 and then analyse what happened before and after this day (Binder 1998). In this study, we use the impairment as our central event. According to Moody's Investors Service, an impairment event is defined by a shortfall in interest or principal payments or by a downgrade to Ca/C (Moody's Investors Service 2009). Referring to variables in event time (e.g. 20 days before impairment) allows us to compare ratings of securities with different impairment dates.

Existing research focuses on ratings at origination or at the beginning of a year to address the question as to how well ratings reflect default risk. Unfortunately, such an approach ignores important parts of the adjustment process. To illustrate this problem, Figure 1 shows the ratings of two sample securities over time relative to their impairment date.

Both securities have the same rating one year prior to default (A1 = 5). While the rating of the security on the left is gradually adjusted over time, the rating of the other security stays constant until the occurrence of impairment. Solely focusing on the rating one year prior to impairment (or similar measures, such as rating at origination or at the beginning of a year) would lead to

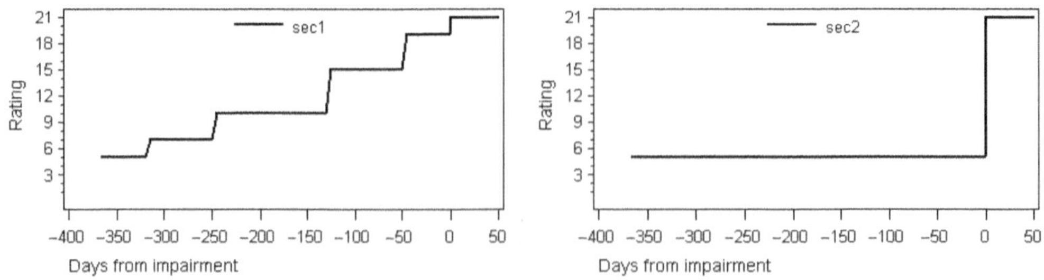

Figure 1. Adjustment processes of two sample securities.
Notes: Both transactions receive the same rating (A1 = 5) one year prior to impairment. However, the adjustment process is completely different, illustrating that solely focusing on the rating one year prior to impairment is not sufficient.

the false conclusion that the rating agency performed equally well in both cases. Obviously, the ratings for the first security are of much greater value.

To take such differences into account, we introduce a new coefficient that measures how well the CRAs anticipate the impairment of the respective (later impaired) tranche. Similar to a Gini coefficient, this 'anticipation coefficient' is defined as the ratio of two areas. Plotting the rating level over time, one can derive this coefficient by dividing the area under the rating curve (Area I) by the area under an optimal[1] rating curve (Area I + Area II) (Figure 2). The optimal rating curve is realised when the CRA assigns the lowest possible rating already one year prior to impairment. For Moody's rating classes, the lowest possible rating is Caa3 = 19 since ratings of Ca = 20 or C = 21 would have already triggered the impairment (compare with Moody's definition of impairment).

Mathematically, the anticipation coefficient (ac_i) is defined as

$$ac_i = \frac{\sum_{t=-365}^{-1} (R_{i,t} - 1)}{365 \cdot (19 - 1)} = \frac{1}{6570} \cdot \sum_{t=-365}^{-1} (R_{i,t} - 1), \qquad (1)$$

where ac_i is the anticipation coefficient of security i and $R_{i,t}$ is the rating of security i at time t relative to impairment. Subtracting one from the ratings ensures that the anticipation coefficient is within an interval between zero and one ($ac_i \in [0; 1]$). To understand the intuition behind this coefficient, it may be helpful to take a look at two extreme examples, an early and a late anticipation of impairment. In the former case, the rating agency anticipates the impairment one year in advance and consequently assigns the lowest rating (Caa3 = 19) for the entire observation period. This results in an anticipation coefficient of one. In the latter case, the rating agency does not anticipate the impairment prior to the event and assigns a very good rating (i.e. Aaa = 1) to the specific tranche until the occurrence of the event. Such a performance results in a very low anticipation coefficient (ac = 0) since the area under the rating curve is very small. In other words, the anticipation coefficient reflects early CRA downgrades.

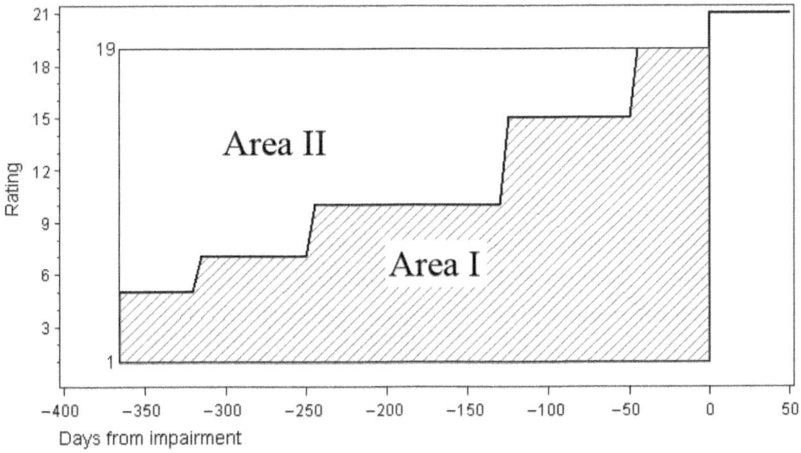

Figure 2. Graphical illustration of the anticipation coefficient.
Notes: To analyse the rating quality, we introduced an anticipation coefficient that can be calculated by dividing Area I by the combined area of Area I and Area II which reflects the best anticipation possible since a CRA would assign the lowest rating (Caa3 = 19) to a security for which it would expect an impairment already one year in advance.

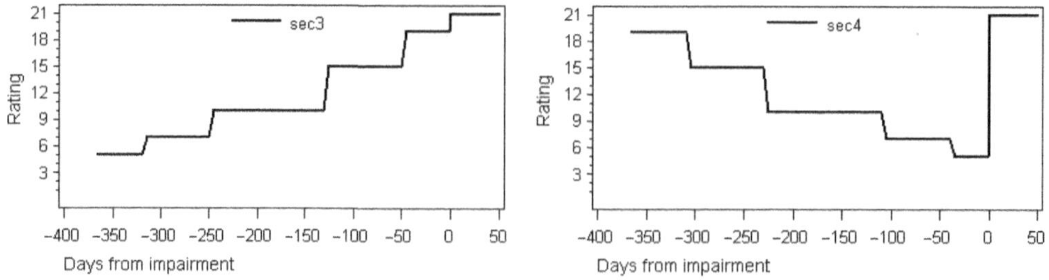

Figure 3. Adjustment processes of two sample securities with equal anticipation coefficients.
Notes: Both transactions result in the same anticipation coefficient since the areas under the rating curves are equal. Nevertheless, the performance of the rating agency is significantly better for the security on the left since the ratings of the second security falsely suggest a decreasing risk of default.

Some problems with the anticipation coefficient may relate to the equal weighting of time and may be relevant when rating agencies upgrade securities prior to impairments. Figure 3 shows two securities with identical anticipation coefficients but completely different rating histories.

The areas below both rating curves are equal and therefore both anticipation coefficients are equal. Without doubt, the ratings of the first security reflect the increased risk prior to impairment better than the ratings of the second security. One possible solution to this problem would be to attach a higher weight to ratings close to impairment. Equation (2) shows how the coefficient could be modified by adding linearly increasing weights:

$$\text{ac}_i = \frac{\sum_{t=-365}^{-1} w_t(R_{i,t} - 1)}{\sum_{t=-365}^{-1} w_t(19 - 1)} \quad \text{with } w_t = \alpha + \beta \cdot t. \tag{2}$$

The parameters α and β determine how much more weight is attached to ratings close to impairment. In the following, however, we use the unweighted approach ($\alpha = 1$ and $\beta = 0$) since the data set we examine in our study does not include any rating upgrades.

3.2 *Hypothesis development*

The following hypotheses aim to answer how the rating quality for structured finance securities changes over time and which factors explain its differences. Based on changes in Moody's anticipation coefficient as a measure for rating quality, the hypotheses are as follows:[2]

- *H*1: Rating quality deteriorated during the GFC.
- *H*2*a*: Rating quality depends on the deal volume of a transaction.
- *H*2*b*: Time since origination has an influence on rating quality.
- *H*2*c*: CRAs perform better when facing competition from other rating agencies.
- *H*2*d*: The impairment type and default amount have an impact on rating quality.
- *H*3: Differences in rating quality can be explained with macroeconomic factors.

H1 is directed towards the general criticism against rating agencies in the financial crisis, H2a–d relate to the influence on the rating quality of tranche-specific factors, and H3 relates to the impact of macroeconomic factors.

H1 addresses the role of credit ratings during the GFC. A substantial amount of criticism has been directed towards CRAs, accusing them of having poorly anticipated the increase in the impairment rate. Coval, Jurek, and Stafford (2009), for example, argued that CRAs have assigned high ratings to very risky assets in the crisis. The hypothesis, therefore, aims to analyse whether empirical data confirm this criticism and show that CRAs performed poorly during the GFC.

H2a addresses a potential conflict of interest of rating agencies. Crouhy, Jarrow, and Turnbull (2008) argued that CRA fees are paid by issuers and that this mismatch could serve as an incentive for rating agencies to assign more issuer-friendly ratings than an independent risk assessment would suggest. Given that rating agencies typically receive a certain proportion of the deal volume, the deal balance may have an influence on overall rating quality. A small deal volume implies low fee revenues and thereby reduces the incentive to distort the rating. In contrast, higher deal volumes are related to higher fee revenues and, possibly, also to a higher willingness to assign issuer-friendly ratings. Conversely, higher fees can also lead to more accurate ratings for two reasons. First, assigning biased ratings to transactions with higher deal volumes can severely damage a rating agency's reputation. Second, higher fee revenues allow CRAs to allocate larger resources (e.g. more financial analysts) to these transactions. As a result, ratings for larger deals may better reflect increased risk in advance of impairments.

H2b addresses the impact of the time since origination on rating quality. The CRAs may be able to accumulate deal-specific knowledge that helps in identifying potential risks in a timelier manner. Furthermore, the risk assessment may become less biased the longer a security has been rated. Rösch and Scheule (2010) showed that an origination rating generates approximately 5.7 times more fee revenues for CRAs than monitoring a rating for one year does. Consequently, credit ratings may be more distorted close to origination.

H2c addresses the degree to which competition with other rating agencies increases overall rating quality. Facing competition from other CRAs can serve as an incentive to perform better to increase the market share. The better a rating agency anticipates impairment, the higher the value of the ratings for investors is. Issuers of securities are interested in having their products rated by a reputable CRA. Another advantage that comes with competition is an increased amount of available information. Rating changes made by other CRAs can, for example, alert a CRA to revise its own assessment of a security (Güttler and Wahrenburg 2007).

H2d analyses the impact of the impairment type and the impairment severity on rating quality. Over 97% of observed impairments are principal impairments, defined as shortfalls in principal payments. The rating agencies aware of this issue may be more careful with their assessments prior to principal payments than in advance of interest payments. Thus, the type of impairment can have an influence on rating quality. Another factor that we analyse in this context is the impact of the severity of impairments. Severe shortfalls in interest payments or principal payments may be easier to anticipate than just minor shortfalls.

H3 identifies the degree to which macroeconomic factors help in explaining differences in the rating quality. Based on the nature of structured finance transactions, one would expect close links to risk parameters of the underlying assets. Identifying such factors not only would be helpful in explaining past differences, but could also contribute to a better understanding as to how reliable future ratings are.

4. Empirical analysis

4.1 *The data set*

This paper analyses a data set provided by Moody's Investors Service covering all Moody's-rated securitisations until 2008. The data contain characteristics of transactions, characteristics of tranches, and ratings of tranches over time, as well as realisations of impairment events. Unfortunately, rating data from other CRAs are not available for this study. However, we hand-collected ratings by Standard & Poor's (S&P) and Fitch for 1000 randomly selected transactions and found very high Spearman correlation coefficients (93.4% between Moody's and S&P, 95.8% between Moody's and Fitch, and 98.5% between S&P and Fitch). Moreover, most of the rating differences are related to a deviation of a single notch. These findings suggest that our results based on Moody's data can be generalised to other major CRAs.

As outlined in the previous section, we first translated Moody's rating classes into 21 numerical values (Aaa = 1, Aa1 = 2, …, C = 21). In addition to the ratings, watchlist entries are available. A watchlist entry indicates that a rating change in the near future is highly probable but that the rating agency has not finished the formal rating review process yet. A rating may be put on review for possible upgrade, downgrade, or change with uncertain direction. Previous studies suggest that the inclusion of the watchlist status significantly improves the accuracy of default predictions (Hamilton and Cantor 2004). Sy (2004) and Güttler and Wahrenburg (2007) made use of the watchlist information by adding (subtracting) a constant to the numerical rating for a negative (positive) watchlist entry. The magnitude of this adjustment factor is, however, subject to discussion. Assuming that a watchlist entry is a weaker statement than an actual rating change suggests that the factor should be less than one. Bannier and Hirsch (2010), however, showed that securities with a negative watchlist entry are, on average, downgraded by 1.65 notches. Given that approximately 65% of the securities placed on review for downgrade are subsequently downgraded, we believe that the adjustment factor should lie somewhere between 0.5 and 1.5. In our study, we used a conservative value of 0.8, which is similar to the adjustment factors used in previous studies.[3]

The second step is inspired by the event study methodology. Following this methodology and defining the day of impairment as the central event allowed us to analyse securitisations over time, independent of their impairment date. In the next step, we extracted for all impaired tranches the daily ratings from 365 days before until 365 days after the impairment. We thereby created a data set with information on ratings from one year before until one year after the impairment.

Finally, deal- and tranche-specific information was combined and merged with the rating file. In addition to the impairment date and the daily ratings before and after the impairment, the final data set includes the following information:

- deal category: asset-backed security (ABS), CDO, residential mortgage-backed security (RMBS), home equity loan (HEL), or commercial mortgage-backed security (CMBS);
- deal balance and tranche balance;
- closing date and date of maturity;
- impairment type (two types exist: shortfalls in principal payments, defined as principal impairments, and shortfalls in interest payments, defined as interest impairments);
- default amount.

Structured finance transactions are very heterogeneous by definition. Various filter rules are aimed at generating a homogeneous data set. The following observations were deleted:

- Transaction observations that cannot be placed into the categories ABS, CDO, RMBS, HEL, and CMBS. These are mainly asset-backed commercial paper, structured covered bonds, catastrophe bonds, and derivative product companies.

- Transaction observations with an impairment date before 2001 due to a limited number of impairment events. Those of the years after 2008 were unavailable at the time of writing this paper.
- Transaction observations not denominated in US dollars and those that did not originate in the USA.
- Transaction observations that had missing ratings for one or more days of the observation period.

The resulting data set comprises 13,679 impaired tranche observations. Table 1 shows the total number of observed impairments over time and the frequency of deal characteristics, as well as the relative impairment rate. The number of observed impairments fluctuated between 90 and 252 for the period 2001–2006. Most observations had impairments in 2007 (1254) and 2008 (11,454), illustrating the severity of the financial turmoil in the securitisation market. Likewise, the impairment rate rose sharply in 2007 and 2008, with RMBSs and HELs especially experiencing a large increase in impairments.

4.2 *Average ratings prior to impairment*

The first question we address is how ratings generally adjust prior to impairments. Do CRA ratings reflect increased default risk prior to the impairment event itself? To shed some light on the adjustment process, we first calculated the means of Moody's ratings at different times in advance of impairments. The results are presented in Table 2.

As expected, ratings were adjusted for the increased risk close to an impairment event. In all the years, we observed a similar upward trend over time, which illustrates that, on average, Moody's has downgraded tranches before impairments. However, differences become evident by separately focusing on three parts of the adjustment process: (i) the rating level at the beginning of the observation period (i.e. 365 days prior to impairment), (ii) the rating adjustment on the impairment day, and (iii) the speed of adjustment in advance of the impairment event.

On focusing on the initial rating level one year prior to impairment, significant differences over time are apparent. In 2006, for example, the average rating was 15.58 (corresponding to a rating between B2 and B3), whereas in 2008 the average rating was 7.65 (corresponding to an investment-grade rating of Baa1). This finding is consistent with the observation that during the GFC, a high number of tranches with investment-grade ratings experienced impairments. A higher proportion of defaults of initially A-rated (Aaa–A3) securities causes the average rating to start at a lower level.

Another striking feature is that the average rating on the impairment day changes over time. In 2001, securities had an average B1 rating (14.27) on day 0. This may seem puzzling at first sight since Moody's defines an impairment event by a shortfall in interest or principal payments or by a downgrade to Ca/C. According to this definition, one would, therefore, expect an average rating that is close to 20 on the impairment day. However, by more closely analysing the adjustment process of randomly selected tranches, we found that, especially in the first few years of the observation period, Moody's did not adjust all ratings immediately on the impairment day. In many cases, the downgrading or the complete withdrawal of ratings did not happen until several weeks after the actual impairment.

Furthermore, we observed differences in the adjustment process. While ratings were adjusted gradually over time in most years, in 2008, significant downgrading took place approximately 180 days prior to impairment (see the upper curve in Figure 4). A reasonable explanation for this

Table 1. Distribution of impairments over time and impairment type.

	Distribution of impairments								
	2001	2002	2003	2004	2005	2006	2007	2008	Total
ABS	29	107	96	137	18	32	27	31	477
CDO	52	111	47	49	23	17	209	2073	2581
RMBS	4	3	3	7	8	6	97	2942	307
HEL	13	14	30	13	21	25	912	6313	7341
CMBS	5	17	23	19	20	22	9	95	210
Total	103	252	199	225	90	102	1254	11,454	13,679
Impairment rate	(0.63%)	(1.34%)	(0.93%)	(0.99%)	(0.32%)	(0.25%)	(2.17%)	(17.26%)	(5.01%)
No. of rated tranches	16,309	18,814	21,416	22,728	28,302	41,247	57,661	66,374	272.851

	Rating one year prior to default							
	2001	2002	2003	2004	2005	2006	2007	2008
Aaa–A3	8 (0.06%)	25 (0.16%)	16 (0.09%)	70 (0.40%)	3 (0.01%)	0 (0.00%)	163 (0.37%)	5388 (10.68%)
Baa1–B3	91 (3.76%)	221 (6.94%)	170 (4.13%)	126 (2.55%)	71 (1.10%)	54 (0.59%)	1,057 (8.20%)	5969 (39.56%)
Caa1–C	4 (12.50%)	6 (26.10%)	13 (23.14%)	29 (28.97%)	16 (13.06%)	48 (17.29%)	34 (16.74%)	97 (77.82%)
Total	103	252	199	225	90	102	1254	11,454
Impairment rate	(0.63%)	(1.34%)	(0.93%)	(0.99%)	(0.32%)	(0.25%)	(2.17%)	(17.26%)
No. of rated tranches	16,309	18,814	21,416	22,728	28,302	41,247	57,661	66,374

Notes: The distribution of impairments in the final data set is given. In the upper part of the table, the distribution of impairments over time and by asset category of the underlying portfolio is given. In the lower part of the table, the rating of impaired securities one year prior to default is given. Especially in 2007 and 2008, a high proportion of transactions with impairment had an initial A rating (Aaa–A3) one year before default. The figures within brackets show relative impairment rates that can be interpreted as an empirical probability of default.

Table 2. Average ratings at different times surrounding the impairment event.

Days relative to impairment	2001	2002	2003	2004	2005	2006	2007	2008
−365	11.99	11.30	11.50	10.30	12.71	15.58	10.10	7.65
−300	12.06	11.45	11.93	10.50	13.18	15.73	10.17	8.04
−240	12.21	11.66	12.18	11.38	13.51	15.95	10.27	8.36
−180	12.23	12.02	12.37	11.91	14.58	16.12	10.39	11.40
−120	12.60	12.61	12.99	12.49	15.30	16.53	10.70	13.26
−90	12.84	12.91	13.22	12.67	15.78	16.67	12.36	13.73
−60	12.98	13.18	13.39	12.85	16.13	16.87	12.80	14.45
−30	13.28	13.88	13.69	12.91	16.39	17.05	13.10	14.69
−5	13.39	14.88	13.79	13.09	16.55	17.14	13.29	14.82
0	14.27	16.39	16.92	18.38	18.23	18.84	18.93	19.76
30	14.27	16.39	16.94	18.38	18.24	18.84	18.93	19.77
90	14.98	17.40	17.28	18.90	18.79	19.05	19.37	20.11

Notes: A heterogeneous adjustment process is given. Differences in the rating level one year prior to impairment as well as differences in adjustment levels can be observed, while ratings decline in all the years over time.

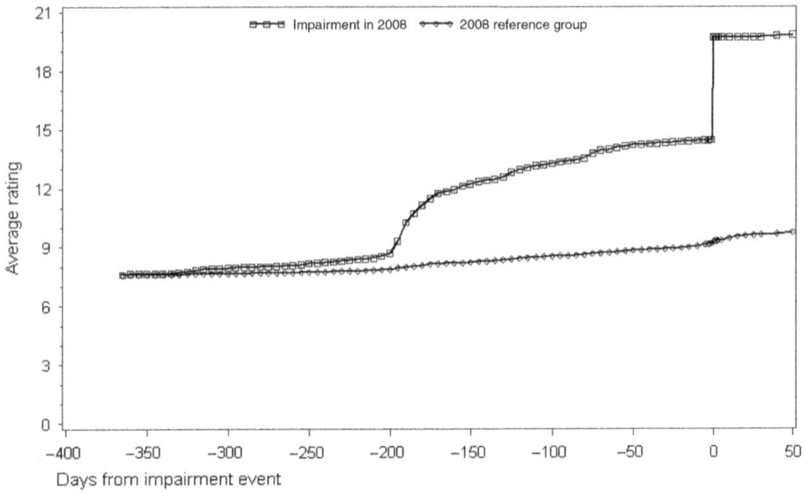

Figure 4. Average ratings of impaired and non-impaired tranches in 2008.
Notes: In contrast to other years, in 2008, securities without impairment were also downgraded.

feature is that in the context of the GFC, rating agencies carried out some systematic adjustments. The sudden increase in the impairment rate, especially for mortgage-backed securities (MBSs), may have raised questions regarding some assumptions (e.g. an underestimation of the correlation between the default risks of MBSs) in the models that CRAs employed. If this is the case, one would expect that not only defaulting tranches but also securities that never experienced impairments would have been downgraded in 2008. To test whether this is the case, we extended the data set by including securities that did not experience any shortfalls in interest or principal payments. Obviously, it is impossible to extract daily ratings relative to an impairment event given that such

Table 3. Average ratings in 2008.

2008	January	February	March	April	May	June	July	August	September	October	November	December
Average rating	11.82	11.71	11.8	**11.99**	12.84	**12.98**	13.62	13.79	13.9	**14.08**	15.02	15.35
Change (%)	−0.93	0.77	1.61	**7.09**	1.09	**4.93**	1.25	0.80	1.29	**6.68**	2.20	0.13

Notes: The average ratings for tranches without impairment in 2008 are given. Significant downgrading took place in April (7.09%), June (4.93%), and October (6.68%).

an event does not exist. We solved this problem by randomly selecting five securities without impairment for every tranche that defaulted. The impaired tranche thereby serves as a reference tranche for the five other securities, which allowed us to use the impairment date of the reference tranche as an imaginary impairment date for the sample securities. Several filters ensure that the securities in the new data set are of the same type (i.e. ABS, CDO, RMBS, HEL, and CMBS) and have the same rating 365 days prior to impairment as their respective reference tranches. The new data set was then used to analyse how ratings changed for products without impairment. Figure 4 shows the adjustment process for impaired tranches in 2008, as well as the rating curves for a group of sample securities without impairment. In contrast to those of the previous years, the rating curve of the 2008 reference group features an upward slope that reveals that not only transactions with impairment but also transactions without impairment were downgraded in that year.

The high density of downgrades over time indicates that rating agencies also revised their models. The analysis of the rating changes in calendar time reveals that a high proportion of downgrades in 2008 took place in April, June, and October (compare Table 3). This finding supports the hypothesis that a revision in the rating models also contributed to the downgrading trend in 2008.

4.3 *Rating quality over time*

4.3.1 H1: Rating quality deteriorates during the GFC

To test the hypothesis of whether rating quality was significantly worse during the GFC, we analysed changes in the anticipation coefficient, introduced in the previous section, over time. The results are shown in Figure 5.

Figure 5 reveals that overall rating quality changed over time. From 2001 to mid-2004, the anticipation coefficient fluctuated between 0.5 and 0.7. In the next two years, the graph followed an upward trend, which indicates that Moody's performed better in that period. However, in 2007, forecasting power fell significantly, reaching a minimum in the beginning of 2008. This finding supports the hypothesis that ratings for securitisations were less predictive during the GFC. It is important to note that the low anticipation coefficients in 2007 and 2008 do not necessarily imply a critique of CRAs. The poor anticipation of impairments may have also been caused by the more turbulent economic environment which made it difficult to predict defaults.

Another aim associated with H1 is to find out what kinds of securities contributed to the observed decline in rating quality. To do so, we analysed which groups of transactions were most affected. The observed impairments can be divided into two groups: transactions with an investment-grade rating (Aaa–Baa3) 365 days before impairment and transactions with a speculative-grade rating (Ba1–C) 365 days before impairment. While the average anticipation coefficients of both groups followed the same overall trend, results are more pronounced for securities that initially received

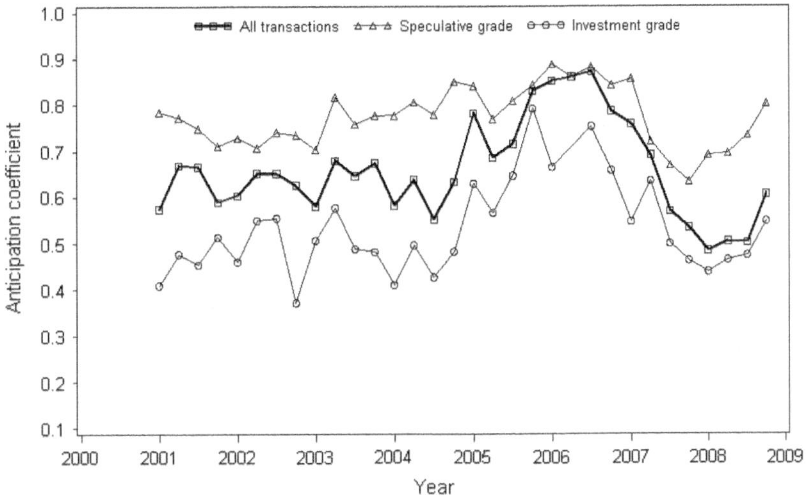

Figure 5. Average anticipation coefficient over time.
Notes: The bold line represents the average anticipation coefficient of all impaired securities. Moreover, the graph shows the changes in the anticipation coefficient separately for securities based on their rating one year prior to default.

an investment-grade rating (Figure 5). Another factor that contributes to the differences in overall rating quality is the composition of impairments. Table 1 (rating one year prior to default) shows that during the GFC, the proportion of highly rated transactions (Aaa–Aa3) with impairment increased. As a result, the overall anticipation coefficient also reflects the changed composition of the impairments.

In summary, the decline in rating quality during the GFC can be explained by two main factors: first, the poorer anticipation of defaults of senior securities and, second, the higher proportion of defaults of initially highly rated securities.

4.4 *Influence of tranche-specific factors on rating quality*

Structured finance transactions are very heterogeneous by definition. Apart from the deal type (ABS, CDO, MBS, etc.), securities vary in many other aspects, such as the deal volume, the subordination level, and the impairment type. H2a–d address the influence of such tranche-specific factors on rating quality. To test the impact of these factors, we used a regression model of the form

$$\phi^{-1}(\mathrm{ac}_i) = \beta' * x_i + \varepsilon_i \tag{3}$$

where Φ^{-1} is the inverse of the normal cumulative distribution function (CDF), x_i is a vector of observable and thus known variables, ac_i is the unweighted anticipation coefficient as described in Section 3, β' is the vector of sensitivities, and ε_i is a normally distributed random error with expectation zero. Transforming the anticipation coefficient with the inverse of the normal CDF accounts for the fact the coefficient is always within an interval between zero and one.

The vector x_i includes the following variables: $x_1 - x_5$ are dummy variables (0 or 1) for the various asset types (ABS, CDO, RMBS, HEL, and CMBS); x_6 is the log of the deal volume in US dollars; x_7 is the years since origination; x_8 is the years to maturity; x_9 is a dummy variable that equals one if at least three CRAs rated this transaction and zero otherwise;[4] x_{10} is a dummy variable that equals one if principal is impaired and zero if interest is impaired; and x_{11} is the log of the default amount in US dollars.

The regression coefficients and significance levels (using heteroskedasticity-robust standard errors) are presented in Table 4. In years with a higher number of impairments, results tend to be statistically more significant as a greater sample size implies lower standard errors.

4.4.1 H2a: Rating quality depends on the deal volume of a transaction

The sensitivity of the anticipation coefficient towards the deal balance is positive in all the years. Consequently, all other things being equal, the ratings of transactions with a higher deal volume reflect increased risk prior to impairment better than ratings for securities with a small volume. The coefficients are statistically significant for the years 2001, 2003, 2004, 2006, 2007, and 2008. The data, therefore, support the assumption that a higher deal volume increases rating quality. One interpretation may be that the risk of severely damaging its reputation seems to outweigh the possible short-term gains a rating agency can achieve by assigning issuer-friendly ratings. Another factor that may contribute to the better anticipation of impairments of high-volume deals is that for such deals typically more information is available. For example, Hung, Lee, and Pai (2009) showed that markets for small-cap stocks are less efficient than those for high-cap stocks. This pattern may also be valid for structured finance securities.

4.4.2 H2b: The time since origination has an influence on rating quality

The variable 'years since closing' is positively correlated with the anticipation coefficient in all the eight observation periods. Thus, Moody's seems to improve its ratings the longer a security exists. A possible explanation for this positive impact on the forecasting quality could be a learning effect. The rating agencies accumulate information about the transactions they rate. Such information on past performance can be helpful in identifying deal-specific risk factors. In addition, the conflict of interest that rating agencies face is weaker in the years after origination. For new ratings, CRAs may tend to assign more issuer-friendly ratings to increase their revenues. Issuers have an incentive to get their securities rated by a CRA that offers high ratings since such ratings facilitate capital access. Bolton, Freixas, and Shapiro (forthcoming), for example, argued that competition between CRAs leads to better initial ratings. Although rating agencies also receive fees for the monitoring of ratings, these fees are considerably lower than those charged for origination ratings (Rösch and Scheule 2010).

4.4.3 H2c: Rating agencies perform better when facing competition from other CRAs

Various authors, including Bolton, Freixas, and Shapiro (forthcoming) and Fons (2008), argued that more competition increases the conflict of interest and thereby exacerbates the problem of issuer shopping. On the other side, Hörner (2002) provided an alternative prediction about the effect of increased competition and argued that greater competition enhances reputational risk and thereby improves the quality of ratings. The latter argument is often used in policy arguments (Becker and Milbourn 2011). Our regression model adds the dummy variable 'number of ratings' to examine the effect of increased competition on rating quality. The variable is zero if a certain transaction is only rated by one or two major CRAs and one if the transaction has three or four ratings. The statistically significant sensitivities in 2002 and 2004 are positive, indicating that Moody's performance was better when facing competition from other CRAs.

However, it is important to distinguish between two different types of competition: an *a priori* competition and an *a posteriori* competition. *A priori* competition relates to the competition

Table 4. Regression results of tranche-specific determinants of the anticipation coefficient.

Variable	2001	2002	2003	2004	2005	2006	2007	2008	All
ABS	0.052	1.265	−0.986	−0.208	1.453	−1.064	0.041	0.022	−0.017
CDO	0.53	1.555	−0.817	0.263	0.919	−1.45	−0.670**	−0.698***	−0.034**
RMBS	−0.549	0.601	−0.892	−0.293	0.736	−1.725*	−0.610*	−0.623***	−0.034**
HEL	0.105	1.287	−1.113	−0.183	0.982	−1.720*	−0.38	−0.184	0.04
CMBS	0.553	1.539	−0.517	0.631	1.478	−1.398	−0.284	−0.092	0.334**
Deal balance	0.213**	0.033	0.077*	0.142*	0.06	0.150**	0.153***	0.167***	0.146***
Years since closing	0.169***	0.116***	0.091***	0.115***	0.090***	0.155***	0.149***	0.062***	0.086***
Years to maturity	0.001	0.002	−0.019***	−0.025	0.001	0.010*	−0.005*	−0.003**	−0.011***
Number of ratings	−0.02	0.227**	−0.059	0.201*	0.019	0.129	−0.002	0.012	0.008
Principal impairment	0.583*	0.165	0.561***	−0.165	−0.07	−0.238	−0.11	0.015	0.125***
Default amount	−0.319***	−0.143***	−0.041	−0.140**	−0.123**	−0.085*	−0.176***	−0.183***	−0.167***
F-statistic	12.6***	14.7***	20.1***	11.4***	32.7***	63.5***	114.7***	607.3***	687.9***
Adjusted R^2	0.579	0.408	0.531	0.352	0.802	0.895	0.507	0.375	0.367
Observations	103	252	199	225	90	102	1254	11,454	13,679

Notes: The results of the regression model using robust standard errors are given. The dependent variable is the unweighted anticipation coefficient discussed in Section 3. Independent variables are dummies for the different transaction types (ABS, CDO, RMBS, HEL, and CMBS) that take on the value of 1 if the security belongs to the respective group and the value of zero otherwise. The deal balance and the default amount are given in their logarithmic forms. Years since closing is the time since origination and years to maturity is the time to legal maturity. Number of ratings is another dummy variable that takes on the value of 1 if at least three major CRAs rated the tranche and the value of zero otherwise. The variable principal impairment is one if the impairment is due to a shortfall in principal payments.

*Two-sided significance levels representing 10%.

**Two-sided significance levels representing 5%.

***Two-sided significance levels representing 1%.

between CRAs before an issuer has selected a rating agency by which the transaction shall be rated. *A posteriori* competition refers to the competition between CRAs that rate the same transactions. The problem of issuer shopping is more relevant for *a priori* competition since rating agencies have an incentive to outbid each other to get the rating job. By contrast, our regression analysis focuses on *a posteriori* competition, that is, on the influence on rating quality of a higher number of CRAs that rate the same transaction.

4.4.4 H2d: The impairment type and default amount have an influence on rating quality

To analyse the influence of the impairment type on rating quality, we added the dummy variable 'principal impairment' to our regression model. The variable takes the value of one for principal impairments and zero for interest impairments. Table 4 shows that the sensitivity of this variable is positive overall. Therefore, transactions with principal impairments generally have higher anticipation coefficients than transactions with shortfalls in interest payments. Given that most impairments belong to the first group (principal impairments), rating agencies may be more careful in assigning ratings in advance of principal payments than in advance of interest payments.

Table 4 also reveals that Moody's ratings better reflected increased risk prior to impairments of securities with a lower default amount. The default amount is negatively correlated with the anticipation coefficient in all the years. One explanation for this behaviour could be that smaller default amounts are typically caused by shortfalls in payments from individual assets, whereas higher default amounts are caused by more general economic downturns that affect a higher proportion of assets. This especially affects highly rated (A region) securities as they require correlated defaults in large numbers to lead to impairment due to over-collateralisation. Possibly, the through-the-cycle approach that most rating agencies use amplifies this effect.

Table 4 also offers information on how the type of underlying asset portfolio influences rating quality. However, the impact was not constant for the whole observation period. Overall, CDO ratings performed poorly. Given that CDOs typically have very broad asset portfolios and in many cases were even restructured from other CDOs (known as CDO-squared transactions), it seems plausible that it was more difficult for CRAs to identify changes in risk for these transactions than for other transaction types.

4.5 *Influence of macroeconomic factors on rating quality*

4.5.1 H3: Differences in rating quality can be explained with macroeconomic factors

After having analysed how tranche-specific factors affect rating quality, this hypothesis addresses the question as to how macroeconomic factors can be used to explain changes in the anticipation coefficient. To do so, we focused on aggregate data (annual average anticipation coefficients) and not on individual tranches. Figure 5 shows that the average anticipation coefficient changed over time. Since the value of a structured finance transaction depends on the value and cash flows of the underlying assets, macroeconomic variables might also affect the predictability of impairments.

To test the impact of macroeconomic factors, we regressed the anticipation coefficient on numerous explanatory variables. These variables include the Case–Shiller US National House Price Index provided by S&P. The Case–Shiller Index serves as a proxy for the housing market. For the calculation of the correlation coefficients, the natural logarithms of the growth rate were used. Furthermore, we added the seasonally adjusted GDP growth rate and the national unemployment rate as reported by the US Bureau of Economic Analysis and the US Bureau of Labor Statistics.

While examining the effect of macroeconomic variables on the anticipation coefficient, it is important to keep in mind that the anticipation coefficient describes the rating adjustments for a

Table 5. Regression of the anticipation coefficient on macroeconomic variables.

Variable	(1)	(2)	(3)
Intercept	0.963***	0.816***	0.625***
Case–Shiller	0.632		
Case–Shiller (lagged by 180 days)		1.565**	
Case–Shiller (lagged by 360 days)			2.602***
GDP growth	0.004		
GDP growth (lagged by 180 days)		0.004	
GDP growth (lagged by 360 days)			0.01
Unemployment level	−0.059		
Unemployment level (lagged by 180 days)		−0.036	
Unemployment level (lagged by 360 days)			−0.002
F-statistic	2.75*	1.9	5.04**
Adjusted R^2	0.145	0.079	0.227
Observations	32	32	32

Notes: The results of the regression models using robust standard errors are given. The dependent variable is the quarterly average anticipation coefficient. Independent variables are the natural logarithms of the Case–Shiller US National House Price Index, the seasonaly adjusted US GDP growth rate, and the US national unemployment rate. All independent variables are additionally specified with a 180-day and a 360-day lag to take into account that the anticipation coefficient describes the rating adjustments for a one-year period.
*Two-sided significance levels representing 10%.
**Two-sided significance levels representing 5%.
***Two-sided significance levels representing 1%.

one-year period and not for a specific point in time. For example, the anticipation coefficient of a security with impairment on 1 July 2007 describes the rating adjustments from 1 July 2006 to 30 June 2007. Consequently, the explanatory variables may better explain changes in the coefficient with a certain lag. In our example, it may be more appropriate to use economic indicators from the end of 2006 rather than from June 2007 (when the impairment eventually occurred). To allow for this effect, the independent variables are specified with a 180-day and a 360-day lag. Table 5 shows the estimated regression coefficients.

The model with the best fit uses the variables lagged by one year. The regression coefficients reveal that the Case–Shiller House Price Index positively affects the anticipation coefficient. A high Pearson correlation coefficient of $\rho = 0.58$ implies that the anticipation coefficient moves in line with the growth of the Case–Shiller Index of the year before. Figure 6 presents both curves: the anticipation coefficient and the logs of the Case–Shiller Index growth rate with a one-year lag.

The positive correlation can be explained by the asset portfolios of structured finance securities that are, in many cases, closely related to the housing market. In the case of a significant downturn in the housing market, many assets will lose their value in a short time, which does not allow CRAs to adjust their ratings in a timely manner. As a result, the average anticipation coefficient falls. However, the positive correlation also suggests that the anticipation coefficient increases if the housing market is in good condition. The explanation for this is straightforward: in a boom period, fewer securities default and those very few that still experience shortfalls in payments very likely belong to the more risky tranches that typically receive a lower rating from CRAs. In good years, the average anticipation coefficient is consequently dominated by risky securities with low ratings. As a result, the anticipation coefficient rises. This effect has already been illustrated in Table 1, which shows the composition of impairments.

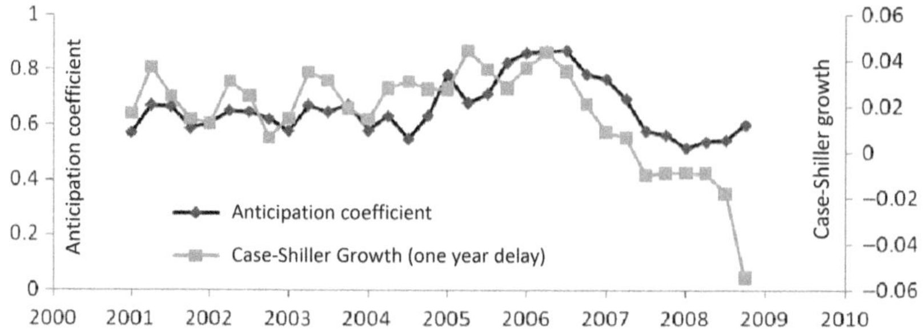

Figure 6. Anticipation coefficient and Case–Shiller growth over time.
Notes: The anticipation coefficient (black) and the logs of the Case–Shiller growth (grey) with a one-year lag are shown. Both curves move in line, which illustrates the high correlation between both the variables.

5. Discussion and outlook

To date, no empirical evidence exists on the information content of ratings for structured finance securities prior to impairment. The main objective of this paper was to analyse rating adjustments prior to impairment events and to reveal and explain differences in rating agency performance along this dimension. Based on an empirical study of 13,679 impairments rated by Moody's, we showed that ratings are generally adjusted prior to default.

This paper developed a new measure that quantifies a CRA's performance in advance of impairments. In contrast to existing research, this new measure, the anticipation coefficient, includes rating information of a whole one-year period. The literature thus far has focused on the rating at origination or the beginning of a year. A high anticipation coefficient signals that ratings were adjusted in a timely manner prior to shortfalls in interest or principal payments and therefore allowed investors to adapt to the increased portfolio risk. The anticipation coefficient may be applied for the analysis of other rating applications.

The anticipation coefficient reveals that the Moody's ability to identify higher levels of impairment risk deteriorated significantly during the GFC. This is consistent with the general criticism put forward against CRAs. However, for the time prior to the crisis, we observed an improvement in rating quality. The low level of the anticipation coefficient during the GFC can be ascribed to the over-proportional increase in impairments of highly rated tranches and the relatively late adjustments for securities that initially received investment-grade ratings. These findings may not be interpreted as a critique of the valuable work CRAs provide. It is reasonable to argue that the forecasting of such a severe downturn is difficult.

Using the anticipation coefficient, we found that differences in Moody's performance can be partially explained by deal-specific and macroeconomic factors. The ratings of securities with a higher deal volume are typically of higher value for investors. Furthermore, ratings better reflect increased risk prior to impairments the longer they have existed, so that CRAs can accumulate deal-specific information over time that they then use to improve their ratings. Another factor that influences rating quality is the competition CRAs face after origination. Transactions that are rated by several CRAs tend to have better risk assessments prior to defaults. Surprisingly, Moody's performed better in anticipating impairments with low default amounts. One possible explanation for this behaviour is that, in their assessments, rating agencies allow for the risk that some of the portfolios' assets will experience shortfalls in payments but do not expect economic downturns that will affect a higher number of assets.

With respect to macroeconomic factors, a significant impact of the housing market on rating quality in the structured finance market became evident. For example, the forecasting quality of ratings highly correlates with the Case–Shiller US National House Price Index.

Unfortunately, our empirical analysis only assesses data from Moody's Investors Service. While previous research suggests that ratings of several CRAs show a high level of agreement, comparing Moody's performance with those of other rating agencies offers potential for further research. In addition, a more thorough analysis as to how to take the watchlist status of a transaction into account may yield further insights.

Overall, the analysis shows that ratings do not consistently reflect increased risk prior to impairments. Investors and regulators should consider further information next to ratings, such as deal volume, asset type, time since origination, and the overall economic situation.

Acknowledgements

The support of the Australian Centre for Financial Studies, the Hong Kong Institute for Monetary Research, and the ThyssenKrupp Foundation is gratefully acknowledged.

Notes

1. Optimal means that the rating agency (in our case Moody's) anticipated the impairment one year prior to impairment and therefore assigned the lowest possible rating (Caa3 = 19) at that time.
2. Section 4.1 shows empirical evidence that the findings may be generalised to other CRAs.
3. Note that our findings are robust with regard to alternative values. Güttler and Wahrenburg (2007) and Sy (2004) used adjustment factors of 1.0 and 0.67, respectively.
4. This variable is based on information about ratings from Moody's, S&P, Fitch Ratings, and the Dominion Bond Rating Service and collected from Bloomberg/Datastream.

References

Acharya, V.V., S.T. Bharath, and A. Srinivasan. 2007. Does industry-wide distress affect defaulted firms? Evidence from creditor recoveries. *Journal of Financial Economics* 85, no. 3: 787–821.

Altman, E., B. Brady, A. Resti, and A. Sironi. 2005. The link between default and recovery rates. *Journal of Business* 78, no. 6: 2203–28.

Altman, E., and D.L. Kao. 1992. Rating drift of high yield bonds. *Journal of Fixed Income* 1, no. 4: 15–20.

Altman, E., and H. Rijken. 2004. How rating agencies achieve rating stability. *Journal of Banking and Finance* 28, no. 11: 2679–714.

Amato, J.D., and H. Furfine. 2004. Are credit ratings procyclical? *Journal of Banking and Finance* 28, no. 11: 2641–77.

Ashcraft, A., P. Goldsmith-Pinkham, and J. Vickery. 2010. MBS ratings and the mortgage credit boom. CentER discussion paper 2010-89S, 1–59, Tilburg University, Tilburg.

Bank for International Settlements. 2009. Enhancements to the Basel II framework. Report submitted by a working group established by the Basel Committee on Banking Supervision. Bank for International Settlements, Basel.

Bannier, C.E., and C.W. Hirsch. 2010. The economic function of credit rating agencies – what does the watchlist tell us? *Journal of Banking and Finance* 34, no. 12: 3037–49.

Becker, B., and T. Milbourn. 2011. How did increased competition affect credit ratings? *Journal of Financial Economics* 101, no. 3: 493–514.

Benmelech, E., and J. Dlugosz. 2009. The alchemy of CDO credit ratings. *Journal of Monetary Economics* 56, no. 5: 617–34.

Binder, J. 1998. The event study methodology since 1969. *Review of Quantitative Finance and Accounting* 11, no. 2: 111–37.

Bolton, P., X. Freixas, and J. Shapiro. Forthcoming. The credit ratings game. *Journal of Finance*.

Calem, P.S., and M. LaCour-Little. 2004. Risk-based capital requirements for mortgage loans. *Journal of Banking and Finance* 28, no. 3: 647–72.

Cantor, R., and F. Packer. 1997. Differences of opinion and selection bias in the credit rating industry. *Journal of Banking and Finance* 21, no. 10: 1395–414.

Committee on the Global Financial System. 2008. Ratings in structured finance: What went wrong and what can be done to address shortcomings? CGFS papers no. 32, Bank for International Settlements, Basel.

Coval, J.D., J. Jurek, and E. Stafford. 2009. The economics of structured finance. *Journal of Economic Perspectives* 23, no. 1: 3–25.

Crouhy, M., R. Jarrow, and S. Turnbull. 2008. The subprime credit crisis of 07. *Journal of Derivatives* 16, no. 1: 81–110.

Duffie, D., and N. Gârleanu. 2001. Risk and valuation of collateralized debt obligations. *Financial Analysts Journal* 57, no. 1: 41–59.

Fama, E.F., L. Fisher, M.C. Jensen, and R. Roll. 1969. The adjustment of stock prices to new information. *International Economic Review* 10, no. 1: 1–21.

Fons, J.S. 2008. Rating competition and structured finance. *The Journal of Structured Finance* 14, no. 3: 7–15.

Griffin, J., and D.Y. Tang. Forthcoming. Did subjectivity play a role in CDO credit ratings? *Journal of Finance*.

Güttler, A., and M. Wahrenburg. 2007. The adjustment of ratings in advance of defaults. *Journal of Banking and Finance* 31, no. 3: 751–67.

Hamilton, D.T., and R. Cantor. 2004. Rating transition and default rates conditioned on outlooks. *Journal of Fixed Income* 14, no. 2: 54–71.

Hörner, J. 2002. Reputation and competition. *American Economic Review* 92, no. 3: 644–63.

Hull, J., and A. White. 2004. Valuation of a CDO and an *n*th to default CDS without Monte Carlo simulation. *Journal of Derivatives* 12, no. 2: 8–23.

Hung, J.C., Y.H. Lee, and T.Y. Pai. 2009. Examining market efficiency for large- and small-capitalization of TOPIX and FTSE stock indices. *Applied Financial Economics* 19, no. 9: 735–44.

Jorion, P., Z. Liu, and C. Shi. 2005. Informational effects of regulation FD: Evidence from rating agencies. *Journal of Financial Economics* 76, no. 2: 309–30.

Kothari, V. 2006. *Securitisation: The financial instrument of the future*. Singapore: Wiley Finance Series.

Leland, H., and K. Toft. 1996. Optimal capital structure, endogenous bankruptcy, and the term structure of credit spreads. *Journal of Finance* 51, no. 3: 987–1019.

Li, D.X. 2000. On default correlation: A copula function approach. *Journal of Fixed Income* 9, no. 4: 43–54.

Löffler, G. 2005. Avoiding the rating bounce: Why rating agencies are slow to react to new information. *Journal of Economic Behavior and Organization* 56, no. 3: 365–81.

Löffler, G. 2009. Can market discipline work in the case of rating agencies? Some lessons from Moody's stock price. Working Paper, Goethe University, Ulm.

Longstaff, F., and A. Rajan. 2008. An empirical analysis of the pricing of collateralized debt obligations. *Journal of Finance* 63, no. 2: 529–63.

Longstaff, F., and E. Schwartz. 1995. Valuing risky debt: A new approach. *Journal of Finance* 50, no. 3: 789–820.

MacKinlay, A.C. 1997. Event studies in economics and finance. *Journal of Economic Literature* 35, no. 1: 13–39.

Mathis, J., J. McAndrews, and J. Rochet. 2009. Rating the raters: Are reputation concerns powerful enough to discipline the rating agencies? *Journal of Monetary Economics* 56, no. 5: 657–74.

Merton, R.C. 1974. On the pricing of corporate debt: The risk structure of interest rates. *Journal of Finance* 29, no. 2: 449–70.

Moody's Investors Service. 2009. Default and loss rates of structured finance securities: 1993–2008. http://www.moodys.com/researchdocumentcontentpage.aspx?docid=PBC_119617.

Porras, E.R. 2008. The role of correlation in the current credit ratings squeeze. IE Business School Working Paper, DF8-126-I, IE Business School, Madrid.

Qi, M., and X. Yang. 2009. Loss given default of high loan-to-value residential mortgages. *Journal of Banking and Finance* 33, no. 5: 788–99.

Rösch, D., and H. Scheule. 2010. Rating performance and agency incentives of structured finance transactions. Working Paper, Leibniz University of Hanover and University of Melbourne, Hannover.

Rösch, D., and H. Scheule. Forthcoming. Capital incentives and adequacy for securitisations. *Journal of Banking and Finance*.

Schönbucher, P.J., and D. Schubert. 2001. Copula-dependent default risk in intensity models. Working Paper, Bonn University, Bonn.

Sy, A.N.R. 2004. Rating the rating agencies: Anticipating currency crises or debt crises? *Journal of Banking and Finance* 28, no. 11: 2845–67.

Violi, R. 2008. Credit ratings transition in structured finance. CGFS Working Group on Ratings in Structured Finance Paper, BIS.

The determinants of bank CDS spreads: evidence from the financial crisis

Laura Chiaramonte[a] and Barbara Casu[b]

[a]*Department of Business Administration, Faculty of Economics, University of Verona, Verona, Italy;* [b]*Cass Business School, City University London, London, UK*

Based on a sample of mid-tier and top-tier internationally active banks with 5-year senior CDS, this paper investigates the determinants of credit default swaps (CDS) spreads and whether CDS spreads can be considered a good proxy of bank performance. The analysis encompasses three time periods: a pre-crisis period (1 January 2005–30 June 2007), a crisis period (1 July 2007–31 March 2009) and a post-crisis period (1 April 2009–30 June 2011) and focuses exclusively on bank-specific balance sheet ratios. The results of the empirical analysis indicate that bank CDS spreads, both in the pre-crisis period, but especially in the crisis period, reflect the risk captured by bank balance sheet ratios. We find that the determinants of bank CDS spreads vary strongly across time, as economic and financial conditions vary. TIER 1 ratio and leverage appear insignificant in all of the three periods considered, while liquidity indicators become significant only during the crisis and post crisis period.

1. Introduction

Banks have played a crucial role in the making and spread of the recent financial crisis. Indeed, at the most critical moment of the crisis, the key player was none other than a bank, Lehman Brothers, whose default sparked the most acute phase, and had a number of immediate repercussions on the whole system.[1] The demise of the American investment bank is considered an important event not only because it was responsible for a sudden collapse in global business confidence – it was the first time that a major bank was allowed to fail – but also because it marked a watershed in the history of credit default swaps (CDS). The bankruptcy of Lehman Brothers in September 2008 and, shortly afterwards, the near downfall of the insurance conglomerate American International Group, both of which were involved in the CDS sector, polarised attention towards the CDS activities of the major international banks.

CDS, the most widespread form of credit derivative, has been, according to some, responsible for exacerbating the effects of the recent financial crisis (Dickinson 2008; Kress 2011; Stulz 2011). CDS were originally created in the 1990s by JP Morgan, and consist of an agreement between two parties, the so-called protection buyer and protection seller. The protection seller undertakes, in exchange for a premium paid by the protection buyer, to pay out if a specific credit event[2] occurs, typically the default of a third debtor, the so-called reference entity. CDS are thus contracts that make it possible to isolate and transfer credit risk (Ashraf, Altunbas, and Goddard 2007; Jarrow 2011). Owing to these constituent features, CDS spreads have become increasingly popular as a simple, direct indicator of a firm's credit risk, especially during the financial crisis.[3] As pointed out by Hart and Zingales (2010), a CDS can be seen as a bet on an institution's strength and therefore its price or spread reflects the probability that the debt will not be repaid in full. Put simply, the CDS spread can be seen as an indication of the risk that the bank will fail. When banks' risk increases, one would expect CDS spreads to increase thus providing direct market discipline and influence bank risk-taking behaviour (and/or trigger regulatory action). However, in practice the functioning of this market discipline mechanism is not clear cut and depends both on the financial system institutional structure (for example, the design of the safety net, the strength of property rights, the incentives to information disclosure) and on investors' behaviour and macroeconomic conditions. Balasubramnian and Cyree (2011) document that the yield spreads on bank-issued subordinated notes and debentures are sensitive to bank risk, but the presence of implicit guarantees such as the too-big-to-fail policy may reduce the levels to which they reflect bank-specific risks. A number of studies seem to indicate that, because of its inherent characteristics, the CDS market is more efficient than the bond market in pricing credit risk and in anticipating rating changes (Di Cesare and Guazzarotti 2010; Zhu 2006). Nonetheless, the recent financial crisis cast doubt on the effectiveness of CDS spreads as an indicator of risk, as it became evident that the dramatic increases in CDS spreads could not be fully explained by increases in banks credit risk. During the period 1 July 2007 to 31 March 2009, CDS spread values grew considerably and displayed record peaks (Figure 1) that can only be explained taking into account the overall market situation.

As pointed out by Annaert et al. (2010), CDS spread changes that are driven by the increased credit risk of individual financial institutions should signal to regulators that they need to pay closer attention to the institution's financial health. On the other hand, when CDS spread changes are not related to fundamentals (as during the crisis period), the market's ability to correctly price for risk becomes questionable.

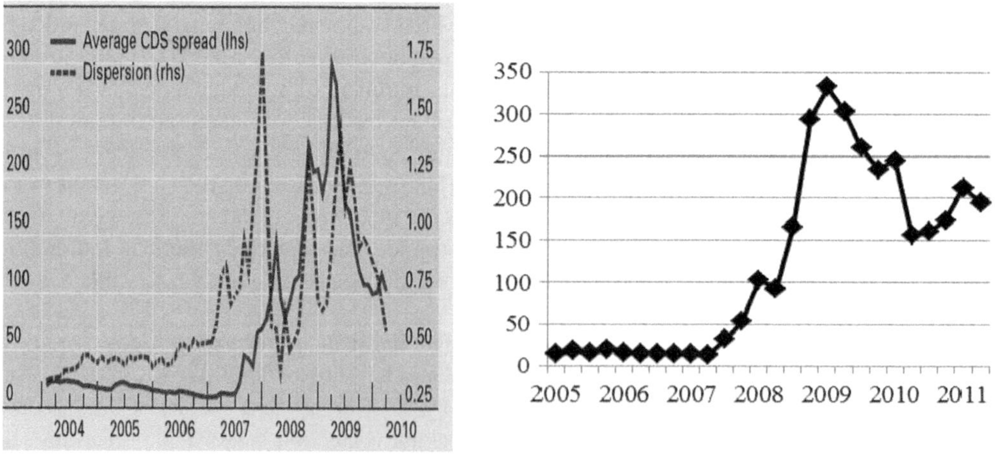

Figure 1. CDS market.
Note: In the figure on the left, taken from the BIS Annual Report (2010), the CDS market is based on the CDS spreads of 34 large banks and 14 large insurance companies in Europe and North America. Average CDS spread (lhs) is in basis points. Dispersion (rhs) is the standard deviation of the cross section of CDS spreads, divided by the contemporaneous average. The figure on the right shows the trend of average CDS spread values for the 57 sample banks. Average values for bank CDS spreads are in basis points.
Source: Bank for International Settlements. 2010. *Annual Report*, Basel, June (for the figure on the left) and Datastream Database (for the figure on the right).

This paper aims to build upon this recent strand of the literature (Annaert et al. 2010; Eichengreen et al. 2009; Constantinos 2010; Demirgüç-Kunt and Huizinga 2010; Hart and Zingales 2010; Huang, Zhou, and Zhu 2009; Raunig and Scheicher 2009; Norden and Weber 2010) by investigating the determinants of CDS spreads to understand whether CDS spreads can be considered a good proxy for bank risk. In particular, we estimate the relationship between bank balance sheet ratios and bank CDS spreads both in the pre-crisis period, in the crisis and post-crisis period.

This paper makes three contributions to the related literature. First, this study is one of the few concerned exclusively with bank CDS spreads at an international level: most other studies examine a mix of industrial and financial firms.[4] A number of reasons led to the decision to consider only CDS spreads in the banking sector. Very little is known about what actually drives credit spreads in general and bank CDS spreads in particular (Annaert et al. 2010). Moreover, variables that are found to affect credit spreads of non-financial companies often lose their explanatory power when applied to financials (Boss and Scheicher 2005; Raunig and Scheicher 2009).

Our second contribution relates to the analysis of the determinants of CDS spreads; we chose to concentrate only on bank balance sheet ratios, rather than considering both market-specific and firm-specific factors; with the sole exception of leverage. To the best of our knowledge, no study in the related literature has used specifically balance sheet variables to explain variation in CDS spreads. Most empirical papers (see, for example, Bystrom 2005; Collin-Dufresne, Goldstein, and Martin 2001; Das et al. 2006; Das, Hanouna, and Sarin 2008; Duffie, Saita, and Wang 2007; Zhang, Zhou, and Zhu 2005) investigating the explanatory power of credit risk variables for bond and CDS include in the model several variables to proxy for business conditions, market conditions and/or uncertainty (term structure of interest rates, market return, market volatility, etc.). We are conscious of the influence market variables have on CDS spreads; however, in this paper, because of the time period considered, we decided to focus only on the correlation between balance sheet ratios and CDS spreads. In periods of financial stress, market data fluctuate wildly; therefore, biasing the relationship with accounting variables. Moreover, changes in market data during a crisis period do not necessarily reflect the changes in credit risk but may be driven by investors' panic and lack of trust. Finally, this paper is one of the first contributions on bank CDS spreads that also takes into account the post-crisis period.

The results of the empirical analysis can be summarised as follows. First, bank CDS spreads reflect the risk captured by bank balance sheet ratios. Hence bank CDS spreads are a good proxy of bank risk. Second, the relationship between bank CDS spreads and balance sheet ratios becomes stronger during the crisis and post-crisis period. Third, bank CDS spreads seem to be influenced by different variables in the pre-crisis and crisis period. Fourth, variables that *a priori* would be considered as determinants of CDSs spread, the TIER 1 Ratio and the Leverage, appear insignificant in all of the periods considered. Finally, as expected, the bank CDS market in the pre-crisis period showed little interest in any of the liquidity indices considered.

The remainder of the paper is organised as follows. Section 2 presents a review of the relevant literature. Sections 3 and 4 discuss data and empirical methodology, respectively. Sections 5 and 6 present empirical results and robustness tests. Finally, Section 7 summarises the major findings and concludes the paper.

2. Literature review

Research on CDS spreads is still limited, mostly because the credit derivatives market in general and the CDS market in particular has only gained a substantial size since the early 2000s.[5]

The CDS literature is composed of two groups of studies, one focusing on the pricing characteristics of CDS spreads, and the other investigating the determinants of CDS spreads and their variation.

To the first group belong the empirical analyses that demonstrate the price leadership of CDS spreads over corporate bond spreads in measuring firm-specific credit risk. Various reasons underlie this claim. Hull, Predescu, and White (2004), Das and Hanouna (2006), Zhu (2006) and Ericsson, Jacobs, and Oviedo (2009) point out that CDS contracts are quoted directly in term of spreads[6], while bond spreads require a number of complicating assumptions and calculations, for example, the specification of a benchmark risk-free yield curve before credit spreads can be calculated. Blanco, Brennan, and Marsh (2005), Zhu (2006), Alexopoulou, Andersson, and Georgescu (2009) and Norden and Weber (2009) show that the CDS market leads the corporate bond market in terms of price discovery. Volz and Wedow (2011), Constantinos (2010), Flannery (2010), Norden and Weber (2010) find that CDS markets convey information on banks' default risk that is suited to play an important role in enhancing market discipline. In particular, they believe that the CDS market is of particular importance for banking supervisors.

The second group comprises the empirical analyses that investigate the determinants of CDS spreads. The credit risk literature identifies two different approaches: the structural approach and the reduced form approach.

The structural models, derived from the option pricing model originally developed by Black and Scholes (1973), are based on firms' structural variables, in other words firm-specific (i.e. rating, leverage, market capitalisation, asset volatility, stock price changes, etc.) and market-specific factors (i.e. term structure of interest rates, market return, market volatility, etc.), and consider default a function of endogenous elements. The first author to apply the option pricing model to insolvency was Merton (1974), who based his formulation on the assumption that insolvency arises solely and exclusively if at bond maturity date a firm's assets are worth less its liabilities. Subsequently, a number of generalisations on Merton's model were proposed, the first by Black and Cox (1976) (cf. also Anderson and Sundaresan 1996; Anderson, Sundaresan, and Tychon 1996; Longstaff and Schwartz 1995; Mella-Barral 1997; Zhou 2001). These considered the possibility of default prior to bond maturity if the value of the firm's assets fell below a certain level, the threshold or default boundary.

The reduced form models emerged in the second half of the 1990s, thanks to contributions from a number of scholars (the most significant were Duffie and Singleton 1999; Jarrow, Lando, and Turnbull 1997; Jarrow and Turnbull 1995; Lando, 1994, 1998; Madan and Unal 1995; and more recently Hull and White 2000, 2001). Reduced form models are a recent approach to credit risk, and treat default as a sudden surprise, a totally exogenous event that is unrelated to the firm's balance sheet. The reason for default is not specified.

The structural models have been widely preferred to the reduced form models by practitioners in the field of credit risk, because the reduced form approach has been criticised on the grounds of the weak economic rationale for the occurrence of a default event (Alexopoulou, Andersson, and Georgescu 2009).

There is a substantial literature that builds on the structural models to analyse movements in CDS spreads.[7] Among the studies focusing on the structural models' theoretical determinants of CDS spreads are Aunon-Nerin et al. (2002), Benkert (2004), Zhang, Zhou, and Zhu (2005) and Abid and Naifar (2006). Recent empirical studies on the determinants of CDS spreads include, among others, Annaert et al. (2010), Eichngreen et al. (2009), Ericsson, Jacobs, and Oviedo (2009) and Di Cesare and Guazzarotti (2010). More recently, alongside the two groups of studies on CDS spreads mentioned above, a new current of research has emerged that examines the relationship between CDS spreads and rating announcements (Blanco, Brennan, and Marsh 2005; Daniels and Shin Jensen 2004; Hull, Predescu, and White 2004; Lehnert and Neske 2006; Norden and Weber 2004). Previously, research had analysed the impact of credit rating announcements on stock prices, bond prices or both.

Loosely following the strand of literature on structural models, this paper investigates the determinants of bank CDS spreads, building upon the works of Annaert et al. (2010), Boss and Scheicher (2005), Raunig and Scheicher (2009), among others.

3. Data sample and descriptive statistics

3.1 *Data description*

The study considers only mid-tier and top-tier international banking groups (by total assets) with 5-year senior CDS spreads. The decision to focus on CDS spreads in the banking sector had a decisive impact on sample size, given that only a limited number of banks are involved in CDS activities, and in credit derivatives in general. Indeed this type of business is highly concentrated among a restricted number of big banks.[8] There are overall 89 international banks with senior CDS spreads at 5 years. In addition, the decision to use quarterly balance sheet data rather than annual data reduced the sample, as not all banks with CDS contracts report financial data on a quarterly basis. For these reasons, the final sample is thus composed of 57 international banks, 43 of which European, 7 are US, 4 are Australian and 3 Japanese banks. See Table A1 in the appendix for details on the final sample.

The overall time horizon comprises the period from 1 January 2005, the year in which International Accounting Standards (IAS/IFRS) became mandatory for the preparation of consolidated financial statements of European banks, to 30 June 2011, the last data available at the time of this study. This time period is then divided into three sub-periods. The first sub-period is the pre-crisis period (from 1 January 2005 through 30 June 2007). This time was typified by very moderate CDS spreads. It is widely accepted that the outbreak of the sub-prime crisis occurred in July 2007. Therefore, we specify our second sub-period, the crisis period (from 1 July 2007 to 31 March 2009). During this time, CDS spread values grew considerably and displayed record peaks. We decided to end the crisis period at March 2009, as in subsequent months bank CDS spreads (and notably peak values), levelled off at values below those seen previously (see Figure 1) but higher than pre-crisis period values (European Central Bank 2009b; Bank for International Settlements 2010). Finally, our third period encompasses the less acute phase of the crisis (or post crisis period) and covers the most immediate aftermath of the crisis to date (from 1 April 2009 to 30 June 211). This period thus examines the beginning of the recovery phase, when bank CDS spreads began gradually to decrease.

3.2 *Dependent variable*

This paper uses as dependent variable 5-year senior CDS spreads in the banking sector. CDS spreads were chosen since they are widely considered an excellent indicator of markets' perception of a firm's default risk. The chosen data category, collected from Datastream, is 'CDS Premium Mid', which corresponds to the average of 'CDS premium bid' and 'CDS premium offered', and shows the mid rate spread between the entity and the relevant benchmark curve. The rate is expressed in basis points (bp). This study uses 5-year quotes insofar as this is the benchmark maturity in the CDS market. Senior CDS spreads were used since senior offers better data coverage than subordinated. Quarterly CDS spreads were used, a choice strictly related to the type of explanatory variables considered (balance sheet variables). The daily frequency of CDS spreads was adjusted to that of the explanatory variables.

Table A1 in the appendix presents descriptive statistics of senior 5-year CDS spreads for the 57 banks comprising our sample in the pre-crisis period (1 January 2005–30 June 2007), for the crisis period (1 July 2007–31 March 2009) and for the post crisis period (1 April 2009–30 June 2011).

Prior to the recent financial crisis, the CDS spreads of sample banks, regardless of geographical area, were moderate and fairly homogeneous. In particular, average CDS spread values ranged from 6.21 bp (Rabobank) to 68.13 bp (Banque Federale des Banques). The standard deviation of CDS spreads of the banks in the study were all below average values. Furthermore, the majority of sample banks recorded very similar minimum values, ranging from 1 to 12 bp. The same is true of peak values that ranged between 20 and 40 bp on average.

Conversely, clear differences between geographical areas emerge from the analysis of CDS spreads in the second period. During the crisis, though all sample bank CDS spreads showed a tendency to grow, in geographical terms such growth was heterogeneous. The Anglo-Saxon countries were worst hit by the financial crisis: first and foremost the USA, followed by Ireland and the UK, due principally to the prevalence of the Originate to Distribute banking model, but also to excessive financial leverage. Average CDS spread values, but in particular exceptionally high peak values, well in excess of average sample bank values, were recorded by US banks: Washington Mutual Inc. (maximum: 6235 bp), National City Corporation (maximum: 2969 bp), Wachovia Corporation (maximum: 1560 bp); by Irish banks: Anglo Irish Bank Corporation (maximum: 950 bp), Bank of Ireland (maximum: 670 bp), Allied Irish Banks (maximum: 646 bp); and by UK banks: Bradford & Bingley (maximum: 1591 bp), HBOS PLC (maximum: 500 bp) and Alliance & Leicester (maximum: 471 bp). All were thrown into crisis due to massive losses on structured financial products and, with the exception of Washington Mutual Inc., were bailed out though take-overs by other more solid banks, governments bailouts (nationalisation or recapitalisation) or cash injections from their respective central banks.

The remaining sample banks recorded more moderate average and peak CDS spread values that were nevertheless above average values in the preceding period, evidence of a reasonable ability to withstand the difficulties that overwhelmed the Anglo-Saxon banks. The sole exceptions were the Spanish banks Caja De Ahorros De Valencia Castellon Y Alicante Bancaja (maximum: 1148 bp) and Caja de Madrid (maximum: 750 bp), the Belgian banks Fortis (maximum: 666 bp) and Dexia SA (maximum: 550 bp) and the Austrian bank Erste Group Bank AG (maximum: 487 bp).

During the crisis the standard deviations of CDS spreads were below average values; in certain cases standard deviations equalled zero when banks formally had a CDS contract but traded very little. This was the case of the French Banque Federale Des Banques, and, in the pre-crisis period, the Spanish Banco de Sabadell SA.

Finally, in the post crisis period (1 April 2009–30 June 2011), Table A1 shows that just under half of sample banks recorded lower average CDS spread values than during the crisis period. Nevertheless, almost all peak values were lower, with the exception of most of Portuguese, Spanish, Irish and Italian banks. In the post crisis period, bank CDS spreads of these countries, due to national debt crisis, grew again despite not to levels reached in the previous acute phase of the crisis.[9] Minimum values were higher than the previous period. The standard deviations of sample bank CDS spreads were almost all below average values.

3.3 *Explanatory variables*

This study uses as explanatory variables eight balance sheet ratios, in order of the analysis profile pre-calculated by Bloomberg on the Global format. Quarterly data were selected rather than annual data to make available a higher number of observations for analysis.

The eight balance sheet ratios by management area and their hypothesed relationship (irrespective of the time horizon considered) with the dependent variable are outlined below and summarised in Table 1.

Table 1. Explanatory variables and predicted sign.

Variable	Description	Predicted sign
Asset quality		
qa1	Loan loss reserve/gross loans (%)	Positive
qa2	Unreserved impaired loans/equity (%)	Positive
Capital		
pat1	TIER 1 Ratio (%)	Negative
pat2	Leverage: equity/total assets (%)	Negative
Operations		
op1	ROA (%) = net income/average total assets	Negative/positive
op2	ROE (%) = net income/average equity	Negative
Liquidity		
liq1	Net loans/deposits and short-term funding (%)	Positive/negative
liq2	Liquid assets/deposits and short-term funding (%)	Negative

3.3.1 Asset quality

Loan Loss Reserve/Gross Loans (%), qa1. This ratio expresses the percentage value of total credits appropriated to the depreciation fund. It is a reserve for losses expressed as percentage of total loans. The higher the ratio, the lower the quality of the loan portfolio. Hence, an increase in qa1 should lead to an increase in CDS spreads.

Unreserved Impaired Loans/Equity (%), qa2. This ratio is also known as the 'capital impairment ratio'. An increase in the ratio should signal a greater probability of default. As such, a positive relationship between change in qa2 and change in CDS spreads are hypothesised.

3.3.2 Capital

TIER 1 Ratio[10] (%), pat1. This ratio measures the capital adequacy of a bank. In particular, TIER 1 capital ratio measures the ability of the bank to absorb losses. The higher the ratio, the higher the risk buffer and the lower should be the CDS spreads. Hence, a negative sign is expected.

Leverage: Equity/Total Assets (%), pat2. There are different definitions of leverage – balance sheet, economic and embedded – and no single measure can capture all dimensions simultaneously. The first definition is based on balance sheet concepts, the second on market-dependent future cash flows and the third on market risk. Balance sheet leverage is the most visible and widely recognised form and it is one adopted in this study. The leverage ratio, defined as Equity/Total Assets, reflects the level of indebtedness of a firm. One would expect that as equity diminishes, with constant total assets, the proportion of debts to total assets should increase, as should the level of indebtedness and hence the risk of default. A negative sign is therefore expected between Leverage and CDS spreads.

With the choice of these two variables, we are close to Almer, Heidorn, and Schmaltz (2008), who investigated the determinants of short- and long-term bank CDS spreads using cross-sectional regressions; the authors also used as explanatory variables the following: 'Insolvency Factors': Loan Loss Reserve (%), Loan Loss Provision (%), % of Problem Loans, Pre-Tax-Profit (%) and Long-term Rating. Furthermore, leverage is the only explanatory variable used in this paper that is also present in Merton's model.

3.3.3 Operations

ROA (*Return on average Assets*) (%), op1. This ratio is an indicator of the return on a firm's investments. The sign linking ROA to CDS spreads is uncertain, as the market may interpret the relationship between these variables either negatively or positively. In particular, a bank that undertakes numerous investments (low ROA) may be perceived by the market as being very risky. In this case, low ROA values would correspond to high CDS spreads. On the other hand, the market may react positively if it assumed that high levels of investment are capable of creating positive income and future cash flows. In this case, moderate ROA values would correspond to low CDS spreads.

Furthermore, a negative relationship between ROA and CDS may be due to a decrease (or an increase) in operating income at the same level of investment. In such case, a decrease (increase) in ROA would correspond to an increase (decrease) in CDS spreads.

ROE (*Return on average Equity*) (%), op2. This ratio is an index of the return on own equity. The higher the ratio, the lower the perceived default risk. Hence, a negative sign is expected.

3.3.4 Liquidity[11]

Net Loans/Deposits and Short-Term Funding (%), liq1. The loan-to-deposit ratio is a measure of liquidity. The relationship linking this index to CDS spreads is uncertain. The relationship can be interpreted positively when banks with fewer deposits, and hence lower liquidity, are not perceived positively by the market. An increase in liq1 should therefore correspond to growth in CDS spreads. On the other hand, the relationship can be interpreted negatively when a high level of loans, for the same level of deposits, is perceived by the market as a positive signal, since sample banks are commercial banks and loans represent their core business. Growth in liq1 should therefore correspond to a decrease in CDS spreads.

Liquid Assets/Deposits and Short-Term Funding (%), liq2. A further measure of liquidity is the ratio of Liquid Assets to Deposits and Short-Term Funding. The higher this percentage, the more liquid the bank and the less vulnerable to a classic run. Hence, a negative sign is expected. An increase in liq2 should decrease CDS spreads. Similarly, Almer, Heidorn, and Schmaltz (2008) considered as 'Illiquidity Factors' also the ratio of Total Money Market Funding to Total Liabilities (the so-called % of Wholesale Funding).

Table 2 reports descriptive statistics relating to the eight balance sheet variables of the sample banks for the pre-crisis period (1 January 2005–30 June 2007), the crisis period (1 July 2007–31 March 2009) and the post crisis period (1 April 2009–30 June 2011).

Unlike CDS spreads, the values of balance sheet variables did not change significantly from the pre-crisis period to the crisis period. The only exception is the average value of qa2. Furthermore, most sample banks recorded homogeneous values for almost all variables in all periods, with the exception of the banks that incurred vast losses during the crisis and/or were bailed out by government intervention (principally the UK, Irish and US banks).

In particular, the average value of qa1 remained substantially unchanged, from the pre-crisis period to the crisis period for almost all banks in the study. Conversely, the other indicator of asset

Table 2. Summary statistics on eight balance sheet indicators for sample banks.

	Pre-crisis period[a]		During the crisis period[a]		Post crisis period[a]	
Variable	Mean (Std. Dev.)	Min.–Max.	Mean (Std. Dev.)	Min.–Max.	Mean (Std. Dev.)	Min.–Max.
Asset quality						
Qa1	0.014 (0.009)	0.000–0.041	0.016 (0.010)	0.001–0.051	0.025 (0.015)	0.001–0.078
Qa2	1.370 (9.505)	0.000–107.945	0.283 (1.951)	−7.866–36.044	0.257 (1.777)	−26.7530–4.569
Capital						
Pat1	0.078 (0.013)	0.047–0.139	0.081 (0.017)	0.051–0.179	0.105 (0.023)	0.043–0.182
Pat2	0.053 (0.021)	0.019–0.104	0.051 (0.042)	−0.036-0.386	0.058 (0.033)	−0.018–0.295
Operations						
Op1	0.008 (0.004)	−0.001–0.025	0.003 (0.011)	−0.091–0.044	0.001 (0.012)	−0.104–0.030
Op2	0.182 (0.060)	−0.071–0.562	0.041 (0.237)	−2.020–1.445	0.018 (0.177)	−1.489–0.422
Liquidity						
Liq1	0.820 (0.351)	0.139–2.031	0.805 (0.418)	0.014–2.488	0.875 (0.677)	0.015–12.948
Liq2	0.484 (0.276)	0.128–1.530	0.464 (0.277)	0.090–1.750	0.487 (0.295)	0.082–1.896

Notes: This table reports summary statistics on eight explanatory balance sheet variables for the sample banks for the pre-crisis period (1 January 2005–30 June 2007), the crisis period (1 July 2007–31 March 2009) and the post crisis period (1 April 2009–30 June 2011).

Source: Datastream Database and authors' calculations.

[a] The number of banks in the period preceding the crisis was 53, in the crisis period 55, and in the post crisis period 47. The independent variables (qa1, qa2, pat1, pat2, op1, op2, liq1 and liq2) are defined in Section 3.3.

quality, qa2, fell considerably, probably due to the numerous capital increases carried out by the banks in difficulty during the crisis. The average qa2 value of the sample banks decreased from 137% in the pre-crisis period to 28% during the crisis. This fall was principally attributable to two banks, Banco Espirito Santo and Credit Suisse, both of which recorded a significant fall in this index. Conversely, other sample banks – principally the UK, Irish and US banks – recorded strong growth in qa2 during the crisis. Such growth was the result of deterioration in the quality of capital, and affected the Belgian banks Dexia and KBC Groep NV, the Austrian Raiffeisen International Bank Holding, the Swedish Swedbank AB and the Japanese Mizuho Financial Group.

The variables relating to the banks' financial structure, pat1 and pat2, remained substantially unchanged from the pre-crisis period to the crisis period. Overall, the majority of sample banks, despite being adversely affected by the crisis, exhibited a capital coefficient (pat1) well above the minimum regulatory threshold both before and during the crisis. The average value of pat2 declined from 5.3% in the pre-crisis period to 5.1% during the crisis. However, while the ratio of Equity to Total Assets remained substantially unchanged during the crisis for the majority of the UK banks, it showed a tendency to increase for large European banks, but above all for US commercial banks. Overall, at a global level, the financial leverage of the sample banks remained high.

The profitability indices, op1 and op2, both declined, but at different rates. In particular, the average op1 value of sample banks fell by three percentage points, while average op2 values halved from 18% to 4%. During the crisis, negative average Return on Assets (ROA) and Return on Equity (ROE) values were recorded principally by UK, Irish and US banks.

The two liquidity indices considered, liq1 and liq2, show fairly similar average values between the pre-crisis period and the crisis period. In particular, the former ratio decreased slightly from 82% to 80%, while the latter decreased slightly from 48% to 46%.

The last panel of Table 2 highlights how in the post crisis period, the average value of all eight balance sheet variables remained substantially unchanged with respect to the previous period. The exceptions were qa1, op1 and op2. In particular, in the post crisis period the average value of qa1 showed a tendency to grow (from 1.6% to 2.5%) principally due to an increase in devaluation of loans. The average value of the two income ratios continued to fall in the post crisis period, principally due to a significant deterioration in the asset quality of most sample banks. From the crisis period to the post crisis period, op1 declined from 0.5% to 0.1%, while op2 fell from 4% to 1.8%. Finally, the average value of the two liquidity indices increased in the post crisis period: liq1 increased from 80% to 87%, principally thanks to a moderate recovery, while liq2 grew from 46% to 48%.

Time-series graphs were plotted to show the relationship between average bank CDS spreads and each explanatory variable (see Figure A1). Furthermore, correlation coefficients were calculated between balance sheet variables and CDS spreads (see Table 3). Figure A1 in the appendix shows the time-series graphs of average CDS spreads versus the eight balance sheet variables for the pre-crisis period (January 2005–June 2007) and the crisis period (July 2007–March 2009).[12] The panels in Figure A1 show a clear reversal in the CDS trend and in that of the majority of explanatory variables at the start of the third quarter of 2007, the time of the outbreak of the financial crisis. Furthermore, for most graphs, the relationships observed in Figure A1 are readily interpreted principally during the crisis period. During this period, the signs predicted in Table 1 were largely confirmed (with the exception of pat1). Panel A shows the relationship between average CDS spreads and average qa1 values, while Panel B presents the relationship between average CDS spreads and average qa2 values. As predicted, the time series of average CDS spreads versus average qa1 values, in the period between July 2007 and March 2009, showed the positive trend expected. Conversely, the relationship between average CDS spreads and average qa2 values showed a negative sign rather than the positive one expected.

Panel C presents the time series of average CDS spreads versus average pat1 values. The relationship is positive in the crisis period, contrary to what was expected. CDS spreads thus tended to increase, rather than to decrease, with growth in pat1.

Panel D presents the time series of average CDS spreads versus average of pat2 values. In this case, during the crisis period, the expected sign (negative) was respected. As equity decreased, with total assets held constant, the incidence of debts on total assets increased, as did the level of indebtedness and consequently the risk of default. Panel D illustrates that sample banks displayed high levels of leverage, not only in the crisis period but also in the pre-crisis period, when bank CDS spreads remained low. This implies that until the onset of the crisis, markets were not concerned by the very high leverage of banks. Only at the outbreak of the crisis (July 2007) did CDS spread values begin to rise significantly. Hence the outbreak of crisis was one of the factors responsible for growth in bank CDS spreads, and not excessive leverage itself, although excessive bank leverage is considered one of the determinants of the crisis. In other words, contrary to what was expected, Leverage was not among the key determinants of bank CDS spreads.

This result seems to contradict those of the structural models' approach in general and the recent conclusions of Di Cesare and Guazzarotti (2010) in particular, who find that leverage remains one of the most significant variables in explaining CDSs spreads for US non-financial firms even during the crisis period. However, it is important to recall that leverage of a bank is fundamentally a different variable from a firm's leverage. Indeed, prior to the crisis, quantitative limits on bank leverage were rare and only post-crisis there are talks of introducing bank leverage limits as an additional prudential tool to complement minimum capital adequacy requirements. Our study underlines the difference between the financial and non-financial sector CDSs and casts doubts on the predicitive value of models and combine both financial and non-financial firms. This outcome confirms the findings of Annaert et al. (2010), according to which variables that are found to affect credit spreads of non-financial companies often lose their explanatory power when applied to financials.

Panel E shows the relationship between average CDS spreads and average op1 values, while Panel F shows the relationship between average CDS spreads and average of op2 values. Panel E highlights a clearly negative relationship during the crisis. Hence, the market gives a negative interpretation to low ROA in times of crisis. Panel F also shows a negative relationship: moderate ROE values increase the perceived probability of default.

Panel G presents the time series of average CDS spreads versus average of liq1 values and highlights a negative relationship during the crisis, particularly from 2008 onwards. The market thus interprets positively a high level of loan activity in times of crisis. Panel H presents the time series of average CDS spreads versus average liq2 values. In this case also the expected sign (negative) is respected.

Table 3 shows the correlations between each explanatory balance sheet variable and CDS spreads, both for the pre-crisis period (January 2005–June 2007) and for the crisis period (July 2007–March 2009). Since results for the post crisis period are not significantly different from the crisis period, these are not reported.

Table 3 shows a reversal in the trend of CDS spreads and the majority of explanatory variables (six variables out of eight) at the start of the third quarter 2007, with the outbreak of the financial

Table 3. Correlations pre-crisis and crisis period.

	CDS spreads	
Variable	Pre crisis period	During the crisis period
Qa1	0.0107	0.1174*
Qa2	−0.0298	0.0133
Pat1	0.0031	0.1592*
Pat2	0.1372*	−0.0441
Op1	0.2041*	−0.3021*
Op2	0.1319*	−0.3214*
Liq1	−0.0146	0.1196*
Liq2	0.1339*	−0.1779*

Notes: The dependent variable (CDS spreads) and the independent variables (qa1, qa2, pat1, pat2, op1, op2, liq1 and liq2) are defined respectively in Sections 3.2 and 3.3. The pre-crisis period spans from 1 January 2005 to 30 June 2007, while the crisis period extends from 1 July 2007 to 31 March 2009.
The variables with no * are independent.

crisis. Furthermore, Table 3 highlights how the expected signs (illustrated in Table 1) are principally respected during the crisis. The sole exception is the sign of the TIER 1 Ratio (qa1), which differs from that expected during the crisis period.[13]

4. Empirical methodology

To determine whether balance sheet data explain bank CDS spreads, we follow a panel data regression. Indeed, as our sample includes banks having both sufficient valid CDS spreads and quarterly accounting data (recall that the sample includes only mid-tier and top-tier international banking groups with 5-year senior CDS spreads) it is not a random sample and it is possible to assume that our results could not be generalised to all banks.

In particular, we specify the following generic model:

$$\mathrm{CDS}_{it} = \alpha + \beta(\mathrm{BankBSratios})_{\mathrm{it}} + d_{\mathrm{crisis}} + \varepsilon_{it}, \tag{1}$$

where i is the subscript identifying the bank and t indicates the time period (the quarter in progress). In this model, we introduce only time-varying bank-specific explanatory variables (balance sheet ratios: BankBSratios) but not time-varying market-wide explanatory variables. d_{crisis} is the dummy variable that identifies the outbreak of the recent financial crisis (1 July 2007) and ε_{it} is the error.

In the first instance, the regressions were conducted covering the entire time horizon (1 January 2005–30 June 2011); a first regression including only the eight balance sheet variables; a second one including the eight variables plus the dummy crisis (from 1 July 2007).

Subsequently, to determine whether the relationship between bank CDS spreads and balance sheet data changes with varying macroeconomic and financial conditions, three further panel regressions were performed: one on the period preceding the crisis (1 January 2005–30 June 2007), one the crisis period (1 July 2007–31 March 2009) and a last one on the post crisis period (1 April 2009–30 June 2011).[14]

In all the regressions, levels rather than differences were used, for both dependent and explanatory variables. Note that the goal of this paper is not to predict but to explain credit spreads, hence, we use contemporaneous dependent and explanatory variables.

5. Results

Table 4 reports the results of the first two panel regressions (without and with the dummy crisis), both conducted on the entire time horizon (1 January 2005–30 June 2011). For both regressions, the final sample consisted of 1256 observations for 57 banks. Table 4 indicates that the balance sheet variables explain nearly 64% of bank CDS spreads (adjusted R^2 value); and that the balance sheet indices and the dummy crisis together explain 67% of bank CDS spreads (adjusted R^2). From the first panel regression it emerges that, with the exception of liq1, all the explanatory variables are significant and have the expected sign (with two exceptions: qa2 is negative rather than positive, and pat1 is positive rather than negative).

In the case of qa2, Panel B in Figure A1 shows how the relationship between this variable and bank CDS spreads was inversely proportionate during both the pre-crisis and the crisis periods. In particular, Panel B highlights how, in the pre-crisis period, high qa2 values corresponded to very low CDS spreads. This implies that in the pre-crisis period, the market was not concerned with the poor quality of bank loan portfolios. Moreover, Panel B shows that in the crisis period, a fall in qa2 resulted in a rise rather than a fall in bank CDS spreads. The abrupt decrease in this relationship is most probably attributable to the numerous capital increases carried out by many

Table 4. Panel regressions.

Variable	Whole period	Whole period and dummy crisis	Pre-crisis period	During the crisis period	Post crisis period
Qa1	3019.194***	3184.293***	339.959*	5841.518***	3578.455***
	(360.622)	(342.706)	(132.078)	(1054.481)	(823.578)
Qa2	−2.383***	−1.798***	−0.101	−1.018	28.410
	(0.394)	(0.377)	(0.069)	(1.747)	(24.794)
Pat1	809.870***	252.133	−38.498	2159.72***	978.256**
	(129.453)	(132.205)	(61.460)	(411.876)	(312.541)
Op1	−4170.813***	−3396.34***	1626.445***	2154.717	−13173.09***
	(906.371)	(863.232)	(349.269)	(1409.976)	(3371.008)
Op2	−206.312***	−152.949***	−3.866	−301.503***	128.771
	(36.052)	(34.546)	(11.552)	(55.877)	(119.554)
Liq1	0.025	−29.542	2.017	−178.760***	−110.261*
	(17.081)	(16.422)	(4.160)	(41.685)	(47.502)
Liq2	−82.940***	−70.733***	−2.357	−26.342	−99.579*
	(19.160)	(18.223)	(4.069)	(40.455)	(48.683)
Dummy crisis		54.940***			
		(4.796)			
Number of observations	1256	1256	506	354	396
Number of sample banks	57	57	53	55	47
Adjusted R^2	0.6386	0.6742	0.6141	0.6627	0.7329
Qa1	3897.548***	3376.869***	285.000*	5491.569***	4250.474***
	(390.638)	(364.000)	(128.170)	(1424.575)	(805.759)
Qa2	−2.273***	−1.520***	−0.036	−0.984	46.202
	(0.462)	(0.431)	(0.070)	(2.436)	(24.959)
Pat2	−312.295	−750.698*	−261.141***	−2493.139*	2141.462*
	(169.897)	(314.818)	(72.162)	(993.529)	(896.981)
Op1	−4731.896***	−4208.07***	1702.289***	−1284.64	−12093.8***
	(1049.319)	(973.519)	(327.702)	(1905.935)	(3354.918)
Op2	−196.451***	−110.0233**	−13.423	−162.507*	119.693
	(41.837)	(39.259)	(11.602)	(77.744)	(120.221)
Liq1	−9.279	−51.343**	4.712	−193.063**	−107.880*
	(20.067)	(18.836)	(4.100)	(41.803)	(47.871)
Liq2	−66.426**	−60.439**	−3.826	−6.090	−86.151
	(22.369)	(20.742)	(3.938)	(55.849)	(49.382)
Dummy crisis		71.185***			
		(4.996)			
Number of observations	1301	1301	525	372	404
Number of sample banks	58	58	56	56	49
Adjusted R^2	0.5556	0.6180	0.6223	0.4911	0.7462

Notes: The dependent variable is CDS spreads which measure the probability of default. The explanatory variables are balance sheet ratios referring to asset quality (qa1 and qa2), capital (pat1 and pat2), operations (op1 and op2) and liquidity (liq1 and liq2). The dummy crisis identifies the start of the crisis (1 July 2007). The dependent variable and the independent variables are defined respectively in Sections 3.2 and 3.3. 'Whole period' denotes the period from 1 January 2005 to 31 March 2010 (latest data available). 'Pre-crisis period' denotes the period from 1 January 2005 to 30 June 2007. 'During the crisis period' denotes the period from 1 July 2007 to 31 March 2009. 'Post crisis period' denotes the period from 1 April 2009 to 30 June 2011. Due to multicollinearity problem between capital explanatory variables (pat1 and pat2), for each time periods considered, the panel regression was performed using alternately the two capital ratios. Standard errors of estimated coefficients are reported in parentheses. Adjusted R^2 derives from areg.

***Denotes coefficient statistically different from zero (1% level, two-tail test).

**5% level.

*10% level.

banks in difficulty during the crisis. Evidently, recapitalisation, particularly through injection of government funds, was perceived negatively by the market, as a sign of crisis in the banking sector. This may have contributed to the increase in bank CDS spreads. For an explanation of the reasons for the unexpected sign of pat1, see the discussion of the crisis period regression panel below.

From the second regression panel it emerges that the dummy crisis is significant and therefore indicates that the crisis was a relevant event in the relationship between bank CDS spreads and balance sheet data, as expected.

To understand whether the relationship between bank CDS spreads and balance sheet data changes with varying macroeconomic conditions, two further panel regressions were conducted, one on the sub-period1 January 2005–30 June 2007 and the other on the sub-period 1 July 2007–31 March 2009. The final sample consisted of 506 observations for 53 banks in the pre-crisis period and 354 observations for 55 banks in the crisis period (Table 4).

Table 4 shows that the explanatory power of the balance sheet variables thus grew 5% with the transition from the pre-crisis period to the crisis period (in terms of adjusted R^2). The lower explanatory power of the balance sheet ratios during the pre-crisis period is simply because bank CDS spreads were flat at that time. As bank CDS spreads grew, so did the explanatory power of the balance sheet variables. Overall, the adjusted R^2 value well in excess of 50% in both periods demonstrates how bank CDS spreads in the pre-crisis period, but above all in the crisis period, reflect a great deal of the risk expressed by the balance sheet variables. These results confirm those reported by Annaert et al. (2010), which suggest that the variables used by structural credit risk models are not significant in explaining bank CDS spread changes in the period prior to the crisis.

In the period preceding the crisis, qa1 and op1 are the only significant variables and the sign respect those predicted. The results in Table 4 show a positive relationship between qa1 and bank CDS spreads. In terms of the relationship between op1 and CDS spreads, in the pre-crisis period the relationship was positive. Hence, in the pre-crisis period, a decrease in op1 brought about a decrease rather than an increase in bank CDS spreads: evidently, the market associated the fall in ROA with a high level of investment capable of generating positive cash and income flows in future.

It also emerges that, as expected, in the pre-crisis period the bank CDS market did not pay attention to any liquidity index. The liquidity crisis (in terms of both market liquidity risk and funding risk) was the last manifestation of the recent financial crisis. This outcome confirms the findings of the study by Almer, Heidorn, and Schmaltz (2008), according to which 'Liquid Factors' did not have a significant impact on bank CDS spreads in the pre-crisis period.

In the crisis period, on the other hand, the number of significant explanatory variables increased with respect to the previous period. This indicates that the CDS market probably pays greater attention to balance sheet indices particularly in periods of financial stress. However, only one of the explanatory variables that was significant during the crisis was significant also during the pre-crisis period: qa1. This implies that the type of variables to which the market pays attention tends to vary as economic and financial conditions vary. This is in line with the finding of Annaert et al. (2010), who finds that the determinants of bank CDS spreads vary strongly across time. This finding also confirms similar results in studies for bond spreads and indicates that models which attempt to explain changes in bank CDS spreads must be re-estimated as macroeconomic conditions change in order to give the 'right' information to regulators and policy-makers. The variables which were significant during the crisis are qa1, pat1, op2 and liq1. Conversely, op1 lost significance during the crisis period. In particular, as predicted, we found a positive relationship between qa1 and bank CDS spreads and a negative relationship between op2 and bank CDS spreads.

An analysis of the signs of two of the four significant variables reveals that the probability of default tends to increase principally for banks that in recent years had a poor-quality loan portfolio and/or lower returns on equity. This outcome confirms the findings of the study by Calice and Ioannidis (2009), according to which Large Complex Financial Institutions with large exposure to problems assets tend to be adversely affected by the widening of credit spreads.

Our results also show that during the crisis period, the relationship between liq1 and CDS spreads was negative. During the crisis period, the decrease in liq1 was due principally to a decrease in loans (the so-called credit crunch phenomena) and was accompanied by an increase in bank CDS spreads.

Pat1, a significant explanatory variable during the crisis, has a different sign from the one expected: positive rather than negative. Pat1 was also positive during the pre-crisis period, although not significant. This positive relationship implies that the growth in pat1 was accompanied, in both the pre-crisis and the crisis period, by an increase rather than a decrease in the perceived probability of bank default. As Panel C of Figure A1 indicates, the positive relationship between pat1 and CDS spreads is particularly evident in the crisis period. The positive (rather than negative) sign of pat1 in Table 4 suggests that the market, above all in the crisis period, lacked faith in this capital index. The banks in difficulty in the final period, with rapidly growing CDS spreads, had a TIER 1 Ratio well in excess of the minimum requirement and also above the average for their geographical area. What emerges is thus the limited efficacy of the capital index TIER 1 Ratio in safeguarding banks from the potential risk of default. This is confirmed, at least in part, by the Basel Committee December 2010 final document (Basel 3), that focuses, among other things, on improving the quality of regulatory capital.[15]

From the results presented Table 4 it is also evident that qa2 and liq2 are not significant variables either in the pre-crisis or in the crisis period.

Finally, to investigate whether the relationship between bank CDS spreads and balance sheet data changes in the post crisis period (1 April 2009–30 June 2011), a fifth panel regression was performed (Table 4).

The final sample consisted of 396 observations for 47 banks. The results show that in the period that takes into account the less acute phase of the crisis (and the beginning of the recovery phase), the relationship between balance sheet variables and bank CDS spreads becomes stronger. In the post crisis period, both liquidity ratios considered (liq 1 and liq2) are significant. This may reflect the increased attention paid by regulators to bank liquidity in the post crisis period. In December 2010, the Basel Committee announced the introduction of two new liquidity standards for banks: the liquidity coverage ratio, rule of short term and the Net Stable Funding Ratio, longer-term structural rule.[16]

6. Robustness tests

As the main goal of this paper is not to predict but to explain credit spreads, in the empirical analysis we used contemporaneous dependent and explanatory variables. However, bank CDS spreads may precede balance sheet data or react to the publication of results. To test this hypothesis, a number of further regressions were carried out (see Table 5).

The first group of regressions considered bank CDS spreads at time $t-1$, the preceding quarter, and balance sheet data at time t, the quarter considered. The second group of panel regressions considered bank CDS spreads at time $t+1$, the quarter following, and balance sheet variables at time t. Both regressions with bank CDS spreads at time $t-1$ and those with bank CDS spreads at time $t+1$ were conducted on the overall period considered (1 January 2005–30 June 2011)

Table 5. Panel regressions (robustness test).

	CDS $t-1$			CDS $t+1$		
Variable	Pre-crisis period	During the crisis period	Post crisis period	Pre-crisis Period	During the crisis period	Post crisis period
Qa1	168.048	4310.54***	3683.421**	334.304	4310.54***	3683.421**
	(181.153)	(1041.466)	(1118.108)	(175.313)	(1041.466)	(1118.108)
Qa2	−0.050	73.594*	−13.973	−0.125	73.594*	−13.973
	(0.765)	(34.942)	(29.081)	(0.092)	(34.942)	(29.081)
Pat1	−117.531*	1128.544**	1270.552**	−32.450	1128.544**	1270.552**
	(58.977)	(1431.283)	(369.058)	(81.598)	(410.269)	(369.058)
Op1	−40.900	997.283	−15088.28**	3727.584***	997.283	−15088.28**
	(349.780)	(1431.283)	(4764.587)	(463.661)	(1431.283)	(4764.587)
Op2	3.715	−217.918***	312.260	−11.628	−217.918***	312.260
	(12.709)	(56.643)	(179.973)	(15.333)	(56.643)	(179.973)
Liq1	1.006	−116.235**	−105.724	3.037	−116.235**	−105.724
	(4.106)	(41.917)	(55.779)	(5.522)	(41.917)	(55.779)
Liq2	−0.524	12.827	−93.834	2.460	12.827	−93.834
	(4.165)	(40.616)	(61.226)	(5.402)	(40.616)	(61.226)
No. of observations	455	301	349	505	301	349
No. of sample banks	53	54	55	53	54	47
Adjusted R^2	0.6460	0.6163	0.6448	0.6191	0.6163	0.6448
Qa1	195.911	2949.261*	4829.115***	154.655	2949.261*	4829.115***
	(178.074)	(1194.255)	(1108.015)	(175.969)	(1194.255)	(1108.015)
Qa2	−0.024	229.261***	19.218	−0.020	229.261***	19.218
	(0.077)	(36.759)	(28.917)	(0.096)	(36.759)	(28.917)
Pat2	−185.803*	−1258.094	4227.542***	−350.036***	−1258.094	4227.542***
	(73.087)	(877.093)	(1107.999)	(99.072)	(877.093)	(1107.999)
Op1	285.546	−1201.006	−13743.28**	3170.933***	−1201.006	−13743.28**
	(337.272)	(1660.659)	(4699.187)	(449.939)	(1660.659)	(4669.187)
Op2	−1.759	−103.864	303.895	−24.423	−103.864	303.895
	(13.023)	(66.038)	(179.230)	(15.928)	(66.038)	(179.230)
Liq1	3.940	−109.317*	−108.554	6.525	−109.317**	−108.554
	(4.139)	(49.553)	(55.669)	(5.630)	(49.553)	(55.669)
Liq2	−2.625	57.716	−68.811	0.188	57.716	−68.811
	(4.060)	(48.108)	(61.665)	(5.407)	(48.108)	(61.665)
No. of observations	471	316	355	524	316	355
No. of sample banks	56	55	49	56	55	49
Adjusted R^2	0.6463	0.5585	0.6730	0.5994	0.5585	0.6730

Notes: The dependent variable is CDS spreads which measure the probability of default. The explanatory variables are balance sheet ratios referring to asset quality (qa1 and qa2), capital (pat1 and pat2), operations (op1 and op2) and liquidity (liq1 and liq2). The dependent variable and the independent variables are defined respectively in Sections 3.2 and 3.3. 'CDS $t-1$' denotes CDS spread values for the quarter preceding the quarter in progress; 'CDS $t+1$' denotes CDS spreads for the quarter following the quarter in progress. The balance sheet data in both panel regressions are at time t (the quarter in progress). 'Pre-crisis period' denotes the period from 1 January 2005 to 30 June 2007. 'During the crisis period' denotes the period from 1 July 2007 to 31 March 2009. 'Post crisis period' denotes the period from 1 April 2009 to 30 June 2011. Due to the multicollinearity problem between capital explanatory variables (pat1 and pat2), for each time periods considered, the panel regression was performed using alternately the two capital ratios. Standard errors of estimated coefficients are reported in parentheses. Adjusted R^2 derives from areg.

***Denotes coefficient statistically different from zero (1% level, two-tail test).

**5% level.

*10% level.

and on all sub-periods. Table 5, however, presents the results of the three sub-periods only: the pre-crisis period (1 January 2005–30 June 2007), the crisis period (1 July 2007–31 March 2009) and the post crisis period (1 April 2009–30 June 2011).[17]

Comparison of the results of the panel regressions in Table 5 with those of the panel regressions of Table 4, which consider both bank CDS spreads and balance sheet variables at time t, reveals that bank CDS spreads did not react in advance to the crisis and required less than a 3-month lag to incorporate balance sheet information. The CDS market is thus an efficient market capable of reacting to information as it is made public. For this reason, it is correct to consider both bank CDS spreads and balance sheet variables at time t. The adjusted R^2 values in Table 4 in all three time periods are higher than those obtained considering bank CDS spreads at time $t + 1$. Moreover, in two of the three periods, the crisis period and the post crisis period, values are marginally higher even than those obtained considering bank CDS spreads at time $t - 1$.

7. Conclusions

This paper investigates whether CDS spreads can be considered a good proxy for bank riskiness. Based on a sample of mid-tier to top-tier international banks with senior CDS spreads at 5 years, we analyse the relationship between bank CDS spreads and balance sheet variables relating to the quality of bank assets, capital, earning potential and liquidity. The analysis was conducted on the period 1 January 2005–30 June 2011. This was then subdivided into three sub-periods: the pre-crisis period (1 January 2005–30 June 2007), the crisis period (1 July 2007–31 March 2009) and the post crisis period (1 April 2009–30 June 2011).

Results indicate that bank CDS spreads in the pre-crisis period, but especially in the crisis and post crisis period, reflecting the risk captured by balance sheet ratios. The lower explanatory power of the balance sheet indices in the pre-crisis period is mainly due to the fact that bank CDS spreads were relatively flat at that time. The crisis was a relevant event in the relationship between bank CDS spreads and balance sheet data. As bank CDS spread grew, so did the explanatory power of the balance sheet variables. The relationship between bank CDS spreads and balance sheet ratios grew stronger during the crisis period, when a number of explanatory variables became significant. Furthermore, bank CDS spreads seem to be influenced by different variables in the pre-crisis and crisis period. This finding confirms similar results in studies for both bond and CDSs spreads and indicates that models which attempt to explain changes in bank CDS spreads must be re-estimated as macroeconomic conditions change in order to give the 'right' information to regulators and policy-makers. Our results also indicate that bank CDS spreads did not react in advance to the crisis and required less than a three-month lag to incorporate the balance sheet information. The CDS market is thus an efficient market capable of reacting to information as it is made public. This casts doubts on the ability of CDS spreads to 'predict' banks probability of default.

In terms of individual predictors, the ratio Loan Loss Reserve to Gross Loans is the only significant variable in all the three sub-periods considered. The probability of default is likely to increase principally for those banks with poor-quality loan portfolios. Contrary to prior expectations, Leverage and the TIER 1 Ratio were not among the determinants of bank CDS spreads in any of the three sub-periods considered. What is more, the sample banks that ran into difficulty almost always had a TIER 1 Ratio well above the statutory minimum. Overall, doubts emerge in relation to the efficacy of the capital index TIER 1 Ratio as a safeguard against the risk of future default.

Finally, as expected, the bank CDS market in the pre-crisis period showed no interest in any of the liquidity indices considered. Only with the outbreak of the sub prime crisis, liquidity indicators become significant and remained significant in the post-crisis period, possibly reflecting the increased attention paid by regulators to bank liquidity in the new Basel proposals.

Acknowledgements

We wish to thank Roberto Bottiglia, Andrea Paltrinieri and Nicola Tommasi for support and assistance. Thanks to Emanuele Maria Carluccio and Francesco Betti, Risk Manager, Accounting & Financial Controls, Aletti Gestielle SGR SpA, for their assistance in gathering balance sheet data. Thanks to Nicolò Bocchin, Gestielle corporate bond manager, for his assistance with CDS data. We are grateful to two anonymous referees for their helpful suggestions that greatly improved the paper. We would like to thank participants to the second Emerging Scholars in Banking and Finance conference, and to the Wo!pertinger 2010 conference for valuable comments and discussions. The usual disclaimer applies. This research was completed while Laura Chiaramonte was a visiting scholar at Cass Business School, City University London.

Notes

1. Allen and Gale (2007a, 2007b), Goodhart (2008), International Monetary Fund (IMF 2008), International Organization of Securities Commissions (IOSCO 2008), Bank for International Settlements (BIS 2008, 2009) and Brunnermeier (2009) offer a detailed analysis of the subprime crisis.
2. The International Swap and Derivatives Association (ISDA) released sets of Credit Derivatives Definitions in 1999 (which were amended in 2001) and 2003. They are Bankruptcy, Obligation Acceleration, Obligation Default, Failure to Pay, Repudiation/Moratorium and Restructuring.
3. See European Central Bank (2009a, 64–70).
4. A limited number of recent studies focus exclusively on CDS spreads in the banking sector, though with different research aims: Kool (2006), Annaert et al. (2009) and Norden and Weber (2010), with a sample of the major European banks; Huang, Zhou, and Zhu (2009), Constantinos (2010) and Hart and Zingales (2010), with a sample of the major US banks; Eichengreen et al. (2009) and Calice and Ioannidis (2009), with a sample of the largest US and European Financial Institutes (LFIs). Almer, Heidorn, and Schmaltz (2008), Volz and Wedow (2011) and Demirgüç-Kunt and Huizinga (2010) with a sample of banks from all over the world.
5. In particular, the national outstanding of credit default swaps, which ISDA began to survey at midyear 2001, grew from \$631.5 billion at midyear 2001 to \$62 trillion in 2007, reaching a peak. In the two subsequent years, the number of CDS diminished to \$38.5 trillion in 2008 and \$30.4 trillion in 2009. Recent reduction in the number of CDS is principally due to trade cancellations (International Swaps and Derivatives Association 2010).
6. The quoting convention for CDSs is the annual premium payment as a percentage of the notional value of the reference obligation. Under certain conditions, this CDS premium should be approximately equal to the credit spread (yield minus risk-free rates) of the reference bond of the same maturity. See, Bank for International Settlements (2003, 84).
7. Initially, the literature concentrated on the structural models' theoretical determinants of corporate bond credit spreads, rather than CDS spreads. See, for example, Collin-Dufresne, Goldstein, and Martin (2001), Campbell and Taksler (2003), Cremers et al. (2004) and, recently, Avramov, Gergana, and Philipov (2007).
8. See Ashraf, Altunbas, and Goddard (2007).
9. See Bank for International Settlements (2011, 8–9).
10. 'TIER 1 Ratio' is shareholder funds plus perpetual non-cumulative preference shares as a percentage of risk-weighted assets and off balance sheet risks measured under the Basel rules.
11. 'Liquid Assets' denotes the sum of Government Securities, Trading Securities, Cash and Due from Banks, and Due from Other Banks. 'Short-Term Funding' denotes the sum of Customer Deposits, Banks Deposits and Total Money Market Funding.
12. Since the results relative to the post crisis period do not differ significantly from the crisis period, to save space, these are not reported but are available upon request from the authors.
13. A possible explanation for this outcome will be offered in the section dedicated to the analysis of regression results.
14. Due to the multicollinearity problem between capital explanatory variables (pat1 and pat2), for each time periods considered, the panel regressions were performed using alternately the two capital ratios.
15. For more details, see Basel Committee on Banking Supervision (2010a).
16. For more details, see Basel Committee on Banking Supervision (2010b).

17. Due to the multicollinearity problem between capital explanatory variables (pat1 and pat2), for each time periods considered, the panel regression was performed using alternately the two capital ratios.

References

Abid, F., and N. Naifar. 2006. The determinants of credit default swap rates: An explanatory study. *International Journal of Theoretical Applied Finance* 9, no. 1: 23–42.

Alexopoulou, I., M. Andersson, and O.M. Georgescu. 2009. An empirical study on the decoupling movements between corporate bond and CDS spreads. European Central Bank (ECB) Working Paper Series, European Central Bank (ECB), Frankfurt, August.

Allen, F., and D. Gale. 2007a. An introduction to financial crises. Wharton Financial Institutions Center Working Paper no. 07–20, Wharton Financial Institutions Center, Pennsylvania, August.

Allen, F., and D. Gale. 2007b. *Understanding financial crises*. Claredon Lecture Series in Finance. Oxford: Oxford University Press.

Almer, T., T. Heidorn, and C. Schmaltz. 2008. The dynamics of short- and long-term CDS-spreads of banks. Frankfurt School Working Paper Series no. 95, Frankfurt School, Frankfurt, April.

Anderson, R., and S. Sundaresan. 1996. Design and valuation of debt contrast. *Review of Financial Studies* 9, no. 1: 37–68.

Anderson, R., S. Sundaresan, and P. Tychon. 1996. Strategic analysis of contingent claims. *European Economic Review* 40, no. 3: 871–81.

Annaert, J., M. De Ceuster, M. Van Roy, and C. Vespro. 2010. What determines euro area bank CDS spreads? National Bank of Belgium Working Paper no. 190, National Bank of Belgium, Brussels, May.

Ashraf, D., Y. Altunbas, and J. Goddard. 2007. Who transfers credit risk? Determinants of the use of credit derivatives by large US banks. *The European Journal of Finance* 13, no. 5: 483–500.

Aunon-Nerin, D., D. Cossin, T. Hricko, and Z. Huang. 2002. Exploring for the determinants of credit risk in credit default swap transaction data: Is fixed-income markets' information sufficient to evaluate credit risk? FAME Working Paper, University of Lausanne, Lausanne.

Avramov, D., J. Gergana, and A. Philipov. 2007. Understanding changes in corporate credit spreads. *Financial Analysts Journal* 63, no. 2: 90–105.

Balasubramnian, B., and K.B. Cyree. 2011. Market discipline of banks: Why are yield spreads on bank-issued subordinated noted and debentures not sensitive to bank risks? *Journal of Banking and Finance* 35, no. 1: 21–35.

Bank for International Settlements (BIS). 2003. Quarterly review. Bank for International Settlements, Basel, December.

Bank for International Settlements (BIS). 2008. Annual report. Bank for International Settlements, Basel, June.

Bank for International Settlements (BIS). 2009. Annual report. Bank for International Settlements, Basel, June.

Bank for International Settlements (BIS). 2010. Annual report. Bank for International Settlements, Basel, June.

Bank for International Settlements (BIS). 2011. Annual report. Bank for International Settlements, Basel, June.

Basel Committee on Banking Supervision (BCBS). 2010a. Basel 3: A global regulatory framework for more resilient banks and banking systems. Basel Committee on Banking Supervision, Basel, December.

Basel Committee on Banking Supervision (BCBS). 2010b. Basel 3: International framework for liquidity risk measurement, standards and monitoring. Basel Committee on Banking Supervision, Basel, December.

Benkert, C. 2004. Explaining credit default swap premia. *Journal of Futures Markets* 24, no. 1: 71–92.

Black, F., and J.C. Cox. 1976. Valuing corporate securities: Some effects of bond indenture provisions. *Journal of Finance* 31, no. 2: 351–67.

Black, F., and M. Scholes. 1973. The pricing of options and corporate liabilities. *Journal of Political Economy* 81, no. 3: 637–54.

Blanco, R., S. Brennan, and I.W. Marsh. 2005. An empirical analysis of the dynamic relationship between investment-grade bonds and credit default swaps. *Journal of Finance* 60, no. 5: 2255–81.

Boss, M., and M. Scheicher, 2005. The determinants of credit spread changes in the euro area. Bank for International Settlements (BIS) Working Paper 12 (part 10), Bank for International Settlements, Basel.

Brunnermeier, M. 2009. Deciphering the liquidity and credit crunch 2007–2008. *The Journal of Economic Perspectives* 23, no. 1: 77–100.

Bystrom, H. 2005. Credit default swaps and equity prices: The iTraxx CDS index market. Working paper, Department of Economics, Lund University, Lund.

Calice, G., and C. Ioannidis. 2009. An empirical analysis of the impact of the credit default swap index market on large complex financial institutions. Working paper, School of Management, University of Bath, Bath, UK.

Campbell, J.Y., and G.B. Taksler. 2003. Equity volatility and corporate bond yields. *Journal of Finance* 58, no. 6: 2321–50.

Collin-Dufresne, P., R.S. Goldstein, and J.S. Martin. 2001. The determinants of credit spread changes. *Journal of Finance* 56, no. 6: 2177–208.

Constantinos, S. 2010. Rethinking market discipline in banking lessons from the financial crisis. World Bank Policy Research Working Paper 5227, World Bank, Washington, March.

Cremers, M., J. Driessen, P.J. Maenhout, and D. Weinbaum. 2004. Individual stock-option prices and credit spreads. Yale International Center for Finance CICF) Working Paper no. 04–14, Yale International Center for Finance (ICF), New Haven, December.

Daniels, K.N., and M. Shin Jensen. 2004. The effect of credit ratings on credit default swap spreads and credit spreads. Centre for Analytical Finance (CAF) Working Paper no. 191, Centre for Analytical Finance (CAF), Aarhus, December.

Das, S., L. Freed, G. Geng, and N. Kapadia. 2006. Correlated default risk. *Journal of Fixed Income Fall* 16, no. 2: 7–32.

Das, S.R., and P. Hanouna. 2006. Credit default swap spreads. *Journal of Investment Management* 4, no. 3: 93–105.

Das, H., P. Hanouna, and A. Sarin. 2008. Accounting-based versus market-based cross-sectional models of CDS spreads. *Journal of Banking and Finance* 33, no. 4: 719–30.

Demirgüç-Kunt, A., and H. Huizinga. 2010. Are banks too big to fail or too big to save? International evidence from equity prices and CDS spreads. Discussion paper no. 59, Center for Economic Research, Tilburg University, Netherlands.

Di Cesare, A., and G. Guazzarotti. 2010. An analysis of the determinants of credit default swap spread changes before and during the subprime financial turmoil. Working Papers Banca d'Italia No. 749, Banca d'Italia, Rome, March.

Dickinson, E. 2008. Credit default swaps: So dear to us, so dangerous. Working Paper Fordham University-School of Law, Fordham University, NY, USA.

Duffie, D., L. Saita, and K. Wang. 2007. Multiperiod corporate default probabilities with stochastic covariates. *The Journal of Financial Economics* 83, no. 3: 635–65.

Duffie, D., and K.J. Singleton. 1999. Modeling term structures of defaultable bonds. *Review of Financial Studies* 12, no. 4: 687–720.

Eichengreen, B., A. Mody, M. Nedeljkovic, and L. Sarno. 2009. How the subprime crisis went global: Evidence from bank credit default swap spreads. National Bureau of Economic Research (NBER) Working Paper Series no. 14904, National Bureau of Economic Research (NBER), Cambridge, April.

Ericsson, J., K. Jacobs, and R. Oviedo. 2009. The determinants of credit default swap premia. *Journal of Financial and Quantitative Analysis* 44, no. 1: 109–32.

European Central Bank (ECB). 2009a. Credit default swaps and counterparty risk. European Central Bank (ECB), Frankfurt, August.

European Central Bank (ECB). 2009b. Financial stability review. European Central Bank, Frankfurt, June.

Flannery, M.J. 2010. Market discipline in banking. In *Oxford handbook of banking*, ed. A. Berger, P. Molyneux, and J.O.S. Wilson, 339–62. Oxford: Oxford University Press.

Goodhart, C.A.E. 2008. The background to the 2007 financial crisis. *International Economics and Economic Policy* 4, no. 4: 331–46.

Hart, O., and L. Zingales. 2010. A new capital regulation for large financial institutions. Working Paper University of Chicago, NBER and CEPR, Cambridge, MA.

Huang, X., H. Zhou, and H. Zhu. 2009. A framework for assessing the systemic risk of major financial institutions. Bank for International Settlements (BIS) Working Papers no. 281, Bank for International Settlements (BIS), Basel, April.

Hull, J.C., M. Predescu, and A. White. 2004. The relationship between credit default swap spreads, bond yields, and credit rating announcements. *Journal of Banking and Finance* 28, no. 11: 2789–811.

Hull, J., and A. White. 2000. Valuing credit default swap II: Modelling default correlations. Unpublished manuscript, University of Toronto, Toronto.

Hull, J., and A. White. 2001. The general hull-white model and super calibration. *Financial Analysts Journal* 57, no. 6: 34–43.

International Monetary Fund. 2008. Global financial stability report. International Monetary Fund, Washington DC, April.

International Organization of Securities Commissions (IOSCO). 2008. Report on the subprime crisis. Working paper, International Organization of Securities Commissions, Madrid, May.

International Swaps and Derivatives Association. 2010. ISDA market survey. http://www.isda.org/statistics/pdf/ISDA-market-survey-historical-data.pdf (accessed August 25, 2010).

Jarrow, R.A. 2011. The economics of credit default swaps. *Annual Review of Financial Economics* 3: 235–57.

Jarrow, R.A., D. Lando, and S.M. Turnbull. 1997. A Markov model for the term structure of credit spreads. *Review of Financial Studies* 10, no. 2: 481–523.

Jarrow, R.A., and S.M. Turnbull. 1995. Pricing derivatives on financial securities subject to credit risk. *Journal of Finance* 50, no. 1: 53–86.

Kool, C.J.M. 2006. Financial stability in European banking: The role of common factors. Discussion paper no. 6, Utrecht School of Economics, Utrecht University, The Netherlands.

Kress, J.C. 2011. Credit default swap clearinghouses and systemic risk: Why centralized counterparties must have access to central bank liquidity? *Harvard Journal on Legislation 48*, no. 1: 49–93.

Lando, D. 1994. Three essays on contingent claims pricing. Unpublished manuscript, Ph.D. diss., Cornell University, Ithaca, NY.

Lando, D. 1998. On Cox processes and credit risky securities. *Review of Derivatives Research* 2, nos. 2–3: 99–120.

Lehnert, T., and F. Neske. 2006. On the relationship between credit rating announcements and credit default swap spread for European reference entities. *Journal of Credit risk* 2, no. 2: 83–90.

Longstaff, F.A., and E.S. Schwartz. 1995. A simple approach to valuing risky and floating rate debt. *Journal of Finance* 50, no. 3: 789–819.

Madan, D., and H. Unal. 1995. Pricing the risks of default. *Review of Derivatives Research* 2, nos. 2–3: 121–60.

Mella-Barral, P. 1997. Strategic debt service. *Journal of Finance* 52, no. 2: 531–56.

Merton, R.C. 1974. On the pricing of corporate debt: The risk structure of interest rates. *Journal of Finance* 29, no. 2: 449–70.

Norden, L., and M. Weber. 2004. Informational efficiency of credit default swap and stock markets: The impact of credit rating announcements. *Journal of Banking and Finance* 28, no. 11: 2813–43.

Norden, L., and M. Weber. 2009. The co-movement of CDS, bond and stock markets: An empirical analysis. *European Financial Management* 15, no. 3: 529–62.

Norden, L., and M. Weber. 2010. When senior meets junior: Information in credit default swap spreads of large banks. Financial Intermediation Research Society (FIRS) meetings paper, Financial Intermediation Research Society (FIRS), Florence, June.

Raunig, B., and M. Scheicher. 2009. Are banks different? Evidence from the CDS market. Oesterreichische National Bank Working Paper no. 152, Oesterreichische National Bank, VielUm, May.

Stulz, R.N. 2011. Credit default swaps and the credit crisis. *Journal of Economic Perspectives* 24, no. 1: 73–92.

Volz, M., and M. Wedow. 2011. Market discipline and too-big-to-fail in the CDS market: Does banks' size reduce market discipline? *Journal of Empirical Finance* 18, no. 2: 195–210.

Zhang, B.Y., H. Zhou, and H. Zhu. 2005. Explaining credit default swap spreads with equity volatility and jump risks of individual firms. Bank for International Settlements (BIS) Working Paper no. 181, Bank for International Settlements (BIS), Basel, September.

Zhou, C. 2001. The term structure of credit spreads with jump risk. *Journal of Banking and Finance* 25, no. 11: 2015–40.

Zhu, H. 2006. An empirical comparison of credit spreads between the bond market and the credit default swap market. *Journal of Financial Services Research* 29, no. 3: 211–35.

Appendix

Table A1. Summary statistics on CDS spreads for sample banks.

	Pre-crisis period		During the crisis period		Post crisis period	
Banks (Country)	Mean (Std. Dev.)	Min.–Max.	Mean (Std. Dev.)	Min.–Max.	Mean (Std. Dev.)	Min.–Max.
Erste Group Bank AG (AT)	19.93 (13.47)	1–75.08	120.46 (103.78)	13.69–487.13	166.49 (46.30)	128.81–275.08
Raiffeisen International Bank Holding (AT)	37.19 (36.53)	1–224.97	171.28 (95.90)	70.90–535	189.28 (51.87)	136.97–306.05
Dexia SA (BE)	9.42 (1.66)	6.50–14	166.55 (122.76)	11.40–550	263.88 (54.99)	183.83–342.01
Fortis (BE)	16.50 (5.26)	8–31.62	74.83 (64.75)	10.80–666.70	86.44 (24.43)	60.99–111.77
KBC Groep NV (BE)	9.60 (1.72)	6.90–15.70	126.33 (76.65)	9.80–343.30	173.83 (54.49)	109.54–266.07
Danske Bank A/S (DK)	7.08 (3.11)	3.50–21	68.67 (61.87)	4.10–225	98.04 (27.70)	69.44–153.06
Banco Bilbao Vizcaya Argentaria (ES)	9.71 (1.36)	7.10–16.50	76.08 (36.76)	11.50–184.95	164.08 (67.34)	78.15–249.35
Banco de Sabadell SA (ES)	24.20 (0)	24.20 (0)	167.02 (97.92)	19.60–371.66	274.95 (83.21)	146.94–406.30
Banco Popular Espanol (ES)	11.27 (3.92)	7.97–31.54	116.50 (112.71)	14.78–340	278.19 (99.07)	139.02–439.06
Banco Santander SA (ES)	10.22 (1.67)	7–17.50	78.21 (37.61)	11.50–183.61	151.97 (60.17)	76.58–239.59
Caja de Ahorros de Valencia Castellon Y Alicante Bancaja (ES)	16.58 (4.06)	9.50–31.36	387.21 (299.71)	28.60–1,148	475.85 (112.84)	368.08–624.91
Caja de Madrid (ES)	21.45 (3.03)	14.80–27.05	284.59 (236.85)	23–750	464.98 (102.51)	345.95–612.50
Banque Federale des Banques (FR)	68.13 (55.44)	1–265.92	14.78 (0)	14.78	24.61 (19.66)	14.78–54.11
BNP Paribas (FR)	7.81 (1.97)	5–14.50	54.99 (25.49)	7.50–143.13	88.51 (21.01)	57.17–107.71
Crédit Agricole SA (FR)	8.06 (1.84)	5.50–13.50	70.69 (32.96)	8–165	119.46 (27.36)	83.66–148.67

Natixis (FR)	9.28 (1.79)	6.30–15	145.67 (93.63)	10.30–390.18	167.18 (48.94)	121.27–283.78
Société Générale (FR)	8.64 (2.30)	5.70–15.50	73.33 (35.83)	8.50–165	113.45 (23.73)	83.29–141.93
Deutsche Bank AG Registered (DE)	13.61 (2.99)	8.70–26.30	82.92 (38.69)	14.50–186.20	103.88 (16.65)	77.40–136.33
Deutsche Postbank AG (DE)	20.50 (3.17)	6.50–28.90	54.73 (23.50)	18.30–105.30	60.41 (12.78)	44.32–74.24
Allied Irish Banks PLC (IE)	8.81 (2.35)	5.70–17.50	151.09 (137.56)	10.40–646.72	637.44 (506.98)	223.69–1,544
Anglo Irish Bank Corporation LTD (IE)	20.20 (5.93)	3–41	279.13 (210.52)	14–950	460.165 (111.09)	340.19–590.63
Bank of Ireland (IE)	8.62 (1.79)	5–14.50	169.04 (147.37)	10.10–670.28	287.81 (73.76)	207.17–377.62
Banca Monte dei Paschi di Siena (IT)	13.70 (4.82)	6–25	75.40 (35.01)	9.50–171.68	151.33 (74.15)	65.80–275.06
Banco Popolare SCARL (IT)	21.98 (5.36)	11–37.79	18.07 (6.62)	14–28.39	227.30 (43.78)	170.72–287.81
Intesa SanPaolo (IT)	11.78 (3.78)	5.40–19.50	66.65 (39.51)	8.50–200	108.57 (42.22)	54.78–173.78
UBI Banca SCPA (IT)	17.63 (2.80)	10–25	70.48 (50.75)	13–190	135.89 (53.92)	67.72–199.23
Unicredit SPA (IT)	12.84 (2.76)	7–20.70	83.64 (50.70)	10–278.74	122.88 (27.96)	90.24–157.84
Rabobank (NL)	6.21 (2.01)	2.50–10	69.21 (50.96)	5–204.30	82.80 (28.95)	65.54–125.85
DNB NOR ASA (NO)	–	–	100.27 (45.30)	37.50–188.11	79.10 (21)	60.57–131.62
Banco Espirito Santo (PT)	13.33 (3.10)	8.20–22.70	91.32 (44.56)	12.50–230	370.90 (245.29)	118.99–700.95
Nordea Bank AB (SE)	11.05 (2.67)	5–19.31	61.43 (42.45)	14.78–165	77.55 (15.69)	58.63–114.04
Skandinaviska Enskilda Banken (SE)	15.59 (9.66)	6.68–31.54	79.72 (69.28)	8.33–281.50	110.91 (35.70)	80.80–189.84
Svenska Handelsbanken (SE)	12.06 (3.34)	5.41–19.31	51.11 (42.08)	14.78–163.40	67.15 (19.57)	51.01–114.41

(Continued)

Table A1. Continued

Banks (Country)	Pre-crisis period		During the crisis period		Post crisis period	
	Mean (Std. Dev.)	Min.–Max.	Mean (Std. Dev.)	Min.–Max.	Mean (Std. Dev.)	Min.–Max.
Swedbank AB (SE)	25.39 (7.82)	10.94–35.24	89.95 (96.55)	14.78–362	131.38 (65.38)	84.57–266.09
Credit Suisse Group AG (SW)	14.90 (3.73)	9.20–25.50	98.42 (55.14)	17.50–262.88	95.13 (19.91)	71.05–130.07
Alliance & Leicester PLC (UK)	14.36 (12.42)	1–78.78	131.33 (88.15)	11.78–471	82.13 (21.15)	65.08–112.84
Barclays PLC (UK)	8.52 (1.94)	5.30–15.80	103.14 (59.44)	11–270	114.41 (28.23)	82.31–164.75
Bradford & Bingley PLC (UK)	25.04 (16.08)	1–84.56	320.93 (298.33)	31.67–1,591	439.34 (80.51)	325.40–610.20
HBOS PLC (UK)	8.44 (2.58)	4.90–16.50	118.43 (69.90)	11.40–500.80	161.76 (20.62)	123.86–183.62
HSBC Holdings PLC (UK)	8.46 (2.19)	4.90–15.50	70.89 (38.04)	10.40–170.59	78.29 (13.62)	56.66–101.19
Lloyds Banking Group PLC (UK)	6.97 (2.43)	3.50–15.50	75.60 (49.77)	6.50–221.05	168.27 (28.20)	120.64–198.72
Royal Bank of Scotland Group (UK)	7.84 (2.50)	3.50–15.50	98.92 (57.50)	9–299.60	169.83 (28.80)	126.14–206.66
Standard Chartered PLC (UK)	16.02 (1.91)	8.50–22.50	40.10 (23.77)	16.20–63.70	72.89 (13.92)	63.70–95.14
Bank of America Corporation (US)	13.59 (3.79)	7.80–23.80	108.99 (71.70)	13.50–400.68	160.30 (34.41)	115.26–233.36
JP Morgan Chase & Co. (US)	20.94 (6.97)	11–43.50	95.17 (44.50)	19.80–242.05	87.95 (21.16)	58.51–132.45
National City Corporation (US)	21.62 (4.80)	10.40–29.44	311.84 (560.67)	18.30–2,969	733 (0)	733
Suntrust (US)	20.03 (13063)	10.30–44.34	69.85 (51.94)	1–115.30	113 (0)	113
Wachovia Corporation (US)	13.69 (2.64)	8.20–21.30	162.16 (124.98)	14.60–1,560	248.80 (3.50)	245.47–253.75

Washington Mutual INC (US)	35.70 (10.51)	18.80–63.20	2,138 (2,580)	41.40–6,235	–	–
Wells Fargo & Co. (US)	11.93 (3.36)	6–19.20	98.95 (57.28)	11.40–307.85	108.07 (28.74)	85.49–182.49
Mitsubishi UFJ Financial Group (JP)	13.67 (5.44)	5.50–29	69.22 (38.50)	6.90–163.80	71.51 (10.25)	53.78–83.14
Mizuho Financial Group Inc. (JP)	28.85 (7.27)	12.21–34.91	37.74 (10.48)	13.50–48.50	62.81 (33.93)	43–135.67
Sumitomo Mitsui Financial Group (JP)	13.87 (5.46)	5.20–25.20	69.97 (39.89)	6.90–150	92.18 (34.90)	57.03–167.38
Aust and NZ Banking Group (AU)	8.31 (1.95)	4.40–13.50	85.10 (51.37)	5.50–228.27	98.59 (15.16)	70.31–113.89
Commonwealth Bank of Australia (AU)	8.54 (2.61)	4.40–19.10	82.15 (48.39)	5–218.30	97.19 (15.94)	67.46–112.36
National Australia Bank LTD (AU)	8.30 (2.01)	4.50–14	85.92 (51.40)	4.90–225	98.88 (15.29)	70.42–115.21
Westpac Banking Corporation (AU)	8.37 (1.93)	4.70–14.20	81.51 (48.52)	5.50–221.73	91.44 (16.69)	67.57–113.36
Country average						
Austria (2)	28.56 (25)	1–150.02	145.87 (99.84)	42.29–511.06	177.89 (49.11)	128.81–306.05
Belgium (3)	11.84 (2.88)	7.13–20.44	122.57 (88.05)	10.66–520	185.75 (85.04)	60.99–342.01
Denmark (1)	7.08 (3.11)	3.50–21	68.67 (61.87)	4.10–225	98.04 (27.70)	69.44–153.06
Espania (6)	15.57 (2.34)	11.76–24.69	184.93 (136.92)	18.16–496.45	272.96 (147.85)	76.58–624.91
France (5)	20.38 (12.66)	4.70–64.88	71.89 (37.58)	9.81–175.61	112.40 (50.07)	14.78–283.78
Germany (2)	17.05 (3.08)	7.60–27.60	68.82 (31.09)	16.40–145.75	82.14 (14.71)	44.32–74.24
Ireland (3)	12.54 (3.35)	4.56–24.33	199.75 (165.15)	11.50–755.66	489.71 (377.49)	207.17–1,544

(Continued)

Table A1. Continued

	Pre-crisis period		During the crisis period		Post crisis period	
Country average	Mean (Std. Dev.)	Min.–Max.	Mean (Std. Dev.)	Min.–Max.	Mean (Std. Dev.)	Min.–Max.
Italy (5)	15.58 (3.90)	7.88–25.59	62.84 (36.51)	11–173.76	142.53 (61.55)	54.78–287.81
Netherlands (1)	6.21 (2.01)	2.50–10	69.21 (50.96)	5–204.30	82.80 (28.95)	65.54–125.85
Norway (1)	–	–	100.27 (45.30)	37.50–188.11	79.10 (21.00)	60.57–131.62
Portugal (1)	13.33 (3.10)	8.20–22.70	91.32 (44.56)	12.50–230	370.90 (245.29)	118.99–700.95
Sweden (4)	16.02 (5.87)	7–26.35	70.55 (62.59)	13.16–242.97	96.74 (45.74)	51.01–266.09
Switzerland (1)	14.90 (3.73)	9.20–25.50	98.42 (55.14)	17.50–262.88	95.13 (19.91)	71.08–130.07
UK (8)	11.95 (5.25)	4.07–33.08	119.91 (85.61)	13.49–448.46	124.80 (47.64)	56.66–206.66
US (7)	19.56 (5.67)	10.33–34.19	486.84 (569.96)	19.58–1,930	191.16 (17.56)	58.51–733
Japan (3)	18.79 (6.05)	7.63–29.70	58.97 (29.62)	9.10–120.76	75.5 (26.36)	43–167.38
Australia (4)	8.38 (2.12)	4.50–15.20	83.67 (49.92)	5.22–223.32	96.52 (15.40)	67.46–115.21

Notes: This table reports quarterly summary statistics on 5-year senior CDS spreads for the 57 sample banks per for the pre-crisis period (1 January 2005–30 June 2007), for the crisis period (1 July 2007–31 March 2009) and for the post crisis period (1 April 2009–30 June 2011). Mean, standard deviation (Std. Dev.), median, minimum (Min.) and maximum (Max.) are expressed in basis points. AT, Austria; AU, Australia; BE, Belgium; DE, Germany; DK, Denmark; ES, Spain; FR, France; IE, Ireland; IT, Italy; NL, Netherlands; NO, Norway; PT, Portugal; SE, Sweden; SW, Switzerland; UK, United Kingdom; US, United States; JP, Japan. With reference to the Country Average, the number of observations is indicated in brackets.
Source: Datastream Database, authors' calculations.

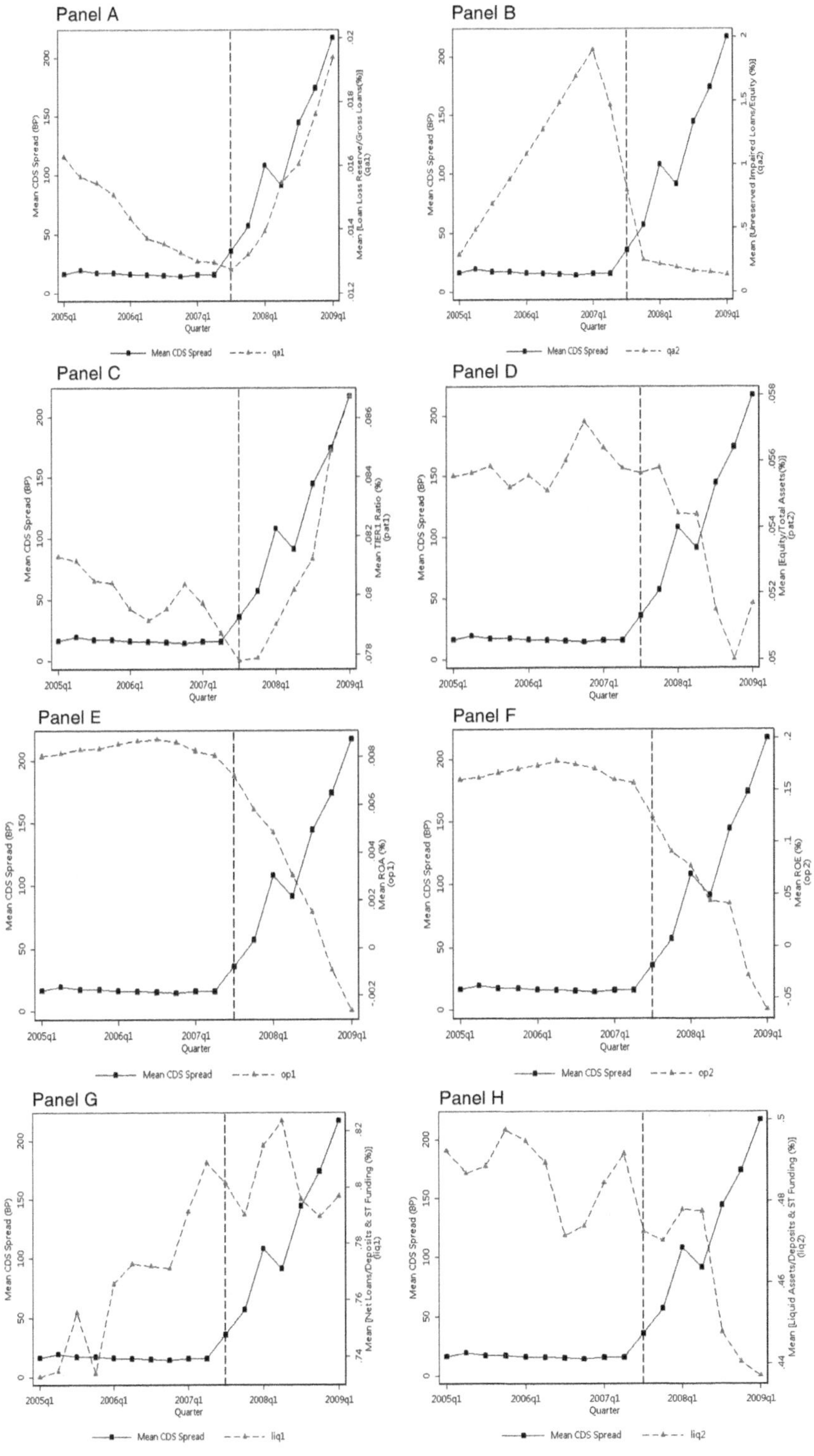

Figure A1. Times-series graphs.

Notes: These figures show the relationship between mean CDS spreads of sample banks and the mean of each balance sheet ratio used (qa1, qa2, pat1, pat2, op1, op2, liq1 and liq2). The sample period is from 1 January 2005 to 31 March 2009. The dashed vertical line coinciding with the start of the third quarter 2007 (July 2007) indicates the outbreak of the crisis.

The impact of market power and funding strategy on bank-interest margins

Mohammed Amidu[a,b] and Simon Wolfe[a]

[a]*School of Management, University of Southampton, SO17 IBJ, UK;* [b]*Department of Accounting, University of Ghana Business School, PO Box LG 78, Legon, Accra, Ghana*

This paper investigates the implications of market power and funding strategies for bank-interest margins, using a sample of 978 banks in 55 emerging and developing countries over an eight-year period, 2000–2007. We provide additional insight by examining the complex interlocking of three key variables that are important for regulators: the degree of market power, funding sources and bank performance. The results show that market power increases when banks use internal funding to diversify into non-interest income-generating activities. We also find that the high net-interest margins of banks in emerging and developing countries can be explained by the degree of market power, credit risk, and implicit interest payments. In addition, our results suggest that interest margins among banks with market power are significantly more sensitive to internally generated funds than they are to deposit and wholesale funding.

1. Introduction

Banks play a key role in financing economic activities in a country. By its very nature, banking is an attempt to manage multiple and seemingly opposing needs. Banks accept deposits and assure savers that their deposits are liquid and secure. They extend credit as well as liquidity to borrowers through lines of credit (Kashyap, Rajan, and Stein 2002). Channelling funds from lenders to borrowers is the primary intermediation function of banks. In order to achieve this greater social welfare, it is important that the intermediation function is carried out with the lowest possible cost. Accordingly, the lower the cost of banks' interest margins, the lower the social cost of financial intermediation. The effectiveness of a banking system in the intermediation process is often measured by examining the spread between lending and deposit rates, as well as assessing the extent of operational efficiencies of the banking system (Taci and Zampieri 1998). In line with this, the banking literature has concentrated on analysing the determinants of bank interest margins and is pioneered by the seminal paper of Ho and Saunders (1981) and the extensions by McShane and Sharpe (1985), Allen (1988), Angbazo (1997), and Wong (1997).

These earlier studies do not reflect the variation of interest margins across-countries and across levels of economic development. A close look at Figure 1 suggests that interest margins vary widely across countries with the interest margin of low and middle income economies being higher than that of high-income countries. For example in 2005, the average interest margin of low-income countries (12.75%) was thrice that of higher income economies (3.89%). The relative

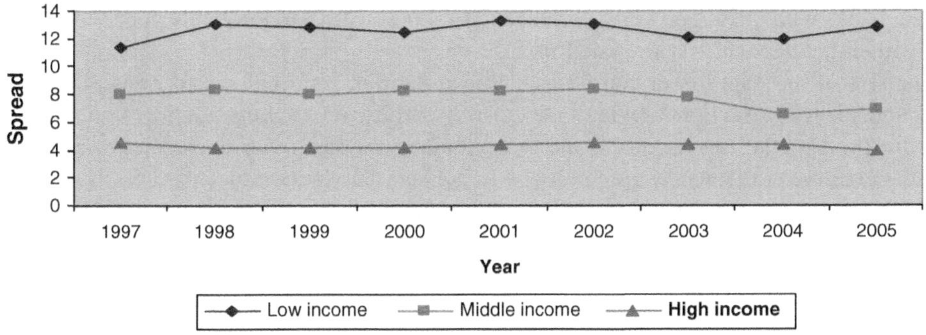

Figure 1. Interest rate spread across countries based on the level of income. Source: World Development indicator (September 2009) and authors' estimation. Note: The spread is the difference between the interest rate charged by banks on loans to prime customers and the interest rate paid by banks for deposits. Low income economies are those in which 2008 Gross National Income (GNI) *per capita* is \$975 or less; the middle economies are those countries whose 2008 GNI *per capita* income is between \$976 and \$11,905 and the high income economies are those in which 2008 GNI *per capita* is \$11,906 or more.

size of cross-economies interest margins appears to be the same over the period 1997–2005. What is not known is whether the higher interest margins in these low income economies are good or bad from a social welfare point of view. On one hand, according to Saunders and Schumacher (2000) narrow margins may be indicative of relatively competitive banking systems; and on the other hand, relatively large margins may bring a degree of stability for a banking system. Our paper therefore investigates the implications of bank market power and funding strategies on interest margins. We conduct this study in the context of developing countries as Figure 1 shows that banks in emerging and developing countries benefit from higher spreads.

The objective of this paper is two-fold: first, we examine the determinants of market power and funding structure of banks in developing countries. It is important from an economic policy perspective to identify the various sources of market power as it is only when these sources are identified that action might be taken to reduce the social inefficiency associated with the existence of market power (Maudos and Nagore 2005). Second, we investigate the implications of bank market power and funding strategies for bank spreads.

We use the Lerner index to construct market power and to avoid any bias emanating from a bank exercising market power in the deposits market, and as there is no consensus in the literature regarding how best to assess the degree of bank market power (Carbó et al. 2009), we employ two different specifications of Lerner: a conventional Lerner (Berger, Klapper, and Turk-Ariss 2009) and a funding-adjusted Lerner (Maudos and Fernandez de Guevara 2007) to investigate the impact of market power on bank performance. Three funding modes have been identified in our sample: deposit funding, non-deposit/wholesale funding and internal capital funding while the net-interest margin (NIM) is used as a measure of bank interest spread.

Our results demonstrate that on average funding-adjusted Lerner index is larger than that of the conventional Lerner index, suggesting that the latter has been underestimating the degree of market power. Moreover, the results reveal that larger, growing and highly capitalised banks have market power. Similarly, diversifying into non-interest income activities using internal capital enhances bank market power. Equally, smaller, highly capitalised and efficiently managed banks employ internally generated funds for their investments. Overall, our results suggest that NIM among banks with market power is significantly more sensitive to internally generated funds than it is with either deposit or wholesale funding.

The rest of the paper is organised as follows: Section 2 provides a theoretical overview of bank spreads while Section 3 reviews the existing empirical literature. Section 4 presents various specifications of the Lerner index, the three funding modes, other explanatory variables used and the estimation methodology employed to achieve our stated objectives. Section 5 contains analysis and the results. Finally, in Section 6 we conclude.

2. Theoretical overview

Theoretical principles explaining bank NIMs can be described either in terms of a 'monopoly', 'dealership' or the 'behavioural' type model. The monopoly model developed by the seminal work of Klein (1971) considers the banking firm's main activity as the production of deposits and loans through intermediation services and is represented by the cost function of the $C(D, L)$ type, where D is the volume of deposits and L is the volume of loans produced by the bank. The rule in line with the cost function is that a banking firm pursues its activities in an environment characterised by the presence of imperfect competition in both deposit and credit markets. That is, the bank has monopolistic power to set interest rates in at least one of the markets where it conducts its operations. Klein (1971) contends that the monopoly power of a bank can then be used to explain the scale of operations, its asset and liability structure as well as its decision to affect the rate of return on liabilities (deposits) and assets (loans). Thus, with this approach, a banking firm's spread reflects primarily its ability to charge a price higher than the marginal cost of providing the services in both loan and deposit markets. Oreiro and de Paula (2010) provide a context where r is the prevailing interest rate on the inter-bank market; r_L is the interest rate charged on loans generated by the bank; and r_D is the interest rate paid to depositors with the bank. α is the reserve requirement expressed as a proportion of the deposits; the ε_L is the interest elasticity of loan demand; ε_D is the interest elasticity of deposit supply; C_L is the marginal cost of loan services; and C_D is the marginal cost of deposit services. Assuming that the banking firm is risk neutral and that its behaviour is directed to maximising profits, the optimal interest margin on loans and deposits according to Freixas and Rochet (1997) is presented as

$$\frac{1}{\varepsilon_L^*} = \frac{r_L^* - (r + C_L)}{r_L^*} \tag{1}$$

$$\frac{1}{\varepsilon_D^*} = \frac{r(1-\alpha) - C_D - r_D^*}{r_D^*}. \tag{2}$$

Equations (1) and (2) suggest that a bank operating in an imperfectly competitive environment sets the prices of its loan and deposit services in a manner equal to the Lerner index which is the inverse of the interest elasticity of the loan demand and deposit supply functions. Equation (1) and (2) are interpreted as, the lesser the sensitivity of loan demand and deposit supply functions to interest rate variations, the greater the bank's margin in both loan- and deposit-taking operations, and, thus the greater the bank spread.

The second model to explain bank spreads is the dealership model introduced by Ho and Saunders (1981). This views the bank as a dynamic dealer, setting interest rates on loans and deposits to balance the asymmetric arrival of loan demand and deposit supplies. The non-synchronous arrival of loans and deposits generates a cost for the bank, given that it will have to hold either a long or short position in the money market. This, therefore, exposes the bank to changes in the money market interest rate (i.e. interest rate risk). In the dealership model, the profit maximising bank is expected to maximise its utility of terminal wealth as

$$s = a + b = \frac{\alpha}{\beta} + \frac{1}{2}R\sigma_i^2 Q, \tag{3}$$

s is the pure margin, a is the mark up on deposits, b is the mark up on loans, α/β measures the relative market power, R is the bank's risk aversion, σ_i^2 is the variance of the interest rate on loans and deposits and the Q is the size of the banks' transaction. According to Ho and Saunders (1981), a large α and a small β will lead to a large α/β and, thus a large spread s. There have been extensions to this model to account for time series/cross-section (McShane and Sharpe 1985), for cross-elasticities of demand between bank products (Allen 1988), for default risk and different size classes of banks (Angbazo 1997), for bank operational cost (Maudos and Fernandez de Guevara 2004), for a multi-product framework that reflects the diversification of banks' output (Carbó Valverde and Rodriguez Fernandez 2007), and for the cost of goods (Wong 1997).

The monopoly model as well as the dealership model and its extensions have two main limitations. According to Hanweck and Ryu (2005), monopoly and dealership models are single-horizon, static models in which bank assets and liabilities are considered homogenous. In practice however, bank portfolios are characterised by heterogeneous assets and liabilities with different security, maturity and re-pricing structure that mostly go beyond a single horizon. The second limitation on these models is that the banking sector is treated as either being homogenous or as having heterogeneous traits that is based only on the assets size of banks. Conversely, banks with different products usually differ in terms of their business models, pricing power and more importantly the funding structure and exogenous shocks. Perhaps, the best known behavioural model on interest margin is one developed by Hanweck and Ryu (2005). The model of bank behaviour in relation to NIMs assume that at each period a bank can significantly, but not completely select the amount of its investment in assets and liabilities of different repricing frequencies, given past choices that are immutable. They argue that 'not only do bank managers have to choose the optimal financial service product mix and geography diversification, they also need to set the lending rate and fees, hedge credit quality and volatility changes, manage their liability structure and gauge the moods of the equity and debt markets to favourable or unfavourable news so as to increase shareholder value'. Given these motivations and the ability of banks to change their portfolios, Hanweck and Ryu (2005) model the determinants of spreads as being the function of changes for different groups of banks in response to credit, interest-rates and term-structural shocks.

3. Empirical literature on bank spreads

The empirical literature on bank spreads suggests that bank interest margins are mostly influenced by the degree of bank market power, administrative and other operating costs, the fraction of non-performing loans, the size of the operating capacity, the level of risk aversion, and regulatory, monetary and macro-economic shocks. Saunders and Schumacher (2000) decompose bank margins of selected OECD countries into a regulatory component, market structure and risk premium component and reveal a trade-off between assuring bank solvency and lowering the cost of financial services to consumers. Claeys and Vander Vennet (2008), investigate the determinants of bank interest margins in the Central and Eastern European (CEE) countries and suggest that relatively high bank margins in CEE countries are influenced by imperfect competitive markets, low operational efficiency, low capital adequacy and a high level of foreign and state ownership. The fall in bank spreads in the European banking sector during 1993–2000 is mainly due to the relaxation of competitive conditions in addition to the reduction of operating costs, interest-rate risk and credit risk (Maudos and Fernandez de Guevara 2004). On the relationship between bank spread and the degree of competition, Carbó Valverde and Rodriguez Fernandez (2007) contend that market power varies significantly across bank specifications with market power increasing as bank output of seven European countries become more diversified towards non-interest activities. Similarly, Demirguc-Kunt, Laeven, and Levine (2004) find that the high NIMs and large overhead costs of banks are closely associated with banks that are smaller, less liquid, less capitalised, have low non-interest income and have a large market share.

Brock and Rojas-Suarez (2000) study bank spread of seven Latin American countries in the 1990s and find that while at a micro-level, liquidity and capital risk affect banks' margin, interest rate volatility, inflation and GDP growth influence bank spreads at the macro-level. Employing a large data from 1999 to 2002, Gelos (2009) found that a prevalence of high bank spreads in 14 Latin American countries is as a result of high interest rates, less efficiency and large reserve requirements. Cross-country studies on sub-Saharan African banking spreads emphasise bank size, activity diversification and private ownership as variables that affect banks return on assets (Flamini, McDonald, and Schumacher 2009). Beck and Hesse (2009) identify NIMs in Uganda to be driven by overhead costs, sectoral composition of loans, and other time invariant bank characteristics. In Brazil, high spreads can be largely accounted for by the policy that requires banks to invest half of their deposits in reserves and mandatory credit (Souza-Sobrinho 2010). These studies are yet to provide reasonable channels through which policy shocks and imperfect competitive environments impact on bank spreads and allocation of resources to the private sector. This is exactly where this paper sheds some light by analysing how funding strategies of banks with market power affect their NIM.

4. Methodology and data

4.1 *Conventional versus funding-adjusted Lerner index of market power*

This paper employs two different specifications of Lerner index: a conventional Lerner (Berger, Klapper, and Turk-Ariss 2009) and funding-adjusted Lerner index (Maudos and Fernandez de Guevara 2007) to measure the degree market power and to analyse its implication on NIM. The conventional Lerner index version of the degree of market power is defined as

$$\text{Lerner index}_{it} = \frac{(P_{\mathrm{TA},it} - \mathrm{MC}_{\mathrm{TA},it})}{P_{\mathrm{TA},it}}. \tag{4}$$

The Lerner index in Equation (4) suggests the extent to which the monopolist's market power allows it to fix a price above marginal cost. The primary assumption is that the flow of goods and services produced by banks is proportional to total assets (Fernandez de Guevara, Maudos, and Perez 2005). With this assumption, the price is constructed to include both interest and non-interest income, where $P_{\mathrm{TA},it}$ is the price of total assets. $\mathrm{MC}_{\mathrm{TA},it}$ is the marginal cost of producing an additional unit of output. The $\mathrm{MC}_{\mathrm{TA},it}$ is derived from the following translog cost function as follows:

$$\ln \text{Cost}_{it} = \beta_0 + \beta_1 \ln \text{TA}_{it} + \frac{\beta_2}{2} \ln \text{TA}_{it}^2 + \sum_{k=1}^{3} \gamma_{kt} \ln W_{k,it} + \sum_{k=1}^{3} \phi_k \ln \text{TA}_{it} \ln W_{k,it}$$
$$+ \sum_{k=1}^{3} \sum_{j=1}^{3} \delta_{ij} \ln W_{k,it} \ln W_{j,it} + \sum_{i=1}^{3} \left(\frac{\delta_i}{2}\right) \ln W_{j,it}^2 + \sum_{k=1}^{2} \eta_k \text{trend}^k$$
$$\times \sum_{i=1}^{3} \varsigma_i \ln W_{j,it} \text{trend} + v \ln \text{TA}_{tj} \text{trend} + \varepsilon_j, \tag{5}$$

where Cost is the bank's total costs, including financial and operating cost; TA_i represents a proxy for bank output measured as total assets, and W_1, W_2, and W_3 indicate the input price of deposit funds, labour and capital and these are, respectively, calculated as the ratio of interest expenses to total deposits and money market funds, labour cost to total assets, and other operating expenses to total assets.[1] The cost function is estimated separately using a panel data for each country in the sample. This allows for the parameters of the cost function to vary from one country to another, reflecting different technologies. Once the cost function is estimated, the marginal cost is evaluated by taking the first derivative with respect to the output for each bank in the sample. Hence, the marginal cost is calculated for each bank as follows:[2]

$$\text{MC}_{it} = \frac{\text{Cost}_{it}}{\text{TA}_{it}} \left[\beta_1 + \beta_2 \ln \text{TA}_{it} + \sum_{k=1}^{3} \phi_k \ln W_{k,it} + v \text{trend}_{it} \right]. \tag{6}$$

There is a possible setback associated with the conventional Lerner index estimated above. The MC estimation following Equation (5) is likely to reflect some form of monopoly power emanating from deposit markets, based on the bank's ability to fund at a relatively low price. In pricing their loans, bank managers cover their funding costs, factor in a risk premium to reflect the uncertainty surrounding the loan-contracting problem and charge an extra premium to reflect their market power Turk-Ariss (2010). Thus, a form of deposit market power is already reflected in the loan pricing. According to Maudos and Fernandez de Guevara (2007), adding financing costs and consequently the price of deposits in the cost function captures the effect of market power in banking and this may bias the results. They add that excluding funding costs in the equation will lead to what they term a 'raw' pricing power that is not biased by market power which had already been obtained in the deposit market while securing funds. We, therefore, estimate a version of Equation (5) that excludes financing costs in the translog cost function. After calculating an operating MC for each bank at each time period following Equation (6), but including only two factors (labour cost and physical cost of capital), we derive a funding-adjusted Lerner index from the structural model specified in Equation (5). Thus, this paper employs two different specifications of Lerner to analyse the impact of market power and funding strategies of banks on NIM: a conventional Lerner (Berger, Klapper, and Turk-Ariss 2009) and a funding-adjusted Lerner (Maudos and Fernandez de Guevara 2007).

4.2 *Determinants of NIM: the dynamic panel model approach*

Our approach not only considers empirically, credit and interest-rate risk in a bank behavioural model, but is also firmly rooted in the new industrial organisation literature on bank-funding strategies. We examine the various funding sources and how they interact with the competitive measure and NIM. The approach is based on the assumption that interest margin, in each of the product service mix of banks' loans and deposits (here include all the funding modes of banks), results from the monopolistic competition among the banks operating in these markets. For a profit maximising bank that faces an inelastic demand function for loans or an inelastic supply function of deposits, the interest margin of a banking firm, financing its asset from various sources in a given period depends on the market structure that the bank operates in, its funding strategies, bank-specific characteristics, as well as the regulatory, macro- and monetary environments of the bank. Our empirical model which investigates these relationships is

$$\mathrm{NIM}_{it,c} = \alpha_1 \mathrm{NIM}_{it,c_{-1}} + \alpha_2 \mathrm{MP}_{it} + \alpha_3 \mathrm{FS}_{it,c} + (\mathrm{MP}_{it,c}{}^{*}\mathrm{FS}_{it,c}) + \sum_{j=3}^{k} \alpha_j X_{ij} + \varepsilon_{it} \tag{7}$$

$$\varepsilon_{it} = \mu_i + \nu_{it}$$

$$E[\mu_i] = E[\nu_{it}] = E[\mu_i \nu_{it}] = 0,$$

where $\mathrm{NIM}_{it,c}$ is the net-interest margin of bank i in country c at period t, and $\mathrm{NIM}_{it,c-1}$ is the observation on the same bank in the same county in the previous year. $\mathrm{MP}_{it,c}$ is the degree of market power of a bank i in country c in period t, $\mathrm{FS}_{it,c}$ is the funding strategy for bank i in country c in period t, $(\mathrm{MP}_{it,c} * \mathrm{FS}_{it,c})$ is the interaction between market power and the funding sources of bank i in country c at period t, the variable $X_{i,j}$ are a set of $\{k\}$ variables controlling for bank-specific characteristics, respective countries' macro-economic environments and contestability variables, α's are the parameter vectors and ε_{it} is the unobserved time-invariant. Here the disturbance term ε_{it} has two components: the μ_i is the unobserved time-invariant bank-specific effect, and ν_{it} is the disturbance term. The estimation of Equation (7) follows the argument put forward by Carbó Valverde and Rodriguez Fernandez (2007) that banks maximise wealth by considering both initial and end-of-period information and that previous values of bank margins may affect current margin values. This is because banks need to match the random deposit supply function and the random demand of lending activities and non-traditional activities across the period. We, therefore, estimate the implication of market power and funding structure on the interest margin, using a dynamic model.

One immediate problem in applying ordinary least squares (OLS) in estimating Equation (7) is that $\mathrm{NIM}_{it,c-1}$ is correlated with fixed effects in the error term which gives rise to the 'dynamic panel bias'. Moreover, there is evidence to suggest that OLS produces biases when an attempt is made to control for unobserved heterogeneity and simultaneity. Therefore, the estimation strategy used in this subsection is based on the methodology proposed by Blundell and Bond (1998), and Alvarez and Arellano (2003) in estimating systems of equations in both first difference and levels. As pointed in Roodman (2009), the system GMM estimator combines the standard set of equations in the first-difference estimator with a suitable lagged level as instruments, and an additional set of equations in level with suitably lagged first differences as instruments. Generally, the linear difference and system GMM estimators have one- and two-step variants. We use a two-step System GMM, Windmeijer (2005) correct standard error, small-sample adjustments, and orthogonal deviation. The two-step variant uses residuals from the one-step estimates and is asymptotically more efficient than the one-step.[3]

4.3 *Variables description*

The dependent variable is the bank interest spread and measured using 'ex-post spread' methodology. The 'ex-post spread' measures the net yield of bank financial intermediation on revenue actually generated by credit operations and the actual cost of deposit taking. The NIM is calculated from the banks' accounting data. It is calculated as the difference between interest revenue and interest expense as a proportion of earning assets.

Three funding modes have been identified in our sample as bank funding strategies: deposits, non-deposits/wholesale and internal funding. Deposits as a source of bank funding includes demand, saving and time deposits. Customer deposits are traditionally considered to be the main funding source of banks and to be cheap relative to other sources of funding, and they allow banks to maintain relatively high interest spreads (Ianotta, Nocera, and Sironi 2007). We measure deposits funding as the total deposits as a percentage of total assets. The Non-deposit funding is the funding resources from other banks and other sources that include notes, debenture, short-term bills and all other related debts not covered in the deposits modes. It is a purchased fund as the banks purchase these funds from other financial institutions. It is a short-term funding with relatively higher interest cost compared with deposits from customers. We measure non-deposit funding as all other debts (except deposits) divided by total assets. The measurement of internally generated funds for banking institutions differs from that of non-financial institutions. Banks are not constrained by cash flows as non-financial institutions, though they are limited by the amount of debt financing they can utilise (Houston, James, and Marcus 1997). We define internal capital similar to that of Houston, James, and Marcus (1997) as the sum of net profits before extraordinary items and loan loss provisions relative to bank loans at the end of the period.

This paper employs a number of control variables that affect the relationship of interest. These controls include bank-specific characteristics and the characteristics of the macro-economic and monetary environments. Following the approach used by Claeys and Vander Vennet (2008); the ratio of banks' equity to total assets is used as a measure of the degree of risk aversion and the level of capitalisation. *Ceteris paribus*, risk-averse bank managers tend to impose an extra premium on interest margin as a compensation for holding systematic risk. A ratio of total loans to assets is used as a proxy for credit risk. The argument put forward for the use of this measurement is that banks charge additional interest margin to compensate for exposure to expected and unexpected credit risk, and therefore the banks NIM will be high. The logarithm of total assets is employed as a proxy of the banks-operating capacity (bank size) as there is no information available to proxy the transaction made. Implicit interest payment is payment of interest on deposits through service-charge remissions and other types of depositor subsidy due to regulatory restrictions on explicit interest payments. Implicit payments are calculated as the difference between operating expenses and non-interest income divided by total assets. The higher the quality of management, the higher the interest margins that the bank imposes, on the basis that a high-quality management translates into a profitable composition of assets and a low-cost composition of liabilities. Operating expenses as a ratio of gross income is used as the proxy of quality of management. Included in our explanatory variables in explaining the determinants of market power and the funding strategies of banks is *non-interest income*. This enables us to assess whether diversification into non-interest activities enhances banks' ability to acquire market power, as well as adopting a particular funding strategy to finance that power. Following Carbó Valverde and Rodriguez Fernandez (2007), the ratio of non-interest income as a percentage of total-operating income is used as a measure of non-interest income.

This paper also controls for the countries' economic development, macro-economic stability, and regulatory framework as these are likely to affect the banking system performance. Inflation and GDP growth are included in the regression to account for differences in macro-economic environments. Inflation is the rate of inflation based on the consumer price index. GDP growth measures business cycle fluctuation. The study employs the respective countries' short-term interest rate as a measure of monetary policy stance. We use the*liberalisation index* constructed by Abiad,

Detragiache, and Tressel (2010) as our regulatory variable. The liberalisation index measures financial reforms that have taken place during the period and it ranges from 0 to 21 with the highest score indicating fully reformed.[4] The banking freedom index provides the overall measures of the openness of the banking sector and the extent to which banks are free to operate their businesses (The Heritage Foundation Index of Economic Freedom 2010). It is scaled from 0 to 100 with higher values indicating greater freedom.

4.4 *Data sources*

We use the micro-bank level and macro-country level data. Bank level data are taken from the Bankscope database maintained by Fitch/IBCA/Bureau Van Dijk. Series are yearly, covering a sample of 978 banks across 55 developing countries during the eight-year period, 2000–2007. As the study focuses on bank intermediation, we opt for the unconsolidated balance sheet data whenever possible even though, in some cases, we have to depend on consolidated statements because of data unavailability. In addition to the commercial banks and to ensure that we do not omit banks that are important players in the deposit and/or loan markets, we also include medium- and long-term credit banks and specialised government institutions as they remain important in these countries. Liberalisation index is obtained from Abiad, Detragiache, and Tressel (2010) while banking freedom index is from the Economic Freedom Indicators of the Heritage Foundation. We obtain our macro-data from the World Bank Development Indicator (World Bank 2008). The series include GDP/GDP *per capita* growth, inflation, average policy interest rates and money market rates.

5. Empirical results

5.1 *Summary descriptive statistics*

Table 1 shows the summary statistics for the key variables used in this study. All bank-specific variables are averaged by the bank during the period 2000–2007, while that of the country-level variables are averaged by country over the period under study. The countries are grouped into regions and this follows the World Bank Developing indicators groupings. The groupings are Africa, Asian, Central, and Eastern European countries (CEEC) and Latin America.

Within the sample period, two varieties of the Lerner index are constructed: a conventional Lerner index and a funding-adjusted Lerner index. The figures from the conventional version vary by more that 25% across the regions, with African banks, on average, pricing their product at around 27% above marginal cost. Similarly, figures from the funding-adjusted version of the Lerner index showing 63% over the marginal cost with the Asian banks being the banks that exhibit the highest market power. These figures demonstrate that, on average, the funding-adjusted Lerner index is larger than that of the conventional Lerner index, suggesting that the latter underestimates the degree of market power. This result justifies the alternative use of both specifications in our analysis. Most of the assets of the banks selected are financed by deposits with 73% being the highest, CEEC assets are financed with deposits. The least deposits funding is for Latin American banks. African banks are most profitable in terms of the NIM. The average NIM of African banks is 7% which is over and above the sample average of 5%. Regarding bank-specific variables, Asian banks are the largest banks in terms of size. The average bank size of the Asian banks is more than $30.12 billion. Latin American banks are the most capitalised. The CEEC demonstrate the highest level of bank growth and on efficiency measured as cost to income ratio, Asian banks are the most

Table 1. Summary statistics on selected bank level variables.

		Mean	Median	SD	Min	Max
Degree of bank market power						
Conventional Lerner index	*Aggregate*	0.246	0.261	0.244	−0.966	0.994
	Africa	0.277	0.296	0.259	−0.966	0.990
	Asia	0.221	0.247	0.209	−0.956	0.989
	CEEC	0.211	0.230	0.219	−0.901	0.880
	Latin America	0.272	0.287	0.267	−0.962	0.994
Funding-adjusted Lerner index	*Aggregate*	0.631	0.655	0.197	−0.981	0.999
	Africa	0.575	0.601	0.227	−0.981	0.995
	Asia	0.684	0.698	0.146	−0.854	0.980
	CEEC	0.611	0.627	0.179	−0.930	0.997
	Latin America	0.666	0.690	0.200	−0.807	0.999
Funding strategy						
Deposits funding	*Aggregate*	0.680	0.764	0.232	0.000	0.999
	Africa	0.682	0.770	0.228	0.001	0.999
	Asia	0.707	0.794	0.227	0.001	0.988
	CEEC	0.733	0.799	0.201	0.000	0.978
	Latin America	0.610	0.682	0.250	0.000	0.975
Non-deposits funding	*Aggregate*	0.170	0.085	0.208	0.000	0.978
	Africa	0.225	0.093	0.273	0.000	0.969
	Asia	0.168	0.072	0.220	0.000	0.978
	CEEC	0.114	0.063	0.141	0.000	0.863
	Latin America	0.184	0.133	0.186	0.000	0.962
Internal funding	*Aggregate*	0.061	0.042	0.116	−0.941	0.990
	Africa	0.093	0.070	0.121	−0.833	0.990
	Asia	0.034	0.029	0.049	−0.423	0.988
	CEEC	0.044	0.035	0.082	−0.846	0.886
	Latin America	0.069	0.049	0.157	−0.941	0.946
Bank spread						
NIM	*Aggregate*	0.057	0.043	0.059	−0.947	0.964
	Africa	0.078	0.063	0.074	−0.063	0.964
	Asia	0.032	0.029	0.032	−0.265	0.661
	CEEC	0.045	0.038	0.031	−0.054	0.237
	Latin America	0.065	0.050	0.069	−0.947	0.840
Bank-specific control variables						
Total assets in US $ billion (size)	*Aggregate*	6.86	0.51	45.37	0.00	1266
	Africa	0.99	0.17	4.63	0.00	68
	Asia	30.12	4.77	104.52	0.02	1266
	CEEC	2.09	0.60	4.55	0.00	51
	Latin America	2.52	0.42	6.59	0.00	100
Ratio of equity to assets (equity)	*Aggregate*	0.151	0.107	0.147	−0.075	0.997
	Africa	0.148	0.114	0.126	−0.075	0.997
	Asia	0.102	0.068	0.106	0.003	0.872
	CEEC	0.139	0.104	0.111	0.015	0.975
	Latin America	0.196	0.123	0.197	0.007	0.988
Bank growth	*Aggregate*	0.214	0.179	0.256	−0.983	0.998
	Africa	0.230	0.199	0.243	−0.967	0.998
	Asia	0.155	0.138	0.171	−0.888	0.983
	CEEC	0.269	0.240	0.270	−0.983	0.995
	Latin America	0.183	0.157	0.283	−0.870	0.997

(Continued)

Table 1. Continued.

		Mean	Median	SD	Min	Max
Cost to income ratio	*Aggregate*	0.445	0.438	0.181	0.002	0.999
	Africa	0.490	0.479	0.182	0.007	0.999
	Asia	0.353	0.333	0.152	0.002	0.996
	CEEC	0.469	0.467	0.157	0.010	0.987
	Latin America	0.440	0.442	0.199	0.005	0.989
Non-interest income	*Aggregate*	0.177	0.127	0.180	0.000	0.997
	Africa	0.179	0.147	0.153	0.000	0.988
	Asia	0.131	0.091	0.147	0.000	0.918
	CEEC	0.172	0.138	0.150	0.000	0.976
	Latin America	0.210	0.115	0.235	0.000	0.997
Loans to assets ratio	*Aggregate*	0.513	0.529	0.205	−0.010	0.999
	Africa	0.480	0.467	0.200	0.006	0.999
	Asia	0.557	0.553	0.159	0.002	0.976
	CEEC	0.534	0.565	0.200	0.000	0.970
	Latin America	0.492	0.514	0.232	−0.010	0.989

Source: Bankscope and authors' own calculation. The data comprises of 978 banks across 55 countries over the period 2000–2007.

Notes: Table 1 presents the summary statistics of selected banks market power, the funding strategy, spread, and bank-specific variables. The degree of market power is proxied by the Lerner index or the price mark-up over marginal cost, with the higher scores, indicating a higher degree of pricing power. Two variants of the Lerner index are reported: a conventional Lerner and a funding-adjusted Lerner. Deposit and non-deposit funding is the share of deposit and non-deposit funding to total assets, respectively. The internal funding is the sum of the net profit before extraordinary items and loan loss provisions relative bank loans at the end the period. We use the bank NIM which is defined as the ratio of the net interest income to total earning assets as a measure of spread. *Bank equity* represents average capitalisation of respective countries' banks and used as a proxy for the degree of risk aversion, *loan to assets* indicate portfolio mix and measures credit risk of the selected banks, the *bank size* is the average total assets, the efficiency of management is proxied by *cost to income ratio*, which is calculated as the operating expenses as a percentage of gross income and *bank growth* is the growth rate of bank assets. *Non-interest income* measured the exposure of a bank to non-interest-generating income. The mean values of the selected banks over the period 2000–2007 are in percentage terms except for bank size which is in billions of US dollars.

efficient. However, Latin American banks are more diversified in terms of generating non-interest incomes. On average 55.7% of Asian banks' assets in the sample are extended as loans, the highest in the sample. The least is the African banks whose total average loan portfolio is 48.0%.

5.2 *The determinants of market power and funding pattern of banks*

This sub-section analyses the empirical results with the aim of identifying various sources of market power as well as explaining variation in funding patterns of banks in emerging and developing countries. It is only when the sources of market power are identified and the variation in funding patterns of banks are analysed that possible action could be taken to reduce the social inefficiency associated with the existence of market power. To begin, Table 2 presents the results of the regressions that use bank-specific variables accounting for the respective countries' level of development and monetary policy stance. Following Demirguc-Kunt and Huizinga (2010), the estimated results include country and year fixed effects, and clustering of the errors at the bank level. Two varieties of the Lerner index are estimated, a conventional Lerner and a funding-adjusted Lerner. Columns 1 and 2 relate to the conventional Lerner, while columns 3 and 4 relate to the funding-adjusted Lerner.

Table 2. Determinants of bank market power.

	Conventional Lerner index		Funding-adjusted Lerner index	
	(1)	(2)	(3)	(4)
Bank size	0.0641***	0.0638***	0.0891***	0.0890***
	(0.0156)	(0.0156)	(0.0064)	(0.0064)
Equity	0.4555***	0.4648***	−0.0787**	−0.0701*
	(0.0958)	(0.0959)	(0.0393)	(0.0393)
Bank growth	0.0658***	0.0665***	0.0001	0.0007
	(0.0218)	(0.0218)	(0.0089)	(0.0089)
Management quality	0.1888**	0.2042**	0.0823**	0.0952***
	(0.0795)	(0.0799)	(0.0329)	(0.0330)
Non-interest income	0.2055***	0.2053***	0.0741***	0.0741***
	(0.0443)	(0.0443)	(0.0181)	(0.0181)
Banking freedom		0.0528*		0.0419***
		(0.0289)		(0.0118)
Inflation	−0.0132	−0.0128	0.0028	0.0032
	(0.0084)	(0.0084)	(0.0034)	(0.0034)
GDP growth	−0.0499*	−0.0459*	0.0013	0.0047
	(0.0276)	(0.0276)	(0.0112)	(0.0112)
GDP *per capita*	0.0311**	0.0307*	−0.0021	−0.0024
	(0.0161)	(0.0161)	(0.0065)	(0.0065)
Monetary policy	0.0730***	0.0734***	0.0692***	0.0694***
	(0.0143)	(0.0143)	(0.0059)	(0.0059)
Constant	−0.7075***	−0.9336***	−0.1430**	−0.3242***
	(0.1534)	(0.1970)	(0.0632)	(0.0811)
Observation	4556	4556	4512	4512
Country fixed effects	Y	Y	Y	Y
Time fixed effects	Y	Y	Y	Y
Clustering level	Bank	Bank	Bank	Bank

Notes: The dependent variable in columns 1 and 2 is the conventional version of the Lerner index, and the dependent variable in columns 3 and 4 is the funding-adjusted version of the Lerner index. The degree of market power is proxied by the Lerner Index or the price mark-up over marginal cost, with the higher scores indicating a higher degree of pricing power. *Bank size* is proxied by the natural logarithm of total assets valued in US dollars. Banks' *equity* is the bank total equity to asset ratio, measured as equity as a percentage of total assets. *Bank growth* is the growth rate of bank assets. Efficiency is the ability of the management to generate more quality assets. It is measured as earning assets as a percentage to total assets with a higher percentage points indicating a higher efficiency. *Non-interest income* measures the exposure of a bank to non-interest-generating income. *Banking freedom* is from the Economic Freedom Indicators of Heritage Founding. It is scaled from 0 to 100 with higher values, indicating greater freedom. *Inflation* is the rate of inflation based on the CPI. *GDP growth* measures business cycle fluctuation while *per capita* GDP accounts for the differences in economic developments across countries. Short-term interest rates are included to capture the stance of *monetary policy*. We estimate all regressions using country and time-fixed effects and clustering at the bank level. Robust standard errors are reported in parentheses.
*Statistical significance at 10% level.
**Statistical significance at 5% level.
***Statistical significance at 1% level.

The size of the bank affects both Lerner indices positively suggesting that larger banks tend to have market power. This result is consistent with the argument that larger banks are efficient, gaining economies of scale and scope and producing at lower cost which enables them to have higher margins (Meon and Weill 2005). Similarly, non-interest income has a positive and significant relationship with the Lerner index, indicating that banks that specialise in generating non-interest income tend to have higher market power. Bank equity is positively related to the conventional version of Lerner and significant and negatively to the funding-adjusted Lerner index. The different coefficient sign between the conventional and funding-adjusted indicate that banks with high levels of capital have higher market power if they exercise power in deposit markets. Also, the positive relationship with the conventional Lerner suggest that such banks are able to pay less for deposits and the depositors consider such banks to be more stable. Another significant factor that affects bank market power is the quality of management. We find that, banks with high quality management have higher market power. The results show that the inflation level does not influence bank market power. Macro-economic variables have a different degree of impact on market power. For instance if the business cycle increases by 1%, the Lerner index decreases by more than 4%, while a 1% increase in the level of economic development transforms to a 3% increase in the level of market power. Conventional and funding-adjusted Lerner indexes are affected with the same variables except *equity ratio* and *bank* and *GDP growth*. While equity has a positive relationship with the conventional Lerner, it associates negatively with the funding-adjusted. In the case of *bank* and *GDP growth*, it is significant with the conventional Lerner and insignificant with funding-adjusted Lerner. We have to emphasise that the rest of the explanatory variables of bank market power maintain their coefficient sign as well as their magnitude after inclusion of the economic and banking freedom variables.

Next we analyse the determinants of bank funding patterns where deposit, non-deposit (wholesale) and internally generated funding are the dependent variables. We present our findings in Table 3 and in columns: 1 and 2 for deposit funding; 3 and 4 for non-deposit funding and 5 and 6 for internal funding. Bank size has negative association with deposit funding; positive with non-deposit funding and negative with internal funding only when a funding-adjusted variable is added to the regression. The result suggests that larger banks rely heavily on wholesale funds in financing their operations. As expected, equity ratio has a negative and statistically significant relationship with both deposit and non-deposit funding and positive coefficient on internal funding; indicating that highly capitalised banks finance their investment, using internal funds and thus reduce their leverage. In addition, banks in developing countries finance their growth with internally generated funds. The results also show that the coefficient of management quality variable is positive and significant in all the funding modes, indicating that efficient banks in developing countries are able to proportionately finance their activities with deposit, non-deposit and internal funds. The conventional version of the Lerner index is included in column 1 for deposit funding, in column 3 for non-deposit funding and column 5 for internal funding. The results show positive and significant association with deposit and internal funding meaning that banks with market power have deposit and internal funds as their sources of funding and these sources are considered safe and cheap (Demirguc-Kunt and Huizinga 2010). Interestingly, the funding-adjusted version of Lerner has no significant relationship with the funding modes except internal funds showing that banks that have not already exercised market power in deposit markets increase their internal capital. In addition to the bank-specific and macro-economic variables, we include the liberalisation index which measures the level of financial reforms that the respective countries have undertaken during the period under study. Liberalisation index has a positive relationship with deposit funding and negative with both non-deposit and internal funds, indicating that in a developing country where the financial sector is fully liberalised, deposit funding tends to increase. All the macro-economic and monetary policy variables included in the regression do not impact on any of the funding modes except *per capita* income. An increase in GDP *per capita* increases deposit funding of the selected banks in developing economies.

Table 3. Determinants of bank funding strategies.

	Deposit funding		Non-deposits funding		Internal funding	
	1	2	3	4	5	6
Bank size	−0.0109**	−0.014***	0.0220***	0.0229***	−0.00003	−0.015***
	(0.0046)	(0.0047)	(0.0059)	(0.0060)	(0.0039)	(0.0040)
Equity	−0.729***	−0.744***	−0.418***	−0.412***	0.1487***	0.2174***
	(0.0310)	(0.0306)	(0.0400)	(0.0393)	(0.0260)	(0.0254)
Bank growth	−0.0140**	−0.0119*	0.0084	0.0080	0.0056	0.0137**
	(0.0066)	(0.0066)	(0.0083)	(0.0082)	(0.0055)	(0.0054)
Management quality	0.0413*	0.0383	0.0596**	0.0553*	0.1290***	0.1303***
	(0.0247)	(0.0247)	(0.0326)	(0.0322)	(0.0210)	(0.0207)
Non-interest income	−0.0264*	−0.029**	0.0003	0.0058	0.0346***	0.0406***
	(0.0139)	(0.0137)	(0.0165)	(0.0161)	(0.0117)	(0.0114)
Conventional Lerner	0.0122**		−0.0038		0.0693***	
	(0.0054)		(0.0066)		(0.0046)	
Funding-adjusted Lerner		0.0130		−0.0084		0.2252***
		(0.0125)		(0.0165)		(0.0104)
Liberalisation	0.1466***	0.1422***	−0.1031**	−0.1000**	−0.088***	−0.092***
	(0.0391)	(0.0390)	(0.0493)	(0.0488)	(0.0330)	(0.0325)
Inflation	−0.0014	−0.0017	0.0005	0.0006	−0.0005	−0.0024
	(0.0026)	(0.0026)	(0.0036)	(0.0036)	(0.0022)	(0.0021)
GDP growth	−0.01067	−0.0107	0.0046	0.0046	0.0066	0.0069
	(0.0082)	(0.0082)	(0.0112)	(0.0110)	(0.0069)	(0.0068)
GDP *per capita*	0.0093*	0.0094*	−0.0093	−0.0090	−0.0029	−0.0028
	(0.0051)	(0.0051)	(0.0072)	(0.0072)	(0.0043)	(0.0042)
Monetary policy	0.0026	0.0018	−0.0066	−0.0065	0.0033	−0.0078**
	(0.0046)	(0.0046)	(0.0063)	(0.0063)	(0.0038)	(0.0038)
Observation	3754	3736	3102	3079	3759	3739
Country fixed effects	Y	Y	Y	Y	Y	Y
Time fixed effects	Y	Y	Y	Y	Y	Y
Clustering level	Bank	Bank	Bank	Bank	Bank	Bank

Notes: The dependent variable in columns 1 and 2 is deposit funding; the dependent variable in columns 3 and 4 is non-deposit funding; and internal funding is for columns 5 and 6. Deposit and non-deposit funding is the share of deposit and non-deposit funding to total assets, respectively. The internal funding is the sum of the net profit before extraordinary items and loan loss provisions relative bank loans at the end the period. *Bank size* is proxied by the natural logarithm of total assets valued in US dollars. Bank *equity* is the bank's total equity to asset ratio, measured as an equity as a percentage of total assets. Efficiency is the ability of the management to generate more earning assets. It is measured as the earning assets as a percentage to total assets with a higher percentage, indicating higher efficiency. *Non-interest income* measures the exposure of a bank to non-interest-generating income. The degree of market power is proxied by the Lerner Index or the price mark-up over the marginal cost, with the higher scores indicating a higher degree of pricing power. Liberalisation is the financial reforms index constructed by Abiad, Detragiache, and Tressel (2010). *Inflation* is the rate of inflation based on the CPI. *GDP growth* measures the business cycle fluctuation while *per capita* GDP accounts for the differences in economic developments across countries. Short-term interest rate is included to capture the stance of *monetary policy*. We estimate all regressions using country and time fixed effects and clustering at the bank level. Standard errors are reported in parentheses.

*Statistical significance at 10% level.

**Statistical significance at 5% level.

***Statistical significance at 1% level.

5.3 *Evaluation of the NIM*

In this sub-section, we analyse the relationship between bank market power and funding patterns of banks on one hand and bank NIM on the other. Table 4 presents the regression result that

Table 4. Evaluation of bank NIM, using a funding-adjusted version of the Lerner index.

	(1)	(2)	(3)	(4)	(5)
NIM_{-1}	0.3946***	0.4514***	0.4623***	0.4538***	0.3648***
	(0.0873)	(0.0652)	(0.0626)	(0.0663)	(0.0589)
Risk aversion	0.0590	0.0452**	0.0403	0.0103	0.0218
	(0.0525)	(0.0226)	(0.0282)	(0.0221)	(0.0183)
Credit risk	0.0694***	0.0497***	0.0426***	0.0299***	0.0525***
	(0.0152)	(0.0102)	(0.0118)	(0.0104)	(0.0096)
Operating size	−0.0093***	−0.005***	−0.005***	−0.004***	−0.0024*
	(0.0029)	(0.0018)	(0.0017)	(0.0015)	(0.0013)
Implicit payment	0.4301***	0.4293***	0.4102***	0.3882***	0.4788***
	(0.1208)	(0.0978)	(0.1286)	(0.1210)	(0.1105)
Cost to income	−0.0473***	−0.0115	−0.0031	0.0068	−0.0133
	(0.0150)	(0.0208)	(0.0168)	(0.0148)	(0.0111)
Funded-adjusted Lerner		0.0397*	0.0452*	0.0417*	0.0077
		(0.0236)	(0.0239)	(0.0221)	(0.0142)
Deposit funding			0.0259*		
			(0.0147)		
Non-deposit funding				−0.0256*	
				(0.0147)	
Internal funds					0.0763***
					(0.0284)
Inflation	−0.0077***	−0.006***	−0.005***	−0.006***	−0.0036**
	(0.0028)	(0.0019)	(0.0018)	(0.0019)	(0.0015)
GDP *per capita*	−0.0092***	−0.007***	−0.0055*	−0.0042*	−0.0047**
	(0.0030)	(0.0029)	(0.0031)	(0.0025)	(0.0022)
Monetary policy	0.0102***	0.0136***	0.0120***	0.0137***	0.0141***
	(0.0034)	(0.0033)	(0.0036)	(0.0036)	(0.0029)
Diagnostics tests					
Number of observations	4297	4658	4521	3699	4547
Number of instruments	89	143	137	137	164
Hansen	64.91	130.63	112.33	115.49	134.44
P-value	(0.739)	(0.371)	(0.654)	(0.574)	(0.744)
AB2	−0.79	−0.66	−0.58	−0.84	0.42
P-value	(0.431)	(0.509)	(0.565)	(0.404)	(0.678)
F-test	28.24***	32.92***	25.09***	20.80***	50.92***

Notes: The dependent variable is the *NIM* which is defined as the ratio of the net interest income to total earning assets. The ratio of banks' capital to total assets is used as a proxy to measure the degree of *risk aversion*. Banks' loan to total assets ratio is used as a measure of *credit risk*. The volume of loans granted is proxied as the *operating size* of the bank. *Implicit payment* is the total-operating expenses net of the non-interest revenue expressed as a percentage of total assets. *Cost to income ratio* is used as a measure of operating efficiency. The degree of market power is proxied by the *Lerner Index* with higher scores indicating a higher degree of pricing power. *Deposit funding* is a ratio of total deposit to assets and *non-deposit funding* is the share of non-deposit funding to total assets. *Internal funds* are internally generated funds. It is measured as the sum of the net profits before extraordinary items and loan loss provisions relative to bank loans at the end the period. *Inflation* is the rate of inflation based on the CPI. *Per capita GDP* accounts for the differences in economic development across countries. Short-term interest rate is included to capture the stance of *monetary policy*. We estimate all regressions, using the dynamic panel-data estimation, the two-step System GMM, Windmeijer-correct standard error, small-sample adjustments, and orthogonal deviation. Standard errors are reported in parentheses. We report the following diagnostic tests: (1) observation (2) the instruments count, (3) the Hansen test for over identification restriction which the null hypothesis is that instruments are exogenous, (4) the Arellano–Bond tests for first- and second-order serial correlation in the residuals which the null hypothesis is that there is no serial correlation, (5) the *F*-test for joint significance of instruments.
*Statistical significance at 10% level.
**Statistical significance at 5% level.
***Statistical significance at 1% level.

has NIM as the dependent variable. The different columns reported relate to different empirical approaches to funding modes (deposit funding, non-deposit funding and internal funding) and the varieties of the Lerner index used (conventional and funding-adjusted). All regressions are estimated, using the dynamic panel-data estimation, two-step System GMM, Windmeijer-correct standard error, small-sample adjustments, and orthogonal deviation. The regression results show that in general, all the variables considered in the study significantly influence the NIM except equity to asset ratio that measures risk aversion of banks. Also the lagged-dependent variable, the NIM among the explanatory variables is positive and statistically significant, illustrating the importance of accounting for previous values of the dependent variable. Credit risk has a positive and significant sign meaning that banks apply a risk premium implicitly to the interest rates charged for their operations. The volume of total loans granted, measuring the operating capacity of the bank is negative, meaning that banks that specialised in lending appear to offer lower margins. The implicit payment has its coefficient as positive and significant. This, according to Maudos and Fernandez de Guevara (2004), shows that banks that charge an extra fee for their services more implicitly through lower remuneration of liabilities, maintain higher interest margins. The cost to income ratio measures the operating efficiency of the management in generating income with a high value, indicating management inefficiency. The sign is negative and significant meaning that an increase in the cost to income ratio by 1% decreases NIM by 4% *ceteris paribus*. Inflation has a negative and statistically significant relationship with the NIM, likewise the GDP *per capita* growth. These results show that banks tend to reduce their interest rates margin during economic turmoil. This result is consistent with Boyd, Levine, and Smith (2001) who show a strong negative correlation between inflation and the amount of bank credit, indicating that NIM decreases as inflation increases. However, the positive sign of the monetary policy stance shows that banks in developing countries profit from increases in monetary policy rates.

In column 2, we incorporate the funding-adjusted version of the Lerner index and the results show that the NIM increases when banks increase their market power. When the deposit funding is added in column 3, the Lerner index is still positive and statistically significant. Likewise for deposit funding, it is positive, indicating that banks with market power finance their investment with low cost of deposit funds and this increases their NIM. These findings suggest that deposit discipline exists more in developing countries (Martinez Peria and Schmukler 1999) and that they (depositors) demand relatively low returns from banks that are more capitalised and stable as well as being perceived to have market power. In addition, the finding is consistent with the findings of Berlin and Mester (1999) that banks with high market power have considerable access to cheap deposit funding through a solid local deposit market penetration that enable them to maintain high interest margins. In column 4, as expected, the non-deposit funding is negative and significant meaning that banks in developing countries, though the capital market is relatively undeveloped, finance their loans with borrowed funds and that reduces their margins. The explanatory capacity of internal funding deserves special mention. Its statistical significance shows the importance of introducing it in the regression. The sign is positive and its coefficient is higher compared with the deposit funding. This means that *ceteris paribus a* 1% increase in internal funding generates additional NIM of 8% with deposit funding increasing by only 3%. The high coefficient and significance of internal funding in contrast to deposit and non-deposit funding helps to support the hypothesis that external financing is expensive relative to internally generated funds. This finding also suggests that banks in developing countries are shifting their asset financing towards internally generated funds which have been the preserve of holding companies in advance economies. Houston, James, and Marcus (1997) find a strong positive relation between loan growth of the US bank holding companies and internally generated funds.

Table 5. Evaluation of bank NIM using a conventional version of the Lerner index.

	(1)	(2)	(3)	(4)	(5)
NIM_{-1}	0.3946***	0.4261***	0.3510***	0.4597***	0.3846***
	(0.0873)	(0.0779)	(0.0663)	(0.0694)	(0.0751)
Risk aversion	0.0590	0.0305	−0.0095	0.0364	0.0058
	(0.0525)	(0.0240)	(0.0217)	(0.0246)	(0.0176)
Credit risk	0.0694***	0.0452***	0.0421***	0.0385***	0.0375***
	(0.0152)	(0.0110)	(0.0088)	(0.0107)	(0.0090)
Operating size	−0.009***	−0.0038**	−0.0040***	−0.0041**	−0.0012
	(0.0029)	(0.0017)	(0.0015)	(0.0018)	(0.0013)
Implicit payment	0.4301***	0.4459***	0.4021***	0.3433**	0.4603***
	(0.1208)	(0.1379)	(0.1269)	(0.1355)	(0.1061)
Cost to income	−0.047***	−0.022**	−0.0211**	−0.0208*	−0.0057
	(0.0150)	(0.0116)	(0.0102)	(0.0126)	(0.0073)
Conventional Lerner		0.0359***	0.0246**	0.0209*	0.0142*
		(0.0123)	(0.0113)	(0.0112)	(0.0084)
Deposit funding			−0.0230*		
			(0.0131)		
Non-deposit funding				0.0052	
				(0.0099)	
Internal funds					0.0639**
					(0.0295)
Inflation	−0.007***	−0.0034	−0.0024	−0.0033	−0.0006
	(0.0028)	(0.0023)	(0.0020)	(0.0026)	(0.0020)
GDP *per capita*	−0.009***	−0.009***	−0.0080***	−0.0011	−0.0033
	(0.0030)	(0.0031)	(0.0028)	(0.0023)	(0.0024)
Monetary policy	0.0102***	0.0157***	0.0173***	0.0191***	0.0153***
	(0.0034)	(0.0040)	(0.0028)	(0.0040)	(0.0025)
Diagnostics tests					
Number of observations	4297	4256	4544	3403	4558
Number of instruments	89	144	164	165	164
Hansen	64.91	146.04	147.38	158.97	165.86
P-value	(0.739)	(0.119)	(0.452)	(0.236)	(0.125)
AB2	−0.79	−0.43	−0.45	−0.50	1.47
P-value	(0.431)	(0.670)	(0.650)	(0.614)	(0.141)
F-test	28.24***	42.43**	32.54	35.75***	46.90***

Notes: The dependent variable is the *NIM* which is defined as the ratio of the net-interest income to total earning assets. The ratio of banks' capital to total assets is used as a proxy to measure the degree of *risk aversion*. Banks' loan to total assets ratio is used as a measure of *credit risk*. The volume of loans granted is proxied as the *operating size* of the bank. *Implicit payment* is the total operating expenses net of non-interest revenue expressed as a percentage of total assets. *Cost to income* is used as a measure of operating efficiency. The degree of market power is proxied by the *Lerner index* with the higher scores indicating a higher degree of pricing power. *Deposit funding* is ratio of total deposit to assets and *non-deposit funding* is the share of non-deposit funding to total assets. *Internal funds* is measured as the sum of the net profit before extraordinary items and loan loss provisions relative bank loans at the end the period. *Inflation* is the rate of inflation based on the CPI. The natural logarithm of the *GDP per capita* accounts for the differences in economic developments across countries. Short-term interest rate is included to capture the stance of *monetary policy*. We estimate all regressions using the dynamic panel-data estimation, two-step System GMM, Windmeijer-correct standard error, small-sample adjustments, and orthogonal deviation. Standard errors are reported in parentheses. We report the following diagnostic tests: (1) observations (2) the instruments count, (3) the Hansen test for over identification restriction which the null hypothesis is that instruments are exogenous, (4) the Arellano–Bond tests for first- and second-order serial correlation in the residuals which the null hypothesis is that there is no serial correlation, (5) the *F*-test for joint significance of instruments.
*Statistical significance at 10% level.
**Statistical significance at 5% level.
***Statistical significance at 1% level.

Table 6. The sensitivity NIM to market power and bank funding strategies.

	(1)	(2)	(3)	(4)
NIM_{-1}	0.4634***	0.5093***	0.3887***	0.4181***
	(0.0632)	(0.0642)	(0.0741)	(0.0938)
Risk aversion	−0.0206	−0.0018	−0.0272	−0.0422
	(0.0269)	(0.0313)	(0.0250)	(0.0310)
Credit risk	0.0326***	0.0234**	0.0403***	0.0317***
	(0.0064)	(0.0119)	(0.0086)	(0.0089)
Operating size	−0.0040**	−0.0030	−0.0020	−0.0006
	(0.0016)	(0.0022)	(0.0014)	(0.0012)
Implicit payment	0.4234***	0.4639***	0.5237***	0.6462***
	(0.1462)	(0.1602)	(0.1184)	(0.1568)
Cost to income	−0.0219*	−0.0005	0.0018	−0.0158***
	(0.0131)	(0.0102)	(0.0067)	(0.0059)
Conventional Lerner	0.0037	0.0241**	0.0065	−0.1104*
	(0.0230)	(0.0110)	(0.0099)	(0.0603)
Deposit funding	−0.0378*			−0.0572**
	(0.0210)			(0.0258)
Lerner X deposit fund	0.0431			0.1205*
	(0.0307)			(0.0709)
Non-deposit funding		−0.0203		−0.0586**
		(0.0194)		(0.0269)
Lerner X non-deposit funding		0.0459		0.1389*
		(0.0505)		(0.0763)
Internal funds			0.1245***	0.1381***
			(0.0348)	(0.0415)
Lerner X Internal funding			0.0501*	0.0892***
			(0.0270)	(0.0298)
Inflation	−0.0028	−0.0062**	−0.0002	−0.0012
	(0.0023)	(0.0022)	(0.0019)	(0.0020)
GDP *per capita*	−0.0078***	−0.0045**	−0.00432**	−0.0007
	(0.0025)	(0.0020)	(0.0021)	(0.0020)
Monetary policy	0.0146***	0.0177***	0.0107***	0.0101***
	(0.0031)	(0.0039)	(0.0030)	(0.0033)
Diagnostics tests				
Number of observations	4126	3425	4013	2994
Number of instruments	186	186	186	280
Hansen	195	194	190.34	276.41
P-value	0.064	0.075	0.104	0.194
AB2	−0.19	−0.28	2.03	1.98
P-value	0.846	0.778	0.042	0.048
F-test	46.03***	57.23***	95.34***	83.72**

Notes: The dependent variable is the NIM. The ratio of bank equity to total assets is used as a proxy to measure the degree of *risk aversion*. Bank loans to total assets ratio measures of *credit risk*. The volume of loans granted is proxied as the *operating size* of the bank. *Implicit payment* is the total operating expenses net of the non-interest revenue expressed as a percentage of total assets. Ratio of *cost to income* is used as a measure of the operating efficiency. The degree of market power is proxied by the *Lerner Index*. *Deposit funding* is the ratio of total deposit to assets and *non-deposit funding* is the share of non-deposit funding to total assets, respectively. *Internal funds* are internally generated capital. *Inflation* is the rate of inflation based on the CPI. The natural logarithm of the *GDP per capita* accounts for the differences in economic development. Short-term interest rate is included to capture the stance of *monetary policy*. We estimate all regressions using the dynamic panel-data estimation. Standard errors are reported in parentheses.
*Statistical significance at 10% level.
**Statistical significance at 5% level.
***Statistical significance at 1% level.

Next, Table 5 reports results of regressions on the same variables as that of Table 4. The difference here is that of the measurement of the Lerner index. In Table 5, we use the conventional version of the Lerner index. We show similar results in terms of sign and magnitude except for column 3 where deposit funding has a negative coefficient. These findings reiterated our earlier argument on the weaknesses of the conventional version of Lerner and also justify the use of other alternative Lerner specifications in measuring the market power.

In Table 6, we report the interaction of the Lerner index and the funding strategies of banks. This is to enable us to investigate whether the Lerner index sensitivity of the NIM depends on the funding strategies of the banks. The results indicate that the sensitivity of the NIM to internally generated funds increases as bank market power increases. However, there is no evidence to suggest that interest margin increases for banks with market power and with deposits and non-deposits funding.[5]

6. Conclusion

This paper contributes to the empirical literature on the banks' NIM in emerging and developing countries. We analyse the relationship between bank market power and the funding pattern of banks on one hand and the bank NIM on the other. We use macro-economic and monetary variables to account for differences in economic development and the monetary policy stance. We use both the micro-bank level and macro-country level data. We sample 978 banks across 55 countries during the eight-year period, 2000–2007. To account for endogeneity, and to provide precise and consistent parameter estimates, we employ the System GMM estimator in Section 2 in the estimation process, while in Section 1, we follow the (Demirguc-Kunt and Huizinga 2010) estimation process to include the country and year fixed effects and clustering of the errors at the bank level.

The main contribution of this paper is to provide empirical evidence on how bank market power and funding patterns perform in terms of producing profitable banks in emerging and developing countries. In particular, we analyse how funding strategies of banks with market power affect their NIM. Our results demonstrate that on average, the funding-adjusted Lerner index is larger than that of the conventional Lerner index, suggesting that the latter has been underestimating the degree of market power. On determining of the Lerner index, our regression results reveal that larger, growing and highly capitalised banks have a degree of market power. This result is consistent with the argument that larger banks are efficient, well resourced and gain economies of scale and scope; have the ability to produce at lower cost and that enables them to have high margins (Meon and Weill 2005). Similarly, diversifying into non-interest income activities enhances bank market power. With the funding strategy, smaller, highly capitalised and efficiently managed banks employ internally generated funds for their investment activities.

With regard to determinants of the NIM, the study reveals that NIM among the explanatory variables is positively and statistically significant illustrating the importance of accounting for previous values of the dependent variable. The operating size and cost to income ratio affect the NIM negatively while credit risk and implicit payment have a positive relationship with the NIM. Our study finds evidence that supports the fact that the banking system structure explains the bank NIM. Overall, our results suggest that the NIM among banks with market power is significantly more sensitive to internally generated funds than it is with deposits and wholesale funding. Regarding economic policy implications, the results allow us to conclude that policies should be targeted at reducing competition, promoting banking freedom, and increasing the use of banks' internally generated funds in emerging and developing countries.

Acknowledgements

We thank Victor Murinde and two anonymous reviewers for their helpful comments. Mohammed Amidu expresses his gratitude to the University of Ghana Business School for financial support.

Notes

1. Owing to the absence of data on total number of employees, the unit cost of labour is expressed in terms of total assets.
2. See Fernandez de Guevara, Maudos, and Perez (2005) for an explanation of the detailed estimation process.
3. Tables 4–6 report the results for the full sample as well as for the regional groups. The diagnostic tests include: (1) the instruments count, (2) the Hansen test for over-identification restriction for which the null hypothesis is that instruments are exogenous (3) the Arellano–Bond tests for first- and second-order serial correlation in the residuals for which the null hypothesis is that there is no serial correlation and (4) the *F*-test for joint significance of instruments.
4. The liberalisation index for 2006–2007 was extrapolated from the 2005 index as financial reform rarely changed over time.
5. Further analysis was conducted on whether there are regional differences in the determinants of bank NIM. The result is similar in magnitude and significant to that of the results of the benchmark. This finding is available from the authors upon request.

References

Abiad, A., E. Detragiache, and T. Tressel. 2010. A new database of financial reforms. *IMF Staff Papers* 57, no. 2: 281–302.

Allen, L. 1988. The determinants of bank interest margins: A note. *Journal of Financial and Quantitative Analysis* 23, no. 2: 231–35.

Alvarez, J., and M. Arellano. 2003. The time series and cross-section asymptotics of dynamic panel data estimators. *Econometrica* 71, no. 4: 1121–59.

Angbazo, L. 1997. Commercial bank net-interest margins, default risk, interest-rate risk, and off-balance sheet banking. *Journal of Banking and Finance* 21, no. 1: 55–87.

Blundell, R.W., and S.R. Bond. 1998. Initial conditions and moment restriction in dynamic panel data models. *Journal of Econometrics* 80, no. 1: 115–43.

Beck, T., and H. Hesse. 2009. Why are interest spread so high in Uganda? *Journal of Development Economics* 88, no. 2: 192–204.

Berger, A., L. Klapper, and R. Turk-Ariss. 2009. Bank competition and financial stability. *Journal of Financial Services Research* 35, no. 2: 99–118.

Berlin, M., and L.J. Mester. 1999. Deposits and relationship lending. *Review of Financial Studies* 12, no. 3: 579–607.

Boyd, J.H., R. Levine, and B.D. Smith. 2001. The impact of inflation on financial sector performance. *Journal Monetary Economics* 47, no. 2: 221–48.

Brock, P.L., and L. Rojas-Suarez. 2000. Understanding the behaviour of bank spreads in Latin America. *Journal of Development Economic* 63, no. 1: 113–34.

Carbó, S., D. Humphrey, J. Maudos, and P. Molyneux. 2009. Cross-country comparisons of competition and pricing power in European banking. *Journal of International Money and Finance* 28, no. 1: 115–34.

Carbó Valverde, S., and F. Rodriguez Fernandez. 2007. The determinants of bank margins in European banking. *Journal of Banking and Finance* 31, no. 7: 2043–63.

Claeys, S., and R. Vander Vennet. 2008. Determinants of bank interest margins in Central and Eastern Europe: A comparison with the West. *Economic Systems* 32, no. 2: 197–216.

Demirguc-Kunt, A., and H.P. Huizinga. 2010. Bank activity, and funding strategies: The impact on risk and return. *Journal of Financial Economics* 98, no. 3: 626–50.

Demirguc-Kunt, A., L. Laeven, and R. Levine. 2004. Regulations, market structure, institutions, and the cost of financial intermediation. *Journal of Money Credit Banking* 36, no. 3: 593–622.

Fernandez de Guevara, J., J. Maudos, and F. Perez. 2005. Market power in European banking sectors. *Journal of Financial Services Research* 27, no. 2: 109–37.

Flamini, V., C. McDonald, and L. Schumacher. 2009. The determinants of commercial banks profitability in sub-Sahara Africa. IMF Working paper, Wp/09/15, Washington DC.

Freixas, X., and J.C. Rochet. 1997. *Microeconomics of banking*. Cambridge, MA: Massachusetts Institute of Technology Press.

Gelos, R.G. 2009. Banking spread in Latin America. *Economic Inquiry* 47, no. 4: 796–814.

Hanweck, G., and L. Ryu. 2005. The sensitivity of bank net-interest margins and profitability to credit, interest-rate and term-structure shocks across bank product specializations. Working Paper 2005-02, Federal Deposit Insurance Corporation, Washington DC.

Ho, T., and A. Saunders. 1981. The determinants of bank interest margins: Theory and empirical evidence. *Journal of Financial and Quantitative Analysis* 16, no. 4: 581–600.

Houston, J., C. James, and D. Marcus. 1997. Capital market frictions and the role of internal capital markets in banking. *Journal of Financial Economics* 46, no. 2: 135–64.

Ianotta, G., G. Nocera, and A. Sironi. 2007. Ownership structure, risk and performance in the European banking industry. *Journal of Banking and Finance* 31, no. 7: 2127–49.

Kashyap, A.K., R. Rajan, and J.C. Stein. 2002. Banks as liquidity providers: An explanation for coexistence of lending and deposit taking. *Journal of Finance* 57, no. 1: 33–73.

Klein, M.A. 1971. A theory of the banking firm. *Journal of Money, Credit and Banking* 3, no. 2: 205–18.

Martinez Peria, S., and S.L. Schmukler. 1999. Do depositors punish banks for bad behaviour? Market discipline in Argentina, Chile and Mexico. World Bank policy research, Working Paper 2058, Washington, DC.

Maudos, J., and F. Fernandez de Guevara. 2004. Factors explaining the interest margin in the banking sectors of the European Union. *Journal of Banking and Finance* 28, no. 9: 2259–81.

Maudos, J., and J. Fernandez de Guevara. 2007. The cost of market power in the European banking sectors: Social welfare cost vs. cost inefficiency. *Journal of Banking and Finance* 31, no. 7: 2103–25.

Maudos, J., and A. Nagore. 2005. Explaining market power differences in banking: A cross-country study. Institute Valenciano de Investigaciones Economicas, SA, WP-EC 2005-10.

McShane, R.W., and I.G. Sharpe. 1985. A time series – cross section analysis of the determinants of Australian trading bank loan – deposit interest margins: 1962–1981. *Journal of Banking and Finance* 9, no. 1: 115–36.

Meon, P., and L. Weill. 2005. Can a merger in Europe help banks hedge against macroeconomic risk. *Applied Financial Economics* 15, no. 5: 315–26.

Oreiro, J.L., and L.F. de Paula. 2010. Macroeconomic determinants of bank spread in Latin America: A recent analysis with special focus on Brazil. *International Review of Applied Economics* 24, no. 5: 573–90.

Roodman, D. 2009. How to do xtabond2: An introduction to difference and system GMM in stata. *The Stata Journal* 9, no.1: 86–136.

Saunders, A., and L. Schumacher. 2000. The determinants of bank interest rate margins: An international study. *Journal of International Money and Finance* 19, no. 6: 813–32.

Souza-Sobrinho, N. 2010. Macroeconomics of bank interest spreads: Evidence from Brazil. *Annals of Finance* 6, no. 1: 1–32.

Taci, A., and E. Zampieri. 1998. Efficiency in Czech banking sector. CERGE-EI, Discussion Paper, No. 4/98, Charles University, Prague.

The Heritage Foundation Index of Economic Freedom. 2010. *The link between economic opportunity and prosperity*. Washington, DC: The Heritage Foundation and Dow Jones and Company.

Turk-Ariss, R.T. 2010. On the implication of market power in banking: Evidence from developing countries. *Journal of Banking and Finance* 34, no. 4: 765–75.

Windmeijer, F. 2005. A finite sample correction for the variance of linear efficient two step GMM estimators. *Journal of Econometrics* 126, no. 1: 25–51.

Wong, K. 1997. On the determinants of bank interest margins under credit and interest rate risks. *Journal of Banking and Finance* 21, no. 2: 251–71.

World Bank. 2008. *World development indicators* (database). www.esds.ac.uk (accessed January 31, 2009).

An examination of investor sentiment effect on G7 stock market returns

Deven Bathia and Don Bredin

UCD Smurfit Graduate Business School, Carysfort Avenue, Blackrock, Co Dublin, Ireland

This paper examines the relationship between investor sentiment and G7 stock market returns. Using a range of investor sentiment proxies, including investor survey, equity fund flow, closed-end equity fund (CEEF) discount and equity put–call ratio, we examine if investor sentiment has a significant influence on value and growth stock returns as well as aggregate market returns. Using monthly data for the period January 1995–December 2007, our results depict a negative relationship between investor sentiment and future returns. We find results that are consistent with previous studies in that when investor sentiment is high (low), future returns are low (high). Our panel results display evidence of commonality across all the sentiment measures with the value stocks having a particularly strong effect relative to growth stocks. Furthermore, the effect of survey sentiment on future returns gradually decreases beyond the one-month forecast horizon. We observe evidence of price pressure on value stocks and the overall market due to increases in concurrent equity fund flow. Finally, the discount of CEEFs is also found to proxy for investor sentiment, with a narrower discount being associated with an increase (decrease) in value (growth) stocks.

1. Introduction

Classical asset pricing theory (CAPM) assumes financial markets to be always efficient, though the degree of efficiency may vary. It rules out the element of investor sentiment in asset pricing. The CAPM states that security prices will be at par with their fundamental value due to the presence of rational investors. It further states that arbitrageurs play a significant role in minimizing security mispricing caused by irrational investors. Doubts about the validity of market efficiency emerged following the October 1987 market crash. It strengthened further as researchers began to find evidence of security prices sometimes underreacting to earnings announcements (Jegadeesh and Titman 1993; Chan, Jegadeesh, and Lakonishok 1996) and overreacting to certain news in a consistent manner (Kothari and Shanken 1997; Lo and MacKinlay 1999). Previous studies have attempted to explain these price anomalies by the presence of investors' underreaction and overreaction (e.g. De Bondt and Thaler 1985, 1987; Barberis, Shleifer, and Vishny 1998; Daniel, Hirshleifer, and Subrahmanyam 1998; Hong and Stein 1999). Security mispricing has also been linked to noise trader theory, where researchers have shown that some investors do indeed trade on noise instead of on fundamentals (Black 1986; De Long et al. 1990).

Recent evidence, including Baker and Wurgler (2006) and Brown and Cliff (2005), has highlighted the role of uninformed demand shocks and limits to arbitrage as potential explanations.

Brown and Cliff (2005) highlighted that investor sentiment is driven by persistent uninformed demand shocks, while limits to arbitrage will deter informed traders from trading. Baker and Wurgler (2006) showed that stocks that have subjective valuations and are difficult to arbitrage are mostly affected by investor sentiment. Shleifer and Vishny (1997) derived a model where they showed that in extreme circumstances, professional arbitrageurs may not be successful in bringing security prices back to their fundamental values. Furthermore, Gallagher and Taylor (2001) found evidence supporting the 'risky arbitrage' hypothesis. They showed that the market log dividend–price ratio adjustment, toward the fundamental equilibrium, varies nonlinearly with the size of the deviation from the fundamental equilibrium. Hirshleifer (2001) highlighted the role that investor psychology plays in determining security prices.

In this study, we examine the level of influence that different sentiment measures have on value and growth stock returns for a sample of international markets using a detailed range of sentiment proxies.[1] The sentiment proxies included in our study are consumer confidence index, equity fund flow, closed-end equity fund (CEEF) discount and equity put–call ratio (PCR). The vast majority of empirical studies have examined the case of the USA and found mixed results for the sentiment–stock return relationship. For instance, Baker and Wurgler (2006) showed that investor sentiment significantly affects the cross-section of stock returns. These stocks usually tend to be small, young, highly volatile, unprofitable, non-dividend-paying, extreme-growth and distressed stocks. However, Lemmon and Portniaguina (2006) showed that the value stocks in the USA are significantly affected by changes in consumer confidence index after allowing conditional market beta to be a function of consumer confidence index. The discount of closed-end funds, which was considered as a measure of small investor sentiment by Zweig (1973) and Lee, Shleifer, and Thaler (1991), has been subsequently challenged by several authors (e.g. Chen, Kan, and Miller 1993; Chordia and Swaminathan 1998; Elton, Gruber, and Busse 1998). Given these mixed findings for the USA, we examine the influence of a range of sentiment measures on value and growth stocks for G7 countries.[2] In particular, we examine the success of consumer confidence index and equity PCR in forecasting future stock returns. We also examine the relationship between equity fund flow and stock returns and determine whether CEEF discount plays any role in the return-generating process. The role of investor sentiment is examined at the level of both individual countries and a panel of G7 countries. The cross-sectional nature of sentiment proxies and the cross-country analysis will provide considerably greater power to our tests and also a natural sensitivity test to the previously reported results using US data. This paper contributes to the existing literature in the following areas. First, we investigate the effect of different sentiment measures on stock returns across G7 nations. To our knowledge, this is the first study to examine the effect of investor sentiment, using an extensive range of sentiment proxies, on stock returns of G7 nations.[3] Besides investor survey, we also examine the effect of equity fund flow, CEEF discount and equity PCR on stock returns. Schmeling (2009) and Verma and Soydemir (2006) have shown that investor survey has a significant effect on international stock returns. We assess whether other sentiment proxies (equity fund flow, CEEF discount and equity PCR) display similar effects on stock returns. Second, we examine the extent of the value–growth relationship for G7 markets. Previous studies have mainly examined the effect of investor sentiment on aggregate market returns. A small number of studies (Brown and Cliff 2004; Lemmon and Portniaguina 2006; Schmeling 2009) have determined investor sentiment relationship with value and growth stocks. As Bird and Casavecchia (2007) have shown price momentum, measure of market sentiment, to be effective in timing the acquisition of value and growth stocks, we investigate whether different sentiment proxies could be considered as useful measures in enhancing the performance of value and growth investment strategies. Furthermore, Barberis and Shleifer (2003) have highlighted that investors pursue style investing, wherein all assets are grouped into different styles (e.g. large-cap stocks, growth stocks, US government bonds, etc.) and later funds are allocated to these styles rather than to an individual security. Given the popularity of these investment management strategies (and/or style investing), it would be informative to indicate how the wave of investor sentiment can influence value and growth stocks as well as the overall market. We believe that our findings will be useful to investors who are willing to consider implementing behavioral factors in their investment strategy. Third, we are motivated to explore the relationship among different sentiment measures across individual G7 countries. As our study consists of stock returns of highly developed and industrialized nations, we expect the sentiment effect on stock returns to be similar across G7 nations. Our cross-country results will provide some insights into whether any commonality exists among different sentiment measures across G7 countries. Finally, our panel study will shed some light on whether certain controversial sentiment measures (e.g. CEEF discount and equity fund flow) can be indeed considered as measures of sentiment.

Our panel results display evidence of commonality across all the sentiment measures, with value stocks having a particularly strong effect relative to growth stocks. We find results that are consistent with those reported in recent studies examining a survey-based measure of sentiment on the US stock returns (Fisher and Statman 2000, 2003). Our results indicate that when the beginning of period survey sentiment is high (low), subsequent returns are low (high). Furthermore, we find that the effect of survey sentiment decreases with an increase in forecast horizon. Our cross-country results are particularly informative in relation to the role of limits to arbitrage. The effect of survey sentiment is stronger for all the countries for the three-month forecast horizon and this effect gradually decreases as the forecast horizon is extended beyond three months. Our results for the equity fund flow effect on stock returns are consistent with the findings of survey sentiment and are particularly noteworthy given the previously reported results (Warther 1995). We find evidence of a positive relationship between concurrent equity fund flow and stock returns and a negative relationship between lagged equity fund flow and stock returns. Our panel study findings indicate the presence of temporary price pressure on value stocks and aggregate market, reflecting the implications of extending the analysis beyond the case of the USA.[4]

Consistent with our investor survey and equity fund flow results, we find a significant relationship between changes in CEEF discount and stock returns, indicating that the size of discount plays a significant role in the return-generating process. Particularly, we observe that a decrease in CEEF discount yields positive returns for value stocks and negative returns for growth stocks. We further find that the significance of CEEF discount does not change when we add industry-return indices as non-systematic asset pricing factors. Finally, we find that information contained in equity options volume data can be used as a sentiment indicator in predicting value stock returns. We find that a low PCR yields positive returns for value stocks by 6 basis points over the next month. However, we do not find any effect of equity PCR on the one-month forecasted returns of growth stocks and overall market. The rest of the paper is structured as follows. In Section 2, we discuss a suitable sentiment proxy. In Section 3, we give details on the data adopted, data sources and the methodology. In Section 4, we discuss empirical results for the USA and other G7 countries. In Section 5, we report panel G7 results for each sentiment measure. Finally, we conclude the paper in Section 6.

2. A suitable sentiment proxy

The behavioral explanation of the presence of investor sentiment causing security mispricing continues to remain a controversial topic in the finance literature.[5] Researchers have shown that investors sometimes base their investment decisions on variables other than the company fundamentals. For instance, Green and Hwang (2009) highlighted that small investors categorize stocks on the basis of price, as they observe the shift in comovement following splits to be greater for large and high-priced stocks when investor sentiment is high. Furthermore, Kumar and Lee (2006) showed that the retail investors' trading activities play a significant role in explaining return comovements of small-cap, value (high book-to-market ratio), lower priced stocks as well as stocks with low institutional ownership. Previous studies have identified different sentiment measures (e.g. investor survey, trading volume, mutual fund flow, dividend premium, insider trading, closed-end fund discount (CEFD), initial public offering (IPO) first-day returns, etc.) that reflect investor optimism and pessimism.[6] However, as noted earlier, the vast majority of research has focused solely on the USA. To our knowledge, only the survey proxies have been examined on an international basis. We examine sentiment–return relationship for individual G7 countries and include a detailed list of sentiment measures in our study.

We first consider investor survey as a measure of individual investor sentiment.[7] Surveys are regularly conducted internationally to determine investors' perception of stock market and the overall economic conditions. The level of confidence determines investor optimism and pessimism. Investor optimism is usually associated with higher returns and vice versa. In the USA, investor surveys are regularly conducted by the following organizations: American Association of Individual Investors (AAII), Investors Intelligence (II), University of Michigan Consumer Confidence Index Survey, the Conference Board and UBS Gallup Survey. These surveys ask investors different questions concerning employment, present and future financial situations, household income, etc. Researchers have shown that information contained in survey results are useful predictors of stock returns. The survey sentiment–return relationship has been extensively researched for the case of the USA. For instance, Fisher and Statman (2003) found that an increase in the consumer confidence index is associated with an increase in the bullishness of individual investors. Lemmon and Portniaguina (2006) found consumer confidence index to be useful in forecasting both small-cap stock returns and also the returns of stocks with low institutional ownership. Using II survey data, Brown and Cliff (2005) found that investor optimism is associated with low subsequent returns as valuation levels return to intrinsic value. Similarly, Qiu and Welch (2006) found consumer confidence index to be a useful predictor of excess returns on small decile stocks.

The findings of survey sentiment–return relationship for the non-US market are in line with the US studies. For instance, Schmeling (2009) examined the effect of consumer confidence index on stock returns of 18 industrialized countries and found a negative relationship between consumer confidence index and future stock returns. They also found the effect of sentiment to be greater for countries where stock markets are less institutionalized, have low market integrity and where investors are more prone to a herd-like behavior. Grigaliuniene and Cibulskiene (2010) found evidence of a negative relationship between consumer confidence index and aggregate market returns of the Scandinavian stock market. They observed that stocks that are hard to value and difficult to arbitrage are mainly affected by investor sentiment. Finter, Niessen-Ruenzi, and Ruenzi (2010) investigated the sentiment–return relationship of German stock market and also found similar results.[8] Verma and Soydemir (2006) studied the spillover effects of the US individual and institutional investor survey sentiment on international stock market returns. They found that the US investor sentiment had significant influence on international stock market returns, though the effect of sentiment on stock market returns was different for countries depending on the trade ties with the USA and its institutional structure.[9] The research to date on the USA and internationally conclusively indicates the existence of a relationship between survey sentiment and stock returns.

However, the evidence on the other sentiment proxies is mixed for the USA and has not been examined to date for the other markets. For example, does CEFD represent investor sentiment? If stock market is considered to be efficient, then the fund net asset value (NAV) should be the same as the fund share price (as there are a fixed number of shares issued in a closed-end fund). However, it has been observed that a closed-end fund starts trading at an average of 10% discount within 120 days of trading (Weiss 1989). Thus, the size of the discount, which is the difference between fund NAV and fund share price, is considered to be a measure of investor sentiment by many practitioners. Zweig (1973) carried out the first study adopting CEFD and found that CEFD can be used as a measure of an individual investor's expectations. The puzzle surrounding CEFD was further explored by Lee, Shleifer, and Thaler (1991), who found that when CEFD is high (low), investors are pessimistic (optimistic) about the future returns. By using three different sentiment proxies (CEFD, the ratio of odd-lot sales to purchases and net mutual fund redemptions), Neal and Wheatley (1998) found CEFD and mutual fund net redemptions to be positively related to small firm expected returns and very little evidence of odd-lot ratio to be a predictor of the small firm returns. Using individual investor survey data from AAII, Brown (1999) found an unusual level of individual investor sentiment to be associated with greater volatility in closed-end funds. However, Elton, Gruber, and Busse (1998) and Doukas and Milonas (2004) found no evidence of small investor sentiment, measured by CEFD, as a priced factor in the return-generating process.[10] Thus, there is mixed evidence about whether CEFD plays any significant role in the return-generating process. An important distinction between our study and previous work is that we only consider 'equity funds' and specifically exclude 'bond funds' within the closed-end fund family.

Many practitioners also consider equity fund flow to be a measure of investor sentiment. Previous studies, including Warther (1995), have shown that the increase in a fund flow is associated with the increase in stock prices. The price pressure effect and the information effect are regularly cited to indicate the existence of a positive relationship between mutual fund flow and stock returns. Warther (1995) left this question open for further research after finding the evidence of a positive relationship between US mutual fund flows and subsequent market returns with weekly data and a negative relationship between returns and subsequent fund flows using monthly data. Similarly, Edelen and Warner (2001) found a positive relationship between daily equity fund flow and concurrent market returns. Using data from the USA and Japan, Brown et al. (2003) showed that daily mutual fund flow can be considered as an instrument of investor sentiment. Frazzini and Lamont (2006) considered mutual fund flows as a sentiment measure and found that high sentiment predicts low future returns and growth stocks tend to be the usual victims of high sentiment.[11] Given the mixed findings cited above and the relevance of fund flow as a measure of investor sentiment, we examine the extent of the price pressure effect on stock prices due to increases in equity fund flow.

Finally, we examine the role of equity options volume in determining the predictability of the security prices. Previous studies have shown that the information contained in the non-price derivative measures is helpful in predicting future stock price movements. Some of these measures include open interest, volatility index (VIX) and equity PCR. Bhuyan and Chaudhury (2001) and Mukherjee and Mishra (2004) found that the information content of the open interest is helpful in determining the future level of the underlying asset prices. Ahoniemi (2008) found that the ARIMA (1, 1, 1) model augmented with generalized autoregressive conditional heteroskedasticity (GARCH) errors produces a forecasted accuracy of directional change in the VIX of up to 58.5%. Researchers have also shown that the information contained in equity options volume data, specifically equity PCR, may be helpful in predicting the direction of the stock market, particularly in the short term. The market would interpret a high equity PCR as an indication of pessimism in the stock market and vice versa. Easley, O'Hara, and Srinivas (1998) developed an asymmetric information model where they showed that the informational content in the volume of directional options trades contains information about future stock prices. Bandopadhyaya and Jones (2008) found PCR to be a better measure than VIX for predicting future returns. Furthermore, Pan and Poteshman (2006) studied the relevance of information content in the equity options volume data in determining the future stock price movement. They observed that the stocks with a low PCR outperform stocks with a high PCR over the next day by 40 basis points and by 1% over 1 week. Finally, Lee and Song (2003) found that value stocks outperform growth stocks when PCR is low and growth stocks marginally outperform or perform equally well with regard to value stocks when the PCR is high.

In summary, an increase in consumer confidence represents investors' bullishness. Therefore, higher confidence is associated with higher stock returns. Similarly, when investor optimism grows, equity PCR is relatively low, which subsequently results in positive performance of stocks. At the same time, the discount on closed-end funds narrows when investors become optimistic about future stock returns. Finally, if fund flow is viewed as a measure of investor sentiment, then an increase in fund flow should depict the price pressure on stocks.

3. Sentiment proxies and methodological issues

To study the effect of investor sentiment on value and growth stocks as well as on the aggregate market of G7 nations, we employed monthly returns data for the period January 1995–December 2007 from the Kenneth French's data library.[12] Table 1 provides a detailed account of different sentiment proxies that were adopted. Consumer confidence index data for the US market were taken from the University of Michigan Surveys of Consumers. The consumer confidence index data for Canada and Japan were obtained from the Conference Board of Canada and the Cabinet Office, Japan, respectively.[13] The data for the UK, France, Germany and Italy were obtained from 'Directorate Generale for Economic and Financial Affairs' (DG ECFIN). The details of consumer confidence index calculations are given in Appendix 1.

We obtained the equity fund flow data for the USA from the Investment Company Institute (ICI) and those for Canada from the Investment Funds Institute of Canada (IFIC). The fund flow data for the UK market were sourced from the Investment Management Association, UK (IMA). The equity fund flow data and total net equity fund assets for Canada and the UK were converted to US dollars by considering the month-end foreign exchange rate. The data for France, Germany, Italy and Japan were all obtained from Lipper, Thomson Reuters, and were made available in the US dollars. The equity fund flow data from Lipper were available from January 2002 onwards, whereas those for the USA, Canada and UK were available from January 1995 onwards.[14] Following Indro (2004), we normalized the equity fund flow for each country by taking the percentage of current equity fund flow to its respective total net equity fund assets.

The CEEF data for G7 nations were obtained from Morningstar.[15] We specifically excluded bond funds within a closed-end fund family. For each country, we obtained monthly NAV and price data in the US dollars and then calculated each fund's discount, which we refer to as the CEEF discount. Following Lee, Shleifer, and Thaler (1991) and Doukas and Milonas (2004), we constructed a value-weighted index of discount (VWD) for each country at monthly level:

$$\text{VWD}_t = \Sigma_{i=1}^{n_t} \text{weight}_t \text{Discount}_{it}, \tag{1}$$

Table 1. Data sources.

Country	Time horizon	Source
Panel A: Consumer confidence index		
USA	January 1995–December 2007	The University of Michigan Consumer Surveys
Canada	January 1995–December 2007	The Conference Board, Canada
UK	January 1995–December 2007	DG ECFIN
France	January 1995–December 2007	DG ECFIN
Germany	January 1995–December 2007	DG ECFIN
Italy	January 1995–December 2007	DG ECFIN
Japan	January 1995–December 2007	The Cabinet Office, Japan
Panel B: Equity fund flow		
USA	January 1995–December 2007	ICI
Canada	January 1995–December 2007	IFIC
UK	January 1995–December 2007	IMA
France	January 2002–December 2007	Lipper, Thomson Reuters
Germany	January 2002–December 2007	Lipper, Thomson Reuters
Italy	January 2002–December 2007	Lipper, Thomson Reuters
Japan	January 2002–December 2007	Lipper, Thomson Reuters
Panel C: CEEF		
USA	January 1995–December 2007	Morningstar, Inc.
Canada	January 1995–December 2007	Morningstar, Inc.
UK	January 1995–December 2007	Morningstar, Inc.
France	January 1995–May 2004	Morningstar, Inc.
Germany	January 1995–December 2007	Morningstar, Inc.
Italy	January 1995–January 2003	Morningstar, Inc.
Japan	January 1995–December 2007	Morningstar, Inc.
Panel D: Individual equity options volume		
USA	January 1995–December 2007	CBOE
Canada	December 2000–December 2007	Bourse De Montreal Inc.
UK	January 2000–December 2007	NYSE Euronext
France	January 2002–December 2007	NYSE Euronext
Germany	January 2001–December 2007	Deutsche Borse Group
Italy	January 2001–December 2007	Borsa Italiana
Japan	July 1997–December 2007	Tokyo Stock Exchange

Notes: A detailed list of data sources of different sentiment proxies (consumer confidence index, equity fund flow, CEEF discount and equity put–call options volume) is given. A list of the time horizons for each data source and for each individual country is also given.

where

$$\text{weight}_i = \frac{\text{NAV}_{it}}{\Sigma_{i=1}^{n_t} \text{NAV}_{it}}; \tag{2}$$

$$\text{Discount}_{it} = \frac{(\text{NAV}_{it} - \text{Price}_{it})}{\text{NAV}_{it}} \times 100, \tag{3}$$

where NAV_{it} is the net asset value of each individual CEEF i at time t; Price_{it} is the market price of each individual CEEF i at time t and n_t is the number of funds with the available NAV_{it} and Price_{it}.

We also constructed the change in value-weighted index of discount (ΔVWD) and used it as a proxy to measure CEEF discount effect on value and growth stock returns:

$$\Delta \text{VWD}_t = \text{VWD}_t - \text{VWD}_{t-1}. \tag{4}$$

To calculate equity PCR, we obtained equity options volume data from various sources. The equity derivatives data for the USA, Italy and Japan were obtained from Chicago Board of Options Exchange (CBOE), Borsa Italiana and Tokyo Derivatives Exchange, respectively, while those for Canada and Germany were obtained from Montreal Derivatives Exchange and Deutsche Borse Group, respectively. The equity derivatives data for both the UK and France were sourced from NYSE Euronext.[16] Following Pan and Poteshman (2006), we calculated equity PCR as follows:

$$\text{Put–Call Ratio}_{it} = \frac{\text{Put Volume}_{it}}{\text{Put Volume}_{it} + \text{Call Volume}_{it}}, \tag{5}$$

where put volume for country i is the total number of put contracts traded in a month t and call volume in country i is the total number of call contracts traded in a month t. In our computation of equity PCR, we considered total equity options volume data (including European and American options). Hence, it takes into account all the four different equity options trades, 'open buys' and 'close buys' initiated by the buyer to open a new long position and close the existing short position, respectively, and 'open sells' and 'close sells' initiated by the seller to open a new position and close the existing long position, respectively. Our constructed equity PCR differs from that reported by Pan and Poteshman (2006), who studied the effect of 'open-buy' PCR on the prediction of t-day-ahead stock returns.

The descriptive statistics of stock market returns, consumer confidence index and equity fund flow are reported in Table 2. In this table, we also report the presence of autocorrelation in the consumer confidence index series at different lags. Due to the presence of a high autocorrelation in the series, we tested for a unit root in the series. Our results of the panel unit root test indicate that we are dealing with stationarity in consumer confidence index series.[17] To study the effect of consumer confidence index on value stock and growth stock returns and aggregate market returns, we estimated a panel fixed-effect regression of the following form:

$$r^i_{t+k} = \delta_0^{i,(k)} + \delta_1^{(k)} \text{CC}^i_t + \delta_2^{(k)} \gamma_t^{i,(k)} + \xi^{i,(k)}_{t+k}, \tag{6}$$

Table 2. Descriptive statistics: stock returns, consumer confidence index and equity fund flow.

	Market		Value		Growth		CC index			Equity fund flow			
Country	μ	σ	μ	σ	μ	σ	μ	σ	$\rho(1)$	μ	σ	$\rho(1)$	AR model
USA	1.00	4.24	1.19	3.86	0.95	4.49	94.63	8.71	0.88	0.53	0.53	0.71	3
Canada	1.41	5.17	1.31	6.13	1.28	6.73	89.07	13.19	0.93	0.80	1.11	0.60	4
UK	1.00	3.70	1.12	4.84	0.97	3.61	−3.74	4.02	0.81	0.23	0.22	0.62	15
France	1.25	5.07	1.40	6.45	1.24	5.32	−14.35	8.26	0.93	0.47	0.58	0.29	2
Germany	1.12	5.78	1.78	6.82	1.08	6.60	−8.61	8.51	0.95	−0.21	0.66	0.21	9
Italy	1.23	6.17	1.29	7.71	1.11	6.33	−11.69	5.66	0.89	−1.13	1.10	0.35	3
Japan	0.20	5.55	0.99	7.51	−0.14	5.67	41.85	4.54	0.95	0.65	2.41	0.08	12

Notes: The descriptive statistics of aggregate market returns, value stock and growth stock returns, consumer confidence index and equity fund flow of G7 countries are reported. μ denotes the average returns of the G7 countries and σ denotes the standard deviation of returns for each country. Autocorrelation (ρ) at Lag 1 is reported for consumer confidence index and equity fund flow for each country. The last column reports the AR model used for each country to predict expected fund flow.

where k is the number of months from time t for each country i. The right-hand side of the equation includes consumer confidence (CC) index for each country i and several other macro-economic variables, including annual percentage change in consumer price index, annual percentage change in industrial production, de-trended six-month certificate of deposit rate, term spread and dividend yield, which are incorporated in γ. These macro-economic variables were considered in our regression so as to remove the effect of common risk factors on returns.[18] We estimated the above equation using the panel fixed-effect approach in which all countries enter the regression jointly. This approach will allow us to have different intercepts for each country and constant slope coefficients. The panel fixed effect was studied over the forecast horizon from 1 to 24 months. To account for biased coefficient estimates and standard errors, we employed the moving-block bootstrap simulation procedure to overcome the predictive nature of regression. The moving-block bootstrap was performed by employing a block length of six observations.[19] The influence of survey sentiment measures of individual G7 countries on their respective stock returns was also examined over the forecast horizon from 1 to 12 months. We estimated its coefficient by employing generalized method of moments (exactly identified) and employed a similar bootstrapping procedure (Schmeling 2009). The coefficient of individual countries for the forecast horizon from 12 to 24 months was insignificant and, therefore, it is not reported here to conserve space.

Due to the presence of a high autocorrelation in fund flow series (refer to Table 2), we tested for a unit root in the series. The null hypothesis of a unit root was strongly rejected, a result which is consistent with the consumer confidence survey results. The presence of a high autocorrelation in the series indicates that fund flow is highly predictable. As a result, we employed the traditional Box–Jenkins method to identify the time-series properties of the equity fund flow and decompose the net equity fund flow into expected and unexpected equity fund flows (Warther 1995). By performing the Breusch and Godfrey test of autocorrelation, we determined different autoregressive time-series (AR) models for each country (refer to Table 2) and used those models to determine the expected fund flow. The unexpected fund flow was then calculated by taking the difference between the actual fund flow and expected fund flow. To study the effect of equity fund flow on value stocks, growth stocks and overall market, we again ran the panel fixed-effect regression of the following form:

$$r_t^i = \delta_0^{i,(k)} + \delta_1^{(k)} \mathrm{FF}_{t-k}^i + \xi_t^{i,(k)}, \tag{7}$$

where k is the number of lags employed from time t for each country i. We adopted different models to study the effect of equity fund flow (FF) at different lags on stock returns. In model^{FF} 1, we regressed returns on equity fund flow at t, $t-1$, $t-2$ and $t-3$. In model^{FF} 2, we regressed returns on equity fund flow at $t-1$, $t-2$ and $t-3$. The sign of the coefficients in model^{FF} 1 and model^{FF} 2 will reveal if equity fund flow is predictable. In model^{FF} 3, we regressed returns on expected fund flow at t and unexpected fund flow at t, $t-1$ and $t-2$. The results of model^{FF} 3 will indicate if an increase in equity fund flow leads to an increase in stock returns. To confirm if the increases in concurrent stock returns are due to increases in fund flow, we performed a test for price pressure hypothesis in model^{FF} 4. In this model, we regressed the unexpected equity fund flow on returns at $t-1$, t and $t+1$. We also ran a similar regression at different lags for each individual country to determine the significance of fund flow on stock returns.

The descriptive statistics of value-weighted index of CEEF discount and equity PCR are reported in Table 3. From this table, it is evident that the Canadian market has the highest mean VWD, 22.84%, with the highest standard deviation, 4.70%, in comparison with the Japanese one. Despite Japan having the highest standard deviation of 5.56%, it is the only country with the lowest mean VWD of 5.15%. In order to determine the effect of CEEF discount on stock returns, we ran

Table 3. Descriptive statistics: VWD and equity PCR.

	Value-weighted discount (%)					Equity PCR				
Country	Mean	Min.	Max.	Std. Dev.	Obsv.	Mean	Min.	Max.	Std. Dev. (%)	Obsv.
USA	7.82	0.47	15.01	3.84	156	0.36	0.24	0.68	9.20	156
Canada	22.84	14.22	34.84	4.70	156	0.28	0.18	0.39	4.44	85
UK	9.72	4.59	14.94	2.37	156	0.45	0.37	0.59	4.62	96
France	15.60	1.98	26.01	3.95	113	0.45	0.33	0.58	5.74	72
Germany	14.71	5.74	25.00	3.93	156	0.45	0.23	0.60	5.83	84
Italy	14.19	3.14	25.69	4.27	97	0.43	0.27	0.53	4.85	84
Japan	5.15	−8.38	19.90	5.56	156	0.49	0.10	0.88	20.32	126

Notes: The descriptive statistics of VWD and equity PCR are reported. The VWD is calculated by taking the sum of individual CEEF's weight multiplied by its discount. The equity PCR is equity put volume divided by equity call volume and equity put volume.

two different models. In model^{VWD}1, we ran a panel fixed-effect regression, where we studied the relation between value stock and growth stock returns against ΔVWD and aggregate market returns (Lee, Shleifer, and Thaler 1991; Doukas and Milonas 2004).

$$r_t^i = \delta_0^i + \delta_1 \Delta\text{VWD}_t^i + \delta_2 \text{Aggregate returns}_t^i + \xi_t^i, \tag{8}$$

where r_t^i are either value stock returns or growth stock returns at time t for each country i and ΔVWD is the change in value-weighted index of discounts for each country i at time t.

Consistent with Elton, Gruber, and Busse (1998) and Doukas and Milonas (2004), in model^{VWD} 2, we adopted industry-return indices, unsystematic components, along with ΔVWD and aggregate market returns. This test will allow us to determine the sensitivity of value stock returns and growth stock returns against ΔVWD, industry-return indices and aggregate market returns.[20] Similarly, we also ran model^{VWD} 1 and model^{VWD} 2 for each individual country so as to determine the significance of investor sentiment, measured by ΔVWD, in the return-generating process.

From the statistics of equity PCR given in Table 3, we can see that the Japanese market is the only market that has the highest mean PCR of 0.49 and highest standard deviation of 20.32%, whereas the Canadian derivatives market has both the lowest mean PCR of 0.28 and the lowest standard deviation of 4.44%.[21] To study the effect of equity PCR on future stock returns, we again ran the panel fixed-effect regression of the following form:

$$r_{t+k}^i = \delta_0^{i,(k)} + \delta_1^{(k)} \text{PCR}_t^i + \xi_{t+k}^{i,(k)}, \tag{9}$$

where k is the number of months from time t for each country i. We ran a panel fixed-effect regression starting from the year January 2002 as for almost all the countries equity derivatives data were available from 2002 onwards (except for the USA and Japan, for which data were available from January 1995 and July 1997 onwards, respectively). We also ran a similar regression for each individual country starting from the date from which the data were first available.[22]

4. Empirical results

4.1 *The US results*

Given the volume of studies examining particular sentiment measures from a US perspective and the ambiguity of the results to date for this market, we began our analysis with the USA. A

Table 4. Cross-country analysis: investor sentiment effect on value stock returns.

	USA		Canada		UK		France		Germany		Italy		Japan	
	Coeff.	R^2	Coeff.	R^2	Coeff.	R^2	Coeff.	R^2	Coeff.	R^2	Coeff.	R^2	Coeff.	R^2
Panel A: Consumer confidence index														
R_{t+1}	−0.02	0.06	−0.13	0.08	0.02	0.04	−0.18	0.07	−0.20	0.04	−0.27	0.09	0.01	0.02
	(0.64)		(0.02)**		(0.76)		(0.04)**		(0.12)		(0.00)***		(0.90)	
R_{t+3}	−0.04	0.08	−0.12	0.07	0.00	0.03	−0.11	0.03	−0.36	0.06	−0.40	0.10	−0.22	0.04
	(0.24)		(0.05)**		(0.95)		(0.17)		(0.00)***		(0.00)***		(0.23)	
R_{t+6}	−0.01	0.10	−0.00	0.04	0.04	0.07	−0.06	0.03	−0.19	0.03	−0.29	0.06	−0.08	0.06
	(0.72)		(0.97)		(0.18)		(0.43)		(0.00)***		(0.00)***		(0.63)	
R_{t+12}	−0.09	0.09	0.02	0.03	0.11	0.08	−0.07	0.04	−0.08	0.02	−0.26	0.09	−0.25	0.06
	(0.00)***		(0.61)		(0.28)		(0.37)		(0.32)		(0.02)**		(0.17)	
Panel B: Equity fund flow														
Expected Fund Flow$_t$	−0.06		−0.73		2.03		−0.09		−0.51		0.32		0.69	
	(0.94)		(0.44)		(0.44)		(0.99)		(0.87)		(0.87)		(0.27)	
Unexpected Fund Flow$_t$	6.63		1.45		5.97		2.21		4.56		2.75		−0.49	
	(0.00)***		(0.01)***		(0.07)*		(0.10)*		(0.00)***		(0.00)***		(0.12)	
Unexpected Fund Flow$_{t-1}$	0.70		−0.01		2.13		−2.42		0.63		−0.27		−0.29	
	(0.38)		(0.98)		(0.53)		(0.34)		(0.61)		(0.75)		(0.36)	
Unexpected Fund Flow$_{t-2}$	0.73		−0.09		−5.53		−1.88		1.67		0.10		−0.38	
	(0.32)		(0.91)		(0.07)*		(0.45)		(0.18)		(0.90)		(0.23)	
R^2		0.40		0.05		0.05		0.11		0.25		0.21		0.09
Panel C: CEEF discount														
Intercept	0.49		0.25		0.10		0.17		0.79		0.49		0.90	
	(0.00)***		(0.29)		(0.67)		(0.55)		(0.00)***		(0.21)		(0.00)***	
ΔVWD	−0.30		−0.17		0.26		−0.02		−0.14		0.09		−0.07	
	(0.01)***		(0.17)		(0.33)		(0.84)		(0.20)		(0.50)		(0.38)	
Aggregate returns	0.33		0.03		0.96		−0.12		0.46		0.28		0.49	
	(0.00)***		(0.73)		(0.00)***		(0.38)		(0.00)***		(0.02)**		(0.00)***	
R^2		0.78		0.79		0.67		0.85	0.79		0.85			0.84

(Continued)

Table 4. Continued

	USA		Canada		UK		France		Germany		Italy		Japan	
	Coeff.	R^2	Coeff.	R^2	Coeff.	R^2	Coeff.	R^2	Coeff.	R^2	Coeff.	R^2	Coeff.	R^2
Panel D: Equity PCR														
R_t	−0.07	0.03	−0.61	0.21	−0.52	0.20	−0.34	0.10	−0.27	0.05	−0.15	0.01	−0.04	0.01
	(0.02)**		(0.00)***		(0.00)***		(0.00)***		(0.04)**		(0.31)		(0.30)	
R_{t+1}	−0.02	0.01	0.09	0.01	−0.11	0.01	−0.16	0.02	−0.02	0.01	0.14	0.01	0.00	0.01
	(0.47)		(0.57)		(0.34)		(0.20)		(0.88)		(0.35)		(0.90)	
R_{t+2}	−0.04	0.01	0.09	0.01	−0.12	0.01	−0.18	0.03	−0.05	0.01	0.15	0.01	0.04	0.01
	(0.23)		(0.54)		(0.33)		(0.16)		(0.70)		(0.32)		(0.22)	
R_{t+3}	−0.02	0.01	−0.08	0.01	−0.31	0.08	−0.23	0.05	−0.13	0.01	−0.19	0.02	0.06	0.02
	(0.46)		(0.59)		(0.00)***		(0.07)*		(0.35)		(0.21)		(0.12)	

Notes: In panel A, we report the value stock returns predictability of consumer confidence index across different forecast horizons. In panel B, we report model^{FF} 3, where value stock returns are regressed on expected equity fund flow at t and unexpected equity fund flow at t, $t-1$ and $t-2$. In panel C, we report model^{VWD} 2, where value stock returns are regressed on ΔVWD, aggregate market returns and four different FTSE indices. The coefficients of FTSE indices are not reported here to conserve space. In panel D, we report the value stock returns predictability of equity PCR across different forecast horizons. The p-values are reported below the coefficient values.
*Statistical significance at the 10% level.
**Statistical significance at the 5% level.
***Statistical significance at the 1% level.

comparison with the other G7 countries will be reported in the next section. Tables 4–6 report cross-country results for different sentiment measures and their effects on value and growth stock returns as well as aggregate market returns, respectively. The results reported in column 1 of Table 4 (panel A) show that US value stocks are not influenced by survey sentiment for the one-month and three-month forecast horizons; however, growth stocks are significantly affected (Table 5, panel A). We observed that a one-standard deviation shock in survey sentiment leads to a decrease in growth stock returns by 12 basis points over the next month. This effect continues to remain over the three-month forecast horizon. Our findings are consistent with the findings of Baker and Wurgler (2006), who found that sentiment has a significant effect on a cross-section of future stock returns and growth stocks, in particular.[23] We also found that survey sentiment has a significant effect on aggregate market returns (Table 6, panel A). In particular, we found that a one-standard deviation shock to survey sentiment results in a fall in aggregate market returns by 10 basis points over the next month and by 12 basis points over the next three months. These results are consistent with the previous findings reported by Brown and Cliff (2005) and Fisher and Statman (2003).[24]

In panel B (Tables 4–6), we report the results using the equity fund flow as a proxy for sentiment. Given that we found a positive and statistically significant coefficient for concurrent equity fund flow and an insignificant coefficient for lagged equity fund flow in model^{FF} 1 and model^{FF} 2, respectively, we tested to determine if concurrent unexpected fund flow has any effect on stock returns.[25] As indicated in model^{FF} 3, we regressed returns on expected fund flow at t and unexpected fund flow at t, $t-1$ and $t-2$. We found a positive and statistically significant coefficient for unexpected fund flow on value stock returns, growth stock returns and aggregate market returns at time t. The results indicate that a one-standard deviation shock in unexpected fund flow results in an increase in value stock returns by 3.51%. An argument could be that this increase is due to the existence of price pressure. We tested the price pressure hypothesis in model^{FF} 4, where concurrent unexpected fund flows were regressed on stock returns at $t-1$, t and $t+1$.[26] The lack of a significant negative coefficient at $t+1$ implies that we cannot identify the source of the increase in returns. The increase in security prices may be either due to the price pressure effect or due to the information effect. Our results are consistent with those reported by Warther (1995), who noted that the fund flow–stock price relationship may be a result of price pressure or information effects.[27] Furthermore, we observed the presence of a significant positive correlation coefficient between investor survey and equity fund flow, indicating that investor optimism is associated with an increase in equity fund flow and vice versa.[28]

In panel C of Tables 4 and 5, we report the results of model^{VWD} 2, where we studied the effect of a change in the index of discount of CEEF on stock returns after considering industry-return indices as non-systematic asset pricing factors.[29] Our results of a change in the index of discount of CEEF on value stock returns are particularly noteworthy. A significant negative coefficient of ΔVWD indicates that a 1% point decrease in ΔVWD is associated with an increase in value stock returns by 30 basis points. However, we found a positive and statistically significant coefficient of ΔVWD for growth stock returns (Table 5, panel C), indicating that a 1% decrease in ΔVWD results in a decrease in growth stock returns by 14 basis points. We further got a significant coefficient of industry-return indices (not reported here) coupled with substantial improvement in R^2. Interestingly, our results differ from those reported by Lee, Shleifer, and Thaler (1991), who found that a narrowing of the discount is associated with a positive performance of small stocks. Besides, we considered only closed-end 'equity' funds that have core investment focus only in the US market. Our findings, therefore, reveal that a change in the index of discount of CEEF does enter the return-generating process, where a decrease in discount is associated with

Table 5. Cross-country analysis: investor sentiment effect on growth stock returns.

	USA		Canada		UK		France		Germany		Italy		Japan	
	Coeff.	R^2	Coeff.	R^2	Coeff.	R^2	Coeff.	R^2	Coeff.	R^2	Coeff.	R^2	Coeff.	R^2
Panel A: Consumer confidence index														
R_{t+1}	−0.12	0.09	−0.09	0.09	0.01	0.06	−0.18	0.06	−0.04	0.03	−0.20	0.03	−0.11	0.01
	(0.01)***		(0.07)*		(0.86)		(0.01)***		(0.52)		(0.00)***		(0.40)	
R_{t+3}	−0.12	0.08	−0.17	0.09	−0.10	0.04	−0.08	0.05	−0.30	0.08	−0.23	0.03	−0.19	0.03
	(0.05)**		(0.00)***		(0.16)		(0.26)		(0.00)***		(0.00)***		(0.15)	
R_{t+6}	−0.10	0.07	−0.04	0.02	0.19	0.13	−0.09	0.03	−0.13	0.05	−0.12	0.01	−0.01	0.03
	(0.07)*		(0.24)		(0.00)***		(0.23)		(0.30)		(0.22)		(0.91)	
R_{t+12}	−0.20	0.12	−0.04	0.07	0.10	0.11	−0.14	0.04	−0.20	0.03	−0.04	0.04	0.07	0.07
	(0.00)***		(0.44)		(0.34)		(0.00)***		(0.11)		(0.64)		(0.43)	
Panel B: Equity fund flow														
Expected Fund Flow_t	0.02		−0.48		−0.50		−0.90		−3.83		−1.05		0.63	
	(0.98)		(0.63)		(0.79)		(0.88)		(0.18)		(0.55)		(0.20)	
Unexpected Fund Flow_t	7.58		2.27		6.55		−0.99		1.61		1.83		−0.53	
	(0.00)***		(0.00)***		(0.00)***		(0.30)		(0.11)		(0.00)***		(0.03)**	
Unexpected Fund Flow_{t-1}	−0.39		0.88		1.68		−0.91		−0.54		0.11		−0.22	
	(0.68)		(0.28)		(0.50)		(0.62)		(0.64)		(0.88)		(0.37)	
Unexpected Fund Flow_{t-2}	0.78		−1.02		−1.72		−1.02		−0.15		−0.17		−0.18	
	(0.37)		(0.23)		(0.45)		(0.57)		(0.89)		(0.79)		(0.47)	
R^2		0.38		0.10		0.06		0.06		0.08		0.16		0.12
Panel C: CEEF discount														
Intercept	−0.09		−0.31		0.02		−0.01		−0.07		−0.22		−0.37	
	(0.20)		(0.03)**		(0.81)		(0.96)		(0.71)		(0.05)**		(0.00)***	
ΔVWD	0.14		0.19		0.34		0.09		−0.04		0.03		0.02	
	(0.01)***		(0.01)***		(0.00)***		(0.28)		(0.64)		(0.48)		(0.50)	
Aggregate returns	1.03		1.68		1.06		1.44		1.60		1.23		1.18	
	(0.00)***		(0.00)***		(0.00)***		(0.00)***		(0.00)***		(0.00)***		(0.00)***	
R^2		0.96		0.94		0.88		0.89		0.87		0.98		0.97

Panel D: Equity PCR														
R_t	−0.13	0.07	−0.25	0.03	−0.30	0.13	−0.12	0.03	−0.28	0.05	−0.07	0.01	0.01	0.01
	(0.00)***		(0.11)		(0.00)***		(0.18)		(0.04)**		(0.57)		(0.59)	
R_{t+1}	−0.08	0.03	0.46	0.09	−0.07	0.01	−0.06	0.01	−0.01	0.01	0.13	0.01	0.03	0.02
	(0.04)**		(0.00)***		(0.41)		(0.52)		(0.94)		(0.30)		(0.17)	
R_{t+2}	−0.07	0.02	0.37	0.06	−0.12	0.02	−0.06	0.01	−0.10	0.01	0.05	0.01	0.03	0.01
	(0.08)*		(0.03)**		(0.17)		(0.50)		(0.46)		(0.67)		(0.22)	
R_{t+3}	−0.03	0.01	0.03	0.01	−0.13	0.03	−0.01	0.01	−0.15	0.02	−0.20	0.03	0.02	0.01
	(0.39)		(0.82)		(0.11)		(0.90)		(0.26)		(0.10)*		(0.43)	

Notes: In panel A, we report the growth stock returns predictability of consumer confidence index across different forecast horizons. In panel B, we report model^{FF} 3, where growth stock returns are regressed on expected equity fund flow at t and unexpected equity fund flow at t, $t-1$ and $t-2$. In panel C, we report model^{VWD} 2, where growth stock returns are regressed on ΔVWD, aggregate market returns and four different FTSE indices. The coefficients of FTSE indices are not reported here to conserve space. In panel D, we report the growth stock returns predictability of equity PCR across different forecast horizons. The p-values are reported below the coefficient values.

*Statistical significance at the 10% level.

**Statistical significance at the 5% level.

***Statistical significance at the 1% level.

Table 6. Cross-country analysis: investor sentiment effect on aggregate market returns.

	USA		Canada		UK		France		Germany		Italy		Japan	
	Coeff.	R^2	Coeff.	R^2	Coeff.	R^2	Coeff.	R^2	Coeff.	R^2	Coeff.	R^2	Coeff.	R^2
Panel A: Consumer confidence index														
R_{t+1}	−0.10	0.07	−0.07	0.08	0.01	0.05	−0.16	0.06	−0.12	0.04	−0.22	0.04	−0.07	0.02
	(0.02)**		(0.08)*		(0.82)		(0.01)***		(0.03)**		(0.00)***		(0.60)	
R_{t+3}	−0.12	0.08	−0.13	0.09	−0.11	0.05	−0.06	0.05	−0.31	0.09	−0.26	0.05	−0.18	0.03
	(0.04)**		(0.00)***		(0.18)		(0.30)		(0.00)***		(0.00)***		(0.17)	
R_{t+6}	−0.09	0.07	−0.03	0.03	0.12	0.11	−0.07	0.04	−0.11	0.05	−0.14	0.02	0.01	0.04
	(0.06)*		(0.25)		(0.04)**		(0.29)		(0.26)		(0.11)		(0.94)	
R_{t+12}	−0.18	0.11	−0.02	0.04	0.10	0.09	−0.12	0.04	−0.17	0.03	−0.09	0.05	0.00	0.08
	(0.00)***		(0.47)		(0.31)		(0.00)***		(0.08)*		(0.30)		(0.97)	
Panel B: Equity fund flow														
Expected Fund Flow$_t$	−0.22		−0.33		−0.10		−1.35		1.82		−0.27		0.53	
	(0.80)		(0.67)		(0.95)		(0.84)		(0.52)		(0.87)		(0.29)	
Unexpected Fund Flow$_t$	7.68		1.77		6.92		0.22		2.68		1.86		−0.54	
	(0.00)***		(0.00)***		(0.00)***		(0.83)		(0.01)**		(0.00)***		(0.04)**	
Unexpected Fund Flow$_{t-1}$	−0.05		0.31		2.06		−1.26		0.17		0.04		−0.25	
	(0.95)		(0.62)		(0.42)		(0.53)		(0.88)		(0.95)		(0.33)	
Unexpected Fund Flow$_{t-2}$	0.77		−0.63		−2.96		−0.68		0.50		−0.27		−0.19	
	(0.32)		(0.34)		(0.21)		(0.73)		(0.66)		(0.67)		(0.47)	
R^2		0.44		0.09		0.07		0.05		0.13		0.17		0.11
Panel C: Equity PCR														
R_t	−0.12	0.07	−0.33	0.09	−0.36	0.18	−0.24	0.08	−0.30	0.07	−0.06	0.01	0.01	0.01
	(0.00)***		(0.00)***		(0.00)***		(0.01)***		(0.01)***		(0.60)		(0.69)	
R_{t+1}	−0.07	0.02	0.25	0.05	−0.04	0.01	−0.07	0.01	−0.00	0.01	0.10	0.01	0.03	0.01
	(0.06)*		(0.04)**		(0.68)		(0.45)		(0.97)		(0.40)		(0.29)	
R_{t+2}	−0.06	0.02	0.23	0.04	−0.06	0.01	−0.12	0.02	−0.05	0.01	0.06	0.01	0.03	0.02
	(0.10)*		(0.07)*		(0.49)		(0.25)		(0.69)		(0.60)		(0.17)	
R_{t+3}	−0.03	0.01	−0.02	0.01	−0.16	0.03	−0.11	0.02	−0.09	0.01	−0.20	0.04	0.03	0.01
	(0.45)		(0.85)		(0.07)*		(0.27)		(0.44)		(0.07)*		(0.27)	

Notes: In panel A, we report the aggregate market returns predictability of consumer confidence index across different forecast horizons. In panel B, we report model^{FF} 3, where aggregate market returns are regressed on expected equity fund flow at t and unexpected equity fund flow at t, $t-1$ and $t-2$. In panel D, we report the aggregate market returns predictability of equity PCR across different forecast horizons. The p-values are reported below the coefficient values.

*Statistical significance at the 10% level.

**Statistical significance at the 5% level.

***Statistical significance at the 1% level.

positive performance of value stocks and negative performance of growth stocks. The difference in performances of value and growth stocks may be due to the fact that owners and traders of CEEF are usually individual investors as documented by Weiss (1989) and Lee, Shleifer, and Thaler (1991). As Kumar and Lee (2006) have shown that the retail investors tend to overweight value stocks than the growth stocks, it, therefore, appears that an increase in investor optimism is associated with a narrowing discount and thus simultaneous increase in value stock returns.

The findings of the equity PCR effect on stock returns (see panel D of Tables 4 and 5 and panel C of Table 6) reveal that a low equity PCR is an indicator of future investor gains in the overall market and growth stocks in months $t + 1$ and $t + 2$. For instance, when equity PCR is low, the overall market outperforms in the next month by 7 basis points and in month $t + 2$ by 6 basis points.[30] Similarly, an investor who buys growth stocks that have a zero equity PCR and sells stocks that have an equity PCR of 1 could yield 8 basis points over the next month and 7 basis points in two months from then onwards. Our results, therefore, indicate that the information contained in the equity options volume data can be helpful in determining future movements in stock prices. Our findings also confirm the previous results that investor sentiment influence on asset returns centers around growth stocks. Our results are consistent with those reported by Pan and Poteshman (2006), who found an evidence of options volume containing information about future stock prices.[31] We also observed the presence of a significant negative correlation coefficient between equity PCR and survey (not reported here), further indicating that investor optimism is associated with a low equity PCR.

4.2 *International comparison*

Panel A of Tables 4–6 also reports the predictive power of survey sentiment of individual G7 countries for value and growth stock returns as well as aggregate market returns for different forecast horizons from 1 to 12 months.[32] Our general findings indicate that there exists a negative survey sentiment relationship where high (low) investor sentiment is associated with subsequent low (high) returns. When compared with the USA where only growth stocks and aggregate market are influenced by survey sentiment, we observed that in Canada the effect exists for the three-month forecasted returns for both value stocks and growth stocks as well as for the overall market. The differences in sample size of survey participants and structure of the survey are considered to be the likely reasons. For instance, Conference Board, Canada, surveys at least 2000 households measuring the index on the basis of only four questions, whereas the University of Michigan surveys at least 500 households asking them 50 questions. However, the index of consumer sentiment is derived from only five questions.[33] As questions asked in sentiment surveys across different countries are similar, the results are comparable across individual G7 countries. Consistent with the USA, we also observed that survey sentiment has a significant effect on the one-month forecasted returns of the overall market for other countries (e.g. France, Germany and Italy). Interestingly, we did not find any effect of survey sentiment on the one-month forecasted returns for the UK and Japan. Specifically for Japan, we observed that although the consumer confidence survey represents the most comprehensive survey (accounting for 6000 households), there is no significant effect of survey sentiment on value stocks, growth stocks and the overall market. The effect of survey sentiment disappears for all the countries beyond the six-month forecast horizon, except for value stocks in Germany and Italy and growth stocks in the UK. We, therefore, conclude that the difference in significance levels across individual countries may be due to the fact that the number of survey respondents may not be the same as that of the equity market participants.

The results of model^{FF} 3, where returns were regressed on concurrent expected fund flow, concurrent unexpected fund flow and lagged unexpected fund flow, for the other countries are reported in Tables 4–6 (see panel B, columns 2–7). Our general findings indicate that an increase in concurrent unexpected fund flow causes an increase in security prices. The lagged component of unexpected equity fund flow for all countries is statistically insignificant, except for the value stock returns of the UK. Both France and Germany display no effect of concurrent unexpected equity fund flow on growth stock returns. Overall, we found the existence of a positive relationship between concurrent unexpected fund flow and security prices. There was no evidence of price pressure in any individual G7 country, with the exception of value stocks in France. This indicates that with an increase in optimism, French investors tend to overweight value stocks causing their price to overshoot. We also found Japan to be the only country where inflow of unexpected equity funds has a negative effect on growth stock returns and aggregate market returns at t and $t + 1$. Furthermore, we also observed a significant negative correlation coefficient between equity fund flow and stock returns for Japan (not reported here), indicating the presence of homogeneity in Japanese investors' outlook about future stock returns. This finding is consistent with the results reported by Brown et al. (2003).[34] We, therefore, conclude that the increase in fund flow results in an increase in stock prices for all individual G7 countries, with the exception of Japan. Our results to date are consistent with those obtained for the USA, where the authors have found a positive relationship between fund flow and stock returns (Warther 1995; Edelen and Warner 2001). With the exception of France, we are unable to explain if the presence of a positive association between fund flow and concurrent security returns is either due to price pressure effect or due to information effect.

We report the results of model^{VWD} 2 in panel C of Tables 4 and 5.[35] For value stock returns, we did not find a statistically significant relationship for ΔVWD in any of the country cases (see Table 4, panel C). However, we found that ΔVWD enters the return-generating process for growth stock returns of Canada and the UK (Table 5, panel C). This indicates that growth stocks of Canada and the UK perform well when discounts on closed-end funds widen and vice versa. Our findings are similar to those for the USA, where we observed that an increase in growth stock returns is associated with an increase in CEEF discount. Model^{VWD} 2 also shows substantial improvement in R^2 over model^{VWD} 1 for both value stocks and growth stocks. Our results differ from the findings of Lee, Shleifer, and Thaler (1991), who found that a narrowing discount of the US closed-end funds is associated with a positive performance of small stocks. Overall, we found that the discount on CEEF enters the return-generating process for growth stocks of Canada and the UK only.

The results of equity PCR effect on stock returns are given in the last panel of Tables 4–6. We did not find any evidence of equity PCR effects on value, growth or overall market returns in $t + 1$ and $t + 2$ for any of the remaining G7 countries, with the exception of Canada. For the Canadian market, we found a result which is inconsistent with the theory and those reported previously for the USA. Our results indicate that growth stocks and the overall market in Canada perform well over the next month when the equity PCR is high. The high PCR generally indicates pessimism in the market as there are more put options traded than call options. However, the reported results indicate that an investment in growth stocks with a high equity PCR can help an investor to fetch 46 basis points in month $t + 1$ and 37 basis points in month $t + 2$. This irrational behavior of Canadian investors seems to be sporadic and unexplainable. We believe that there may be some form of herding behavior among Canadian investors and they indeed follow a contrarian strategy as it is highly unlikely that a high equity PCR can lead to subsequently higher returns. We also observed the presence of a significant positive correlation coefficient between Canadian investor survey and equity PCR (not reported here), further strengthening our belief that investor optimism is associated with a high equity PCR. Therefore, the findings of Canadian equity options volume data are not consistent with the previous studies on the US equity options volume data.[36]

5. G7 panel analysis

5.1 *Consumer confidence index*

The results of the panel fixed-effect regression of stock returns on consumer confidence index are reported in Table 7. It can be seen that there is a negative survey sentiment–return relationship for value, growth and aggregate market returns over different forecast horizons from 1 to 24 months. The results indicate that a one-standard deviation shock in survey sentiment leads to a decrease in aggregate market returns (refer to panel C) by 48 basis points over the next month. The effects of survey sentiment on value stock returns and growth stock returns are similar. For instance, we found that a one-standard deviation shock in survey sentiment decreases value stock returns (refer panel A) by 59 basis points over the next month. Furthermore, we also found the effect of survey sentiment to be greater on the three-month forecasted returns of value stocks, growth stocks and aggregate market. This effect is gradually reduced over the forecasted returns of 6, 12 and 24 months.

The reductions in persistence of sentiment on returns for value stocks, growth stocks and aggregate market are similar across all the forecast horizons. We also found that consumer confidence has a consistently greater impact on value stocks than on growth stocks and the aggregate market for all forecasting horizons. For instance, at 1% significance level, growth stocks and aggregate market returns decrease by an average of 60 basis points over the next three months, whereas value

Table 7. The results of panel fixed-effect regression: onsumer confidence index.

Forecast horizon	1 month	3 months	6 months	12 months	24 months
Panel A: Value stock returns					
Survey sentiment	−0.59	−0.79	−0.66	−0.49	−0.16
p-Value	(0.00)***	(0.00)***	(0.03)**	(0.09)*	(0.63)
R^2	0.02	0.02	0.02	0.02	0.03
Obs.	1085	1071	1050	1008	924
Panel B: Growth stock returns					
Survey sentiment	−0.49	−0.60	−0.47	−0.32	−0.30
p-Value	(0.00)***	(0.00)***	(0.06)***	(0.28)	(0.27)
R^2	0.02	0.02	0.02	0.02	0.04
Obs.	1085	1071	1050	1008	924
Panel C: Aggregate market returns					
Survey sentiment	−0.48	−0.60	−0.44	−0.33	−0.26
p-Value	(0.00)***	(0.00)***	(0.05)**	(0.22)	(0.27)
R^2	0.02	0.03	0.02	0.02	0.04
Obs.	1085	1071	1050	1008	924

Notes: The results of panel fixed-effect regression of value stock returns, growth stock returns and aggregate market returns on consumer confidence index and different macro-economic variables are reported. The coefficients of macro-economic variables are not reported here for the sake of brevity.
*Statistical significance at the 10% level.
**Statistical significance at the 5% level.
***Statistical significance at the 1% level.

stocks decrease by 79 basis points for the same time horizon. Our results are consistent with the previous studies, where authors have found both negative survey sentiment–return relationship and value stocks to be more influenced by a survey sentiment than growth stocks (Schmeling 2009). Lemmon and Portniaguina (2006) also showed that survey sentiment has a significant effect on value stock returns for the USA after controlling for conditional market betas. Previous studies on the US market have shown that an increase in investors' confidence is associated with higher stock returns followed by lower returns (see Fisher and Statman 2000, 2003; Brown and Cliff 2005; Baker and Wurgler 2006). Our panel findings, therefore, strengthen the belief that investor optimism (pessimism) is associated with subsequent lower (higher) returns.

5.2 *Equity fund flow*

In Table 8, we report the results of all the four models used in our panel study of equity fund flow effect on stock returns. As noted earlier, in model^{FF} 1, we regressed stock returns at t on equity fund flow at t to $t-3$. The results show that the stock returns are significant and positively related to concurrent equity fund flow and significant and negatively related to lagged equity fund flow.[37] It can be seen that a one-standard deviation shock, 0.95%, to equity fund flow is associated with an increase in aggregate market returns by 59 basis points in the same month (see panel C). The increase in returns is greater for value stocks than that for the growth socks. For instance, value stocks increase by 84 basis points at time t, whereas growth stocks increase by only 56 basis points. However, value stocks, growth stocks and the overall market decrease in subsequent months, indicating the presence of a negative relation between returns and lagged equity fund flows.

Warther (1995) pointed out that the negative coefficient of lagged fund flow could be due to the possibility of stock prices overreacting to net sales at time t and then reverting in the subsequent months or the lagged fund flow could be responsible for the expected concurrent equity fund flows, thus affecting returns in the subsequent months. Therefore, in model^{FF} 2, we regressed returns at t on equity fund flow at $t-1$ to $t-3$. The insignificant negative coefficients at all lags of model 2 indicate the presence of a lagged fund flow effect on expected concurrent equity fund flow. We, therefore, examined model^{FF} 3, where we regressed returns at time t on expected and unexpected concurrent equity fund flows and unexpected equity fund flow at $t-1$ and $t-2$. The results of model^{FF} 3 show that the coefficient on unexpected concurrent equity fund flow is highly significant and has a positive effect on value stocks, growth stocks and aggregate market returns. For instance, a one-standard deviation shock, 0.95%, to the unexpected concurrent equity fund flow will power up the aggregate stock market returns by 0.82% and value stock returns and growth stock returns by 1.02% and 0.81%, respectively. However, we observed that the coefficients of expected concurrent net equity fund flow and unexpected lagged equity fund flow are insignificant. Our panel results, therefore, imply the possibility of the presence of temporary price pressure on stocks due to an increase in concurrent unexpected fund flow.

If the increase in unexpected equity fund flow causes a temporary price pressure on concurrent returns, then we should find a significant negative coefficient of subsequent returns. We report the results of price pressure hypothesis in the final column of Table 8. From the results, it can be seen that there is no evidence to support the feedback trader hypothesis, which states that fund flow should lag returns, as mutual fund investors are generally considered to be feedback traders. The results further show evidence of price reversals for value stock returns and aggregate market returns as we found a significant negative coefficient of subsequent returns. Therefore, we note that the causality running from equity fund flow to returns for value stocks and overall market is due to

Table 8. The results of panel fixed-effect regression: equity fund flow.

	Model^{FF} 1		Model^{FF} 2		Model^{FF} 3		Model^{FF} 4	
Independent variables	Coeff.	*p*-Value	Coeff.	*p*-Value	Coeff.	*p*-Value	Coeff.	*p*-Value
Panel A: Value stock returns								
Fund Flow$_t$	0.88	(0.00)***						
Fund Flow$_{t-1}$	−0.40	(0.06)*	−0.21	(0.32)				
Fund Flow$_{t-2}$	−0.46	(0.03)**	−0.34	(0.11)				
Fund Flow$_{t-3}$	−0.49	(0.01)***	−0.37	(0.08)*				
Expected Fund Flow$_t$					0.17	(0.68)		
Unexpected Fund Flow$_t$					1.07	(0.00)***		
Unexpected Fund Flow$_{t-1}$					−0.31	(0.22)		
Unexpected Fund Flow$_{t-2}$					−0.30	(0.25)		
Value Stock Returns$_{t-1}$							−0.05	(0.92)
Value Stock Returns$_t$							2.27	(0.00)***
Value Stock Returns$_{t+1}$							−1.42	(0.01)***
R^2	0.04		0.02		0.03		0.03	
Panel B: Growth stock returns								
Fund Flow$_t$	0.59	(0.00)***						
Fund Flow$_{t-1}$	−0.30	(0.13)	−0.17	(0.37)				
Fund Flow$_{t-2}$	−0.34	(0.08)*	−0.26	(0.18)				
Fund Flow$_{t-3}$	−0.38	(0.05)**	−0.29	(0.13)				
Expected Fund Flow$_t$					0.10	(0.78)		
Unexpected Fund Flow$_t$					0.85	(0.00)***		
Unexpected Fund Flow$_{t-1}$					−0.09	(0.71)		
Unexpected Fund Flow$_{t-2}$					−0.39	(0.10)*		
Growth Stock Returns$_{t-1}$							1.01	(0.12)
Growth Stock Returns$_t$							1.61	(0.01)***
Growth Stock Returns$_{t+1}$							−0.88	(0.17)
R^2	0.02		0.01		0.03		0.02	
Panel C: Aggregate market returns								
Fund Flow$_t$	0.62	(0.00)***						
Fund Flow$_{t-1}$	−0.32	(0.07)*	−0.18	(0.29)				
Fund Flow$_{t-2}$	−0.30	(0.10)*	−0.21	(0.24)				
Fund Flow$_{t-3}$	−0.40	(0.02)**	−0.31	(0.08)*				
Expected Fund Flow$_t$					0.12	(0.73)		
Unexpected Fund Flow$_t$					0.86	(0.00)***		
Unexpected Fund Flow$_{t-1}$					−0.17	(0.41)		
Unexpected Fund Flow$_{t-2}$					−0.30	(0.17)		
Aggregate Returns$_{t-1}$							0.87	(0.22)
Aggregate Returns$_t$							2.14	(0.00)***
Aggregate Returns$_{t+1}$							−1.30	(0.06)*
R^2	0.03		0.01		0.03		0.02	

Notes: The results of panel fixed-effect regression of G7 countries' value stock returns, growth stock returns and aggregate market returns on equity fund flow at different lags are reported. Model^{FF} 1 reports the regression of stock returns on equity fund flow at t, $t-1$, $t-2$ and $t-3$. Model^{FF} 2 reports the regression of stock returns on equity fund flow at $t-1$, $t-2$ and $t-3$. Model^{FF} 3 reports the regression of stock returns on expected fund flow at t and unexpected fund flow at t, $t-1$ and $t-2$. Model^{FF} 4 reports the regression of unexpected equity fund flow on returns at $t-1$, t and $t+1$.

*Statistical significance at the 10% level.

**Statistical significance at the 5% level.

***Statistical significance at the 1% level.

the price pressure effect. We also found a positive correlation coefficient between equity fund flow and investor survey sentiment (result not reported here), indicating that an increase in consumer confidence is associated with corresponding increase in flow of money into mutual funds.

5.3 *Closed-end equity funds*

The panel results of CEEF discount as a measure of investor sentiment are reported in Table 9. The results of model^{VWD} 1, where we regressed value and growth stock returns at time t on ΔVWD and aggregate market returns, show that a 1% decrease in ΔVWD is associated with an increase in value stock returns by 19 basis points and a decrease in growth stock returns by 11 basis points. The significant coefficient suggests that investor sentiment, as measured by ΔVWD, has a significant influence on both value stocks and growth stocks. If we were to assume that discount on CEEF plays a systematic role in asset pricing, then we need to find its relativeness to non-systematic asset pricing factors in the return-generating process. Hence, we examined the significance of ΔVWD by incorporating industry-return indices along with aggregate market returns (see model 2 in Table 9).[38] We found significant ΔVWD for both value stocks and growth stocks at 5% and 1% levels, respectively. The decrease in ΔVWD by 1% increases value stock returns by 10 basis points and decreases growth stock returns by 7 basis points. Our panel study, therefore, reveals that CEEF discount does enter the return-generating process.

As Kumar and Lee (2006) documented that the US retail investors tend to overallocate value stocks than growth stocks in their portfolio, it, therefore, appears that investor optimism is associated with a narrowing discount and thus an increase in value stock returns.[39] This conclusion is based on the assumption that closed-end funds are primarily owned and traded by individual investors. Previous studies, including Lee, Shleifer, and Thaler (1991), found average institutional ownership of US closed-end funds to be only 6.6%, thus concluding that closed-end funds are primarily owned and traded by individual investors. Weiss (1989) also found that after two calendar

Table 9. The results of panel fixed-effect regression: CEEF discount.

	Model^{VWD} 1				Model^{VWD} 2			
	Value stock returns		Growth stock returns		Value stock returns		Growth stock returns	
	Coeff.	p-Value	Coeff.	p-Value	Coeff.	p-Value	Coeff.	p-Value
Intercept	0.09	(0.78)	−0.04	(0.80)	0.13	(0.67)	−0.04	(0.79)
ΔVWD	−0.19	(0.00)***	0.11	(0.00)***	−0.10	(0.05)**	0.07	(0.00)***
Aggregate returns	1.00	(0.00)***	1.03	(0.00)***	0.36	(0.00)***	1.29	(0.00)***
Banking					0.25	(0.00)***	−0.12	(0.00)***
Basic materials					0.29	(0.00)***	−0.11	(0.00)***
Industrials					0.08	(0.00)***	−0.01	(0.26)
Consumer goods					0.02	(0.29)	−0.01	(0.38)
R^2	0.67		0.89		0.76		0.91	

Notes: The results of panel fixed-effect regression of value stock returns and growth stock returns on change in the index of CEEF discount (ΔVWD) and aggregate market returns in model^{VWD} 1 and change in the index of CEEF discount (ΔVWD), aggregate market returns, FTSE Banking, FTSE Basic materials, FTSE Industrials and FTSE Consumer goods indices in model^{VWD} 2 are reported.

*Statistical significance at the 10% level.

**Statistical significance at the 5% level.

***Statistical significance at the 1% level.

quarters of the IPO of closed-end funds, institutional ownership of US closed-end funds is about 5% when compared with 26.02% of control sample of equity IPOs. We, therefore, assumed that individual ownership remains more or less similar across other G7 countries. The lack of availability of individual ownership data of CEEF restricted us to arrive at actual individual ownership of CEEF for other G7 countries. Thus, the persistence of ΔVWD significance coupled with an increase in R^2 for both value stocks and growth stocks indicates that the discount on CEEF plays a systematic role in the return-generating process.

5.4 *Equity PCR*

The panel results of equity PCR effect on value stocks, growth stocks and aggregate market returns are reported in Table 10. We observed a significant negative coefficient of equity PCR in month t, indicating that a low equity PCR is associated with higher returns in the same month t. The presence of a significant negative correlation coefficient between equity PCR and survey (not reported here) further adds to the fact that investor optimism is associated with a low equity PCR. Our panel results show that only value stocks are significantly affected over the next month $t+1$. The negative coefficient of equity PCR for value stocks at $t+1$ (see panel A) indicates that if an investor buys value stocks when the PCR is 0 or close to 0 and sells value stocks when the PCR is 1 or close to 1, a yield of 6 basis points over the next month could be achieved. Our results show consistency with the previously reported results for the USA by Lee and Song (2003), who showed that value stocks in the USA outperform growth stocks when the PCR is low. We also noted that investors can yield very low returns (6 basis points) in $t+1$ and this may be due to the information content in options volume being incorporated in the stock price in the same month t.[40]

Table 10. The results of panel fixed-effect regression: equity PCR.

	R_t	R_{t+1}	R_{t+2}	R_{t+3}
Panel A: Value stock returns				
PCR	−0.12	−0.06	−0.02	−0.07
p-Value	(0.00)***	(0.04)**	(0.49)	(0.01)***
R^2	0.04	0.01	0.01	0.01
Obs.	504	497	490	483
Panel B: Growth stock returns				
PCR	−0.05	−0.02	−0.01	−0.03
p-Value	(0.02)**	(0.38)	(0.72)	(0.29)
R^2	0.02	0.01	0.01	0.01
Obs.	504	497	490	483
Panel C: Aggregate market returns				
PCR	−0.07	−0.03	−0.01	−0.04
p-Value	(0.00)***	(0.26)	(0.78)	(0.13)
R^2	0.02	0.01	0.01	0.01
Obs.	504	497	490	483

Notes: The results of panel fixed-effect regression of value stock returns, growth stock returns and aggregate market returns on equity PCR for the period January 2002–December 2007 are given. The equity PCR is equity put volume divided by equity call volume and equity put volume.
*Statistical significance at the 10% level.
**Statistical significance at the 5% level.
***Statistical significance at the 1% level.

Pan and Poteshman (2006) found the effect of PCR on stock returns to be decreasing beyond 18 days and showed that stocks with a low PCR outperform stocks with a high PCR over the next day by 40 basis points and by 1% over the next week. The insignificant coefficient on equity PCR for growth stocks and aggregate market for month $t + 1$ indicates that equity PCR is not useful in predicting returns for growth stocks and overall market. The implication is that the information contained in equity options volume data gets fully incorporated in security prices as we move further to month $t + 2$ and beyond.

6. Conclusion

In this paper, we have examined the effect of investor sentiment on value and growth stocks as well as aggregate market returns of G7 nations. The vast majority of previous studies on sentiment–return relationship have only examined the case of the USA, examined the sentiment variable in isolation, generally considered sentiment–aggregate market return relationship and generally found mixed results. Very few studies have examined non-US data, restricting their analysis to survey sentiment measure (Verma and Soydemir 2006; Schmeling 2009). In our study, we adopted a range of sentiment proxies (including consumer confidence index, equity fund flow, CEEF discount and equity PCR) and examined their influence on value stocks, growth stocks and overall G7 market returns. We examined the influence of investor sentiment on stock returns of individual countries as well as a panel of G7 country cases. Our panel findings indicate that value stocks, in particular, are consistently affected by investor sentiment. We observed that when investor sentiment is high (low), future returns are low (high).

We found evidence that survey sentiment has the strongest effect on value stocks rather than on growth stocks. This finding is particularly noteworthy, as the vast majority of researches to date have examined the case of the USA and found sentiment effects mainly driving growth stock returns. We also found evidence of price pressure on value stocks and the overall market due to an increase in fund flow and we conclude that fund flow can indeed be considered a measure of investor sentiment. Our finding is informative to investors who maintain a global portfolio of stocks and want to decide on timing the acquisition of stocks based on the level of confidence in the international markets. Particularly, investors should exercise caution while investing in value stocks during the period of high sentiment as these stocks will generally yield negative returns in the subsequent months. Unlike previous evidence for the USA (Elton, Gruber, and Busse 1998, etc.), our international perspective provides evidence that the discount of CEEFs does enter the return-generating process. We observed that a narrowing of the CEEF discount is associated with an increase (decrease) in value (growth) stock returns. An increase in investor optimism is associated with an increase in value stock returns, as individual investors (considered to be primary holders of closed-end funds) tend to overweight value stocks than growth stocks (Kumar and Lee 2006). Therefore, similar to equity fund flow, we conclude that a discount of CEEFs reflects the level of investor sentiment and it indeed enters the return-generating process. Our results of the equity PCR effect on stock returns are particularly informative to investors trying to seek an information edge from equity options volume data. We observed that when equity PCR is low, value stocks outperform by only 6 basis points over the next month, although no effect was found for either growth stocks or the overall market. We, therefore, note the minimal usefulness of equity PCR in forecasting stock returns, as the effect disappears beyond the one-month forecasted returns.

Having observed the evidence of commonality across different sentiment measures with value stocks being strongly affected by investor sentiment, we believe that the investors' behavior is consistent with the 'adaptive expectation hypothesis'. As studies have shown that value stocks outperform growth stocks for samples of data consistent with those studied here, investor tend to overweight value stocks when sentiment is high, expecting that it would continue to yield positive returns.[41] Therefore, investor optimism is followed by an increase in demand of value stocks, putting pressure on its prices and thereby leading to its rise. After the wave of positive sentiment has passed, the value stock prices would decline in subsequent months, returning to the valuation levels.

Finally, as well as extending the analysis of investor sentiment to an international perspective and the implications of our results for the behavioral finance literature, there are a number of practical investment implications. In particular, we believe that our findings in relation to the extent of influence of different sentiment measures on value and growth stocks as well as overall market will be helpful to investors who are willing to incorporate sentiment inputs in their investment strategies. Of the sentiment measures that we have examined in our study, we believe that investor would be better served if they base their investment decisions on the outcome of consumer confidence index, as the effect of survey sentiment is consistently observed across all the countries. The other sentiment measures (equity fund flow and CEEF discount) may be used in conjunction with a survey sentiment measure to determine the potential outcome of investment decisions. The consistent findings of our panel study for each sentiment measure suggest the development of potential investment strategies in value and growth stocks.

Notes

1. We considered stock returns of G7 nations which consist of the USA, Canada, the UK, France, Germany, Italy and Japan.
2. Aggregate market results are also presented for all countries and sentiment proxies.
3. Schmeling (2009) and Verma and Soydemir (2006) examined the influence of sentiment on international stock returns using only survey-based measures.
4. Warther (1995) and Edelen and Warner (2001) did not find any evidence of price pressure on US stocks due to an increase in concurrent fund flow.
5. See Subrahmanyam (2007) for a detailed survey of literature on behavioral finance.
6. See Baker and Wurgler (2007) for a detailed explanation of each of these sentiment measures.
7. Details about different types of surveys conducted by G7 countries are given in Appendix 1.
8. By employing vector autoregressive models and Granger causality tests, Canbas and Kandir (2009) found that previous stock portfolio returns of the Turkey stock market influence investor sentiment. They further observed that only the turnover ratio seems to have a forecasting potential, whereas CEFD, mutual fund flows, odd-lot sales-to-purchases ratio and repo holdings of mutual funds are not significant in forecasting future stock returns.
9. Also see the work of Zouaoui, Nouyrigat, and Beer (2011), who found the significance of investor sentiment in predicting the stock market crisis of 15 European countries and the USA. They further showed that the impact of sentiment is more pronounced on the countries that are culturally prone to a herd-like behavior and less institutionalized.
10. Also see Chen, Kan, and Miller (1993), Chopra et al. (1993a, 1993b), Brauer (1993), Chordia and Swaminathan (1998), Spiegel (1999) and Russel (2005) for a detailed study of CEFD.
11. Indro (2004) examined the relationship between net aggregate equity fund flow and investor survey and found that when net aggregate equity fund flow is higher during any given week, individual investors become more bullish in the same week.
12. The returns were sourced from http://mba.tuck.dartmouth.edu/pages/faculty/ken.french/data_library.html. Stock market returns are from the value-weighted portfolio including dividends in the US dollars. We segregated the aggregate stock market returns into value and growth stocks returns by considering the top 30% of stocks sorted by book-to-market ratio as value stocks and the bottom 30% of stocks sorted by book-to-market ratio as growth stocks.
13. The consumer confidence index data for Canada (until December 2001) and Japan (until March 2004) were available on a quarterly frequency. Monthly observations were estimated via interpolation by adopting a piecewise cubic spine methodology.

14. We have used net equity fund flow data including distributions for the reasons given in Appendix 2. This appendix also details the procedure of collecting and maintaining equity fund flow data by different sources.
15. Refer to Appendix 3 for a detailed data description of CEEFs considered in our research.
16. Data on the end-of-the-month total equity call and put options traded have been adopted for the USA, Italy and Japan. For Canada and Germany, data on the end-of-the-month total call and put options traded for each individual security have been adopted. The end-of-the-day equity put and call options traded for each individual security were made available for the UK and France. To arrive at the total equity call and put options traded in any given month, we did a summation of the end-of-the-day call and put contracts traded for each individual security.
17. We do not report the results of panel unit root test to conserve space.
18. The macro-economic variables have also been considered in sentiment–return relationship study by Baker and Wurgler (2006), Lemmon and Portniaguina (2006) and Schmeling (2009).
19. A range of block length have been implemented with similar results in all cases.
20. FTSE industry returns (e.g. FTSE Banking, FTSE Basic materials, FTSE Industrials and FTSE Consumer goods) were chosen for two reasons, viz. (a) they represent, almost, more than three-quarters of the stocks in which CEEF invests for each of the respective markets and (b) the ease in data availability for the same time horizon. FTSE industry indices were sourced from Datastream.
21. Liu (2010) found evidence of equity options listing in Japan reflecting significant increase in price and volatility and concluded that this increase may be due to the difference in regulatory environments across different markets.
22. Refer to Table 1 for detailed data source and time horizon for which equity derivatives data are available.
23. By allowing conditional market beta to be a function of consumer confidence, Lemmon and Portniaguina (2006) showed that value stocks are significantly affected by changes in consumer confidence.
24. Brown and Cliff (2005) showed that a higher level of investor optimism is associated with subsequent lower aggregate market returns and higher capitalization growth stocks are the main victims of survey sentiment. Fisher and Statman (2003) also found that investor optimism is associated with higher stock prices.
25. The results of model^{FF} 1 and model^{FF} 2 are not reported here to conserve space but are available from the authors upon request.
26. We do not report the results of model^{FF} 4 to conserve space.
27. Edelen and Warner (2001) attributed the presence of positive association between daily fund flow and concurrent market returns to either price pressure or information effect.
28. We calculated the correlation coefficient between equity fund flow and stock returns using the Spearman pairwise correlation test. The results are not reported here to conserve space.
29. We also tested model^{VWD} 1, where we regressed returns on change in the index of discount of CEEF and aggregate market returns. The results of model^{VWD} 1 are not reported here for the sake of brevity.
30. We do not report coefficients of equity PCR beyond three months as they are insignificant.
31. However, our results differ from those reported by Lee and Song (2003), who found that value stocks outperform growth stocks when equity PCR is low. The different results may be due to the different approach adopted by Lee and Song (2003) in calculating the equity PCR. They calculated equity PCR by dividing trading volume of equity put options by trading volume of equity call options.
32. The coefficients of survey sentiment are not statistically significant for the forecast horizon greater than 12 months. Hence, they are not reported here to conserve space.
33. Refer Appendix 1 for a detailed description of surveys conducted across G7 countries.
34. Also see the work of Ihara, Kato, and Tokunaga (2001), who found evidence of the existence of herding behavior in the Japanese stock market.
35. We do not report the coefficients of industry-return indices to conserve space.
36. Pan and Poteshman (2006) have shown that stocks with a low PCR outperform stocks with a high PCR by 1% over the next week.
37. We do not report the insignificant coefficient at lags greater than 3 to conserve space.
38. Industry-return indices were also considered as non-systematic asset pricing factors in the study by Elton et al. (1998) and Doukas and Milonas (2004).
39. The significant negative correlation coefficient between survey and discount on CEEF (not reported here) further indicates that investor optimism is associated with a lower discount.
40. We were unable to test how frequently the information contained in equity options volume data gets incorporated in the security prices due to lack of availability of daily and weekly equity derivatives data for other countries (except for the USA).
41. A number of studies have reported the outperformance of value stocks over growth stocks (see Capaul, Rowley, and Sharpe 1993; Bauman, Conover, and Miller 1998; Lee and Song 2003).

References

Ahoniemi, K. 2008. Modeling and forecasting the VIX index. Helsinki Center of Economic Research, Helsinki. Unpublished Working Paper.

Baker, M., and J. Wurgler. 2006. Investor sentiment and the cross-section of stock returns. *Journal of Finance* 61, no. 4: 1645–80.

Baker, M., and J. Wurgler. 2007. Investor sentiment in the stock market. *Journal of Economic Perspectives* 21, no. 2: 129–51.

Bandopadhyaya, A., and A. Jones. 2008. Measures of investor sentiment: A comparative analysis Put–Call ratio vs. volatility index. *Journal of Business & Economics Research* 6, no. 8: 27–34.

Barberis, N., and A. Shleifer. 2003. Style investing. *Journal of Financial Economics* 68, no. 2: 161–99.

Barberis, N., A. Shleifer, and R. Vishny. 1998. A model of investor sentiment. *Journal of Financial Economics* 49, no. 3: 307–43.

Bauman, S., M. Conover, and R. Miller. 1998. Growth versus value and large-cap versus small-cap stocks in international markets. *Financial Analysts Journal* 54, no. 2: 75–89.

Bhuyan, R., and M. Chaudhury. 2001. Trading on the information content of open interest: Evidence from the US equity options market. McGill University, Montreal, QC. Unpublished Working Paper.

Bird, R., and L. Casavecchia. 2007. Sentiment and financial health indicators for value and growth stocks: The European experience. *European Journal of Finance* 13, no. 8: 769–93.

Black, F. 1986. Noise. *Journal of Finance* 41, no. 3: 529–43.

Brauer, G. 1993. Investor sentiment and the closed-end fund puzzle: A 7 percent solution. *Journal of Financial Services Research* 7, no. 3: 199–216.

Brown, G. 1999. Volatility, sentiment and noise traders. *Financial Analysts Journal* 55, no. 2: 82–90.

Brown, G., and M. Cliff. 2004. Investor sentiment and the near term stock market. *Journal of Empirical Finance* 11, no. 1: 1–27.

Brown, G., and M. Cliff. 2005. Investor sentiment and asset valuation. *Journal of Business* 78, no. 2: 405–40.

Brown, S., W. Goetzmann, T. Hiraki, N. Shiraishi, and N. Watanabe. 2003. Investor sentiment in Japanese and US daily mutual fund flows. National Bureau of Economic Research, Cambridge, MA. Unpublished Working Paper 9470.

Canbas, S., and S. Kandir. 2009. Investor sentiment and stock returns: Evidence from Turkey. *Emerging Markets Finance and Trade* 45, no. 4: 36–52.

Capaul, C., I. Rowley, and W. Sharpe. 1993. International value and growth stock returns. *Financial Analysts Journal* 49, no. 1: 27–36.

Chan, L., N. Jegadeesh, and J. Lakonishok. 1996. Momentum strategies. *Journal of Finance* 51, no. 5: 1681–713.

Chen, N., R. Kan, and M. Miller. 1993. Are the discounts on closed-end funds a sentiment index? *Journal of Finance* 48, no. 2: 795–800.

Chopra, N., C. Lee, A. Shleifer, and R. Thaler. 1993a. Yes. Discounts on closed-end funds are a sentiment index. *Journal of Finance* 48, no. 2: 801–08.

Chopra, N., C. Lee, A. Shleifer, and R. Thaler. 1993b. Summing up. *Journal of Finance* 48, no. 2: 811–12.

Chordia, T., and B. Swaminathan. 1998. Market segmentation, imperfect information, and closed-end fund discounts. Vanderbilt University, Nashville, TN. Unpublished Working Paper.

Daniel, K., D. Hirshleifer, and A. Subrahmanyam. 1998. Investor psychology and security market under and overreactions. *Journal of Finance* 53, no. 6: 1839–85.

De Bondt, W., and R. Thaler. 1985. Does the stock market overreact? *Journal of Finance* 40, no. 3: 793–805.

De Bondt, W., and R.H. Thaler. 1987. Further evidence on investor overreaction and stock market seasonality. *Journal of Finance* 42, no. 3: 557–81.

De Long, J.B., A. Shleifer, L. Summers, and R. Waldmann. 1990. Noise trader risk in financial markets. *Journal of Political Economy* 98, no. 4: 703–38.

Doukas, J., and N. Milonas. 2004. Investor sentiment and the closed end fund puzzle: Out of sample evidence. *European Financial Management* 10, no. 2: 235–66.

Easley, D., M. O'Hara, and P. Srinivas. 1998. Option volume and stock prices: Evidence on where informed traders trade. *Journal of Finance* 53, no. 2: 431–65.

Edelen, R., and J. Warner. 2001. Aggregate price effects of institutional trading: A study of mutual fund flow and market returns. *Journal of Financial Economics* 59, no. 2: 195–220.

Elton, E., M. Gruber, and J. Busse. 1998. Do investors care about sentiment? *Journal of Business* 71, no. 4: 477–500.

Finter, P., A. Niessen-Ruenzi, and S. Ruenzi. 2010. The impact of investor sentiment on the German stock market. Center for Financial Research, Cologne. Unpublished Working Paper 10-03.

Fisher, K., and M. Statman. 2000. Investor sentiment and stock returns. *Financial Analysts Journal* 56, no. 2: 16–23.

Fisher, K., and M. Statman. 2003. Consumer confidence and stock returns. *Journal of Portfolio Management* 30, no. 1: 115–27.

Frazzini, A., and O. Lamont. 2006. Dumb money: Mutual fund flows and the cross section of stock returns. *Journal of Financial Economics* 88, no. 2: 299–322.

Gallagher, L., and M. Taylor. 2001. Risky arbitrage, limits of arbitrage, and non-linear adjustment in the dividend–price ratio. *Economic Inquiry* 39, no. 4: 524–36.

Green, C., and B. Hwang. 2009. Price-based return comovement. *Journal of Financial Economics* 93, no. 1: 37–50.

Grigaliuniene, Z., and D. Cibulskiene. 2010. Investor sentiment effect on stock returns in Scandinavian stock market. *Economics and Management* 15: 929–40.

Hirshleifer, D. 2001. Investor psychology and asset pricing. *Journal of Finance* 56, no. 4: 1533–597.

Hong, H., and J. Stein. 1999. A unified theory of underreaction, momentum trading and overreaction in asset markets. *Journal of Finance* 54, no. 6: 2143–184.

Ihara, Y., H. Kato, and T. Tokunaga. 2001. Investors' herding on the Tokyo stock exchange. *International Review of Finance* 2, no. 1: 71–98.

Indro, D. 2004. Does mutual fund flow reflect investor sentiment? *Journal of Behavioral Finance* 5, no. 2: 105–15.

Jegadeesh, N., and S. Titman. 1993. Returns to buying winners and selling losers: Implications for stock market efficiency. *Journal of Finance* 48, no. 1: 65–91.

Kothari, S., and J. Shanken. 1997. Book-to-market, dividend yield and expected market returns: A time series analysis. *Journal of Financial Economics* 44, no. 2: 169–203.

Kumar, A., and C. Lee. 2006. Retail investor sentiment and return comovements. *Journal of Finance* 61, no. 5: 2451–486.

Lee, C., A. Shleifer, and R. Thaler. 1991. Investor sentiment and the closed end puzzle. *Journal of Finance* 46, no. 1: 75–109.

Lee, Y., and Z. Song. 2003. When do value stocks outperform growth stocks? Investor sentiment and equity style rotation strategies. University of Rhode Island, Kingston, RI. Unpublished Working Paper.

Lemmon, M., and E. Portniaguina. 2006. Consumer confidence and asset prices: Some empirical evidence. *Review of Financial Studies* 19, no. 4: 1499–529.

Liu, S. 2010. Equity options and underlying stocks' behavior: Further evidence from Japan. *International Review of Finance* 10, no. 3: 293–312.

Lo, A., and C. MacKinlay. 1999. *A nonrandom walk down Wall Street*. Princeton, NJ: Princeton University Press.

Mukherjee, K., and R. Mishra. 2004. Impact of open interest and trading volume in option market on underlying cash market: Empirical evidence from Indian equity option market. Indian Council of Social Science Research (ICSSR), Hyderabad. Unpublished Working Paper.

Neal, R., and S. Wheatley. 1998. Do measures of investor sentiment predict returns? *Journal of Financial and Quantitative Analysis* 33, no. 4: 523–47.

Pan, J., and A. Poteshman. 2006. The information in option volume for future stock prices. *Review of Financial Studies* 19, no. 3: 871–908.

Qiu, L., and I. Welch. 2006. Investor sentiment measures. National Bureau of Economic Research, Cambridge, MA. Unpublished Working Paper 10794.

Russel, P. 2005. Closed-end fund pricing: The puzzle, the explanations, and some new evidence. *Journal of Business and Economic Studies* 11, no. 1: 34–49.

Schmeling, M., 2009. Investor sentiment and stock returns: Some international evidence. *Journal of Empirical Finance* 16, no. 3: 394–408.

Shleifer, A., and R. Vishny. 1997. The limits of arbitrage. *Journal of Finance* 52, no. 1: 35–55.

Spiegel, M. 1999. Closed-end fund discounts in a rational agent economy. Yale University, New Haven. CT. Unpublished Working Paper.

Subrahmanyam, A. 2007. Behavioral finance: A review and synthesis. *European Financial Management* 14, no. 1: 12–29.

Verma, R., and G. Soydemir. 2006. The impact of US individual and institutional investor sentiment on foreign stock market. *Journal of Behavioral Finance* 7, no. 3: 128–44.

Warther, V. 1995. Aggregate mutual fund flows and security returns. *Journal of Financial Economics* 39, no. 2: 209–35.

Weiss, K. 1989. The post-offering price performance of closed-end funds. *Financial Management* 18, no. 3: 57–67.

Zouaoui, M., G. Nouyrigat, and F. Beer. 2011. How does investor sentiment affect stock market crisis? Evidence from panel data. *The Financial Review* 46, no. 4: 723–47.

Zweig, M. 1973. An investor expectations stock price predictive model using closed-end premiums. *Journal of Finance* 28, no. 1: 67–78.

Appendix 1. Consumer confidence index calculation

Consumer surveys have been carried out in almost all the developed countries for more than 20 years. These surveys are conducted to study consumers' present and future financial situations and their outlook on the economy over the next year. The questions in the surveys are very much similar across all the countries. For instance, the University of Michigan surveys at least 500 consumers households about their present and future financial situations, their business and economic outlook over next 1 and 5 years, respectively, and also about their willingness to spend on durable goods in the near future. Similarly, the Conference Board of Canada surveys Canadian households about their present and future financial situations and their level of optimism about the current economic conditions and over the next six months. Besides studying the consumers' current and future financial situations and their outlook on the economy, DG ECFIN also seeks to find the likelihood of consumers' ability to save money over the next 12 months. DG ECFIN conducts consumer survey on at least 2000 households of the UK, Germany and Italy each and 3300 households of France. Of all the countries, Japan surveys maximum households, that is, 6000 households. Its survey questionnaire consists of questions similar to that of the USA and Canada, for example, consumers' perception of the economy, price expectation and their present and future financial situations. Overall, the consumer survey questions are similar across the G7 countries and hence the outcome of the survey is easily comparable. However, the calculation of index differs across countries. For instance, DG ECFIN employs 'Dainties' method, while Japan employs X-11 of the Census Bureau USA. For ease of comparison, we standardized consumer confidence survey measures across all the countries.

Appendix 2. Equity fund flow data calculation

Here, the reasons for using the net equity fund flow data including distributions are detailed. The procedure in which the data are maintained by different sources is also discussed. The ICI of the USA is the national trade association for the investment company industry. Almost all the mutual funds, CEEFs, exchange-traded funds and unit investment trust domiciled in the USA are the members of ICI. For each fund, ICI collects the following information – net new sales, reinvested dividends, net redemptions and net switches between the funds. To determine the significance of net fund flow, previous studies (Warther 1995; Indro 2004) have used net sales excluding distributions. A similar breakdown of net sales including and excluding distributions is maintained by IFIC. The IMA maintains the net sales of equity funds of all the mutual fund managers domiciled in the UK. The net sales data maintained by the IMA include distributions and are net of switches made between the funds and net redemptions. We sourced equity fund flow data for France, Germany, Italy and Japan from Lipper, subsidiary of Thomson Reuters. Lipper maintain the database of fund flow with effect from January 2002. They calculate net sales of a given fund as a difference between total equity fund assets between two months after stripping the performance of all the assets within the fund. The fund flow data maintained by them include reinvested distributions and also take into account both the net redemptions and the net switches between the funds. In order to have consistent data across all the countries, we decided to use net equity fund flow data including distributions valued in the US dollars. For this reason, we have employed value-weighted stock returns including reinvested distributions provided by Kenneth French.

Appendix 3. Details of CEEFs data

Here, different types of closed-end funds collected by Morningstar that are considered in our research are discussed. For each fund, Morningstar gathers NAV and price data. NAV data are sourced directly from the fund manager, whereas price data are obtained from trading exchanges. In our research, we have considered only conventional CEEFs. Bond funds are specifically excluded. Also within CEEFs, we did not consider fund warrants, C-shares and split funds in our analysis. Fund warrants were not considered as they do not have NAV, whereas C-shares are a way of raising money by an existing fund and hence are not considered as conventional closed-end funds. Split funds are investment trusts with a fixed life, where the shares are divided into more than one category. The simplest form of split funds is a split between capital shares and income shares. The other variations of closed-end funds, which are not in their conventional form, include zero dividend preference shares, highly geared shares, participating income shares and stepped preference shares. These funds have been specifically excluded from our discount calculation. Lastly, CEEFs for which neither NAV data nor price data were available were excluded from our VWD calculation.

Index

aggregate market returns 1, 3, 99, 100, 101, 102, 104, 106, 108, 110, 111, 113–22
Alliance & Leicester plc 56, 74
Allied Irish Banks plc 56, 73
American International Group (AIG) 51
Anglo Irish Bank Corporation Ltd 56, 73
anticipation coefficient 2, 32, 35–6, 46, 48; and Case-Shiller growth 47, 48; and deal balance 44; definition 35; determinants of 45; and macroeconomic variables 47; time-related effects 42–3; and years since closing 44
arbitrage 1, 11, 29, 99–102
Asia 87–8
asset class 5, 9, 10, 16–19, 21–2, 24–6, 28, 32
asset quality 57–8, 59, 60, 63, 66
asset-backed securities (ABS) 8, 38, 40, 45
Australia and New Zealand Banking Group 75
average correlation evaluation 20–1

BaFin 7
Banca Monte dei Paschi di Siena 73
Banco Bilbao Vizcaya Argentaria 72
Banco de Sabadell SA 56, 72
Banco Espirito Santo 59, 73
Banco Popolare SCARL 73
Banco Popular Espanol 72
Banco Santander SA 72
Bank of America Corporation 18, 74
bank growth 86, 87; and funding strategy 91; and market power 89, 90
Bank for International Settlements 31–2
Bank of Ireland 56, 73
bank market power *see* market power
bank size 82, 85, 86, 88, 90; and funding patterns 91; and market power 89
bank spreads 79, 80, 81–2, 87
bank-interest margins 78–98; literature review 81–2; *see also* net interest margins
bank-specific control variables 87
Bankscope database 86, 88
Banque Federale des Banques 56, 72
Barclays plc 74
Barroso, Jose Manuel 7
block correlations 7, 20, 25–7, 28
BNP Paribas 26, 72
bootstrap resampling 15, 21, 25
Bradford & Bingley plc 56, 74

Caja de Ahorros de Valencia Castellon Y Alicante Bancaja 56, 72
Caja de Madrid 56, 72
calendar spread 14
Canada 105, 106, 109–10, 112–13, 115
capital 57
capital impairment ratio 57
capital risk 29
capital structure arbitrage 1, 11, 29, 99–102
capitalisation 16, 17, 54, 56, 64, 85, 88
Case-Shiller Index 46–8, 49
Central and Eastern European countries 81, 87–8
classical asset pricing theory (CAPM) 99
closed-end equity fund (CEEF) 3, 99, 100, 101, 105, 120–1
closed-end fund discount (CEFD) 102, 103
collateralised debt obligation (CDO) 8, 29, 33, 38, 40, 45
commercial mortgage-backed security (CMBS) 38, 40, 45
commodities 10, 16, 18, 19, 21–2, 26
Commonwealth Bank of Australia 75
competition among rating agencies 33, 44, 46
consumer confidence index 105, 106, 107, 117–18
corporate bonds 10, 11, 16, 17, 18, 19
cost to income ratio 3, 86, 88, 92, 94, 95
covariance estimation 19–20
Crédit Agricole SA 72
credit default swap (CDS) spreads 1–2, 18, 19, 33; balance sheet indicators 57–9; geographical differences 56; global financial crisis 51–77; literature review 53–5; mark-to-market returns 6, 11–15; naked 5–30; pre-crisis period 61, 63,

64; robustness tests 65–7; sample banks 72–6; time-series graphs 77
credit risk 88, 92, 94, 95
credit risk transfer (CRT) 7
Credit Suisse 59, 74
credit-rating agencies 2, 31–50; average ratings prior to impairment 39–42; competition 33, 44, 46; conflict of interest 37; literature review 33–4; rating quality *see* rating quality
cumulative distribution function (CDF) 43

Danske Bank 72
deal balance 37, 38, 44, 45
deal category 38
deal volume 2, 32, 36, 37, 43, 44, 48, 49
default amount 36, 38, 45, 46, 48
default events 31–50
default probability 33
default risk 6, 7, 39, 41, 54, 55, 58, 81
deposit funding 85, 87, 92, 94, 95
Deutsche Bank AG Registered 11, 73
Deutsche Postbank AG 73
Dexia SA 59, 72
DNB NOR ASA 73
dynamic panel model 83–4

empty creditor problem 7, 9
equities 7, 17, 18, 19
equity fund flow 103, 105, 106, 118–20
equity put-call ratio (PCR) 100, 101, 103–4, 108, 121–2
equity ratio: and funding patterns 91; and market power 89, 90
equity to asset ratio 57, 87, 89, 91, 93
equity to unreserved impaired loan ratio 57
Erste Group Bank AG 56, 72
European Monetary Union 9
ex-post spread 84–5
exchange-traded funds (ETFs) 9, 17, 127

Financial Markets and Institutions, Special Interest Group (FMI-SIG) 1
firm-specific credit risk 54
Fitch 38, 86
foreign exchange (FOREX) 10, 16, 18, 19, 26
Fortis 56, 72
France 105, 106, 108, 109–10, 112–13, 115
Frank, Barney 7
fund net asset value (NAV) 103
funding strategy 87, 90–1; determinants of 91; sensitivity of NIM to 95
funding-adjusted Lerner index 82–3

G7 countries 99–127; *see also individual countries*
GDP growth: and funding patterns 91; and market power 89, 90
GDP *per capita*: and funding patterns 91; and market growth 89; and NIM 92, 94, 95
Germany 105, 106, 108, 109–10, 112–13, 115
global financial crisis 31–2
Goldman Sachs 8, 18
gross domestic product *see* GDP
gross loans 57, 67
growth stock returns 112–13, 117, 119, 120, 121

HBOS plc 56, 74
home equity loans (HEL) 38, 40, 45
HSBC Holdings plc 74

impairment 31–50; average ratings prior to 39–42; rating quality over time 42–3
implicit interest payment 85, 94, 95
inflation: and funding patterns 91; and market power 89; and NIM 92, 94, 95
initial public offering (IPO) 102
interest rate spreads 79
interest risk rate 81
internal funds 85, 87, 92, 94, 95
International Accounting Standards 55
Intesa SanPaolo 73
investor sentiment 99–127; cross-country analysis 108–17; sentiment proxies 104–8
issuer shopping 32, 33, 44, 46
Italy 105, 106, 108, 109–10, 112–13, 115

Japan 105, 106, 108, 109–10, 112–13, 115
JP Morgan Chase & Co. 51, 74

KBC Groep NV 59, 72

Latin America 82, 87–8
Lehman Brothers 7, 26, 51
Lerner index 79, 80, 82–3, 86, 87, 89, 90, 91, 92, 94, 95
leverage 7, 15, 51, 57, 60, 61
leverage cycle 6, 9, 28, 29
liberalisation index 85–6, 91
liquidity 57, 58–60
liquidity indices 53, 60, 64, 68
Lloyds Banking Group plc 74
loan loss provision 58, 85, 88, 91, 92, 94
loan loss reserve 57, 58, 67
loan reserve to gross loans ratio 57, 67
loans to assets ratio 88
long-term rating 58

macroeconomic factors 46–8
management quality: and funding patterns 91; and market power 89
mark-to-market returns 6, 11–15; complete market 12–13; trading protection 13–14; trading strategies and unit of account 14–15

market failures 3
market power 78–98; and bank growth 89, 90; determinants of 88–90; sensitivity of NIM to 95; *see also* Lerner index
market returns, aggregate 1, 3, 99, 100, 101, 102, 104, 106, 108, 110, 111, 113–22
Merrill-Lynch 18
Mitsubishi UFJ Financial Group 75
Mizuho Financial Group 59, 75
monetary policy: and funding patterns 91; and market growth 89; and NIM 92, 94, 95
Moody ratings 2, 34
Moody's Investors Service 31–50

naïve portfolios 21–2, 25
naked credit default swaps 1, 5–30; ban on trading 7–8
National Australia Bank 75
National City Corporation 56, 74
Natixis 73
net interest margin (NIM) 3, 79–80, 85, 87; behavioural model 80, 81; dealership model 80–1; determinants of 83–4; evaluation of 91–6; and market power 95; monopoly model 80, 81
net loans/deposits 58
NIM *see* net interest margin
non-deposit funding 85, 87, 92, 94, 95
non-interest income 85, 88; and funding patterns 91; and market power 89
Nordea Bank AB 73

operating size 92, 94, 95, 96; *see also* bank size
operations 57, 58
optimisation problem 15–16, 17
option pricing model 54

portfolio compression 12, 16
portfolio construction 17–19
portfolio diversification 7, 10
portfolio performance 20–1; block correlations 25–7
pre-tax profit 58
problem loans 58

Rabobank 56, 73
Raiffeisen International Bank Holding 59, 72
rating agencies *see* credit-rating agencies
rating quality 32, 34–7; and deal volume 44; impairment type and default amount 46; macroeconomic factors 46–8; over time 42–3; prior to impairment 39–42; time since origination 44; tranche-specific factors 43–6
recapitalisation 56, 64
reference entity 5, 6, 10, 13, 19, 51
reference portfolio 17; risk-adjusted returns 22; weighted correlations test 22–5
residential mortgage-backed security (RMBS) 38, 39, 40, 42, 43, 45
return on average assets (ROA) 58, 60
return on average equity (ROE) 58, 60
risk aversion 16, 81, 85, 88, 92, 93, 94, 95
risk-adjusted returns 10, 20; vs. reference portfolio 22
Royal Bank of Scotland Group 74

securitisation 31, 32, 33, 37–9, 42
short-term funding 57, 58–9
Skandinaviska Enskilda Banden 73
Société Générale 73
sovereign bonds 10, 16, 17, 18, 19
Standard & Poor's 38
Standard Chartered plc 74
stock returns 99, 100–4, 106–13, 115–21
structured finance market 31–50; literature review 33–4
sub-Saharan Africa 82, 87–8
Sumitomo Mitsui Financial Group 75
Suntrust 74
Svenska Handelsbanken 73
Swedbank AB 59, 74

TIER 1 ratio 51, 53, 57, 62, 65, 67, 68
time since origination 2, 36, 44, 49, 3745
total return 11, 17, 18, 20
trading protection 13–14, 15; *see also* credit default swaps
tranche balance 38
tranche-specific factors 43–6

UBI Banca SCPA 73
UK 105, 106, 108, 109–10, 112–13, 115
Unicredit SPA 73
unit of account 14–15
unreserved impaired loans 57
USA 105, 106, 108–15

value stock returns 109–10, 117, 119, 120, 121
value-weighted discount 108
volatility index (VIX) 103

Wachovia Corporation 56, 74
Washington Mutual Inc. 56, 75
weighted correlations test 22–5
Wells Fargo & Co. 75
Westpac Banking Corporation 75

years since closing 44, 45
years to maturity 43, 45

For Product Safety Concerns and Information please contact our EU representative GPSR@taylorandfrancis.com Taylor & Francis Verlag GmbH, Kaufingerstraße 24, 80331 München, Germany

Batch number: 10732714

Printed by Printforce, the Netherlands